The Language(s) of Politics

THE LANGUAGE(S) OF POLITICS

*Multilingual Policy-Making
in the European Union*

Nils Ringe

University of Michigan Press
Ann Arbor

Copyright © 2022 by Nils Ringe
Some rights reserved

This work is licensed under a Creative Commons Attribution-NonCommercial-NoDerivatives 4.0 International License. *Note to users:* A Creative Commons license is only valid when it is applied by the person or entity that holds rights to the licensed work. Works may contain components (e.g., photographs, illustrations, or quotations) to which the rightsholder in the work cannot apply the license. It is ultimately your responsibility to independently evaluate the copyright status of any work or component part of a work you use, in light of your intended use. To view a copy of this license, visit http://creativecommons.org/licenses/by-nc-nd/4.0/

For questions or permissions, please contact um.press.perms@umich.edu

Published in the United States of America by the
University of Michigan Press
Manufactured in the United States of America
Printed on acid-free paper
First published January 2022

A CIP catalog record for this book is available from the British Library.

Library of Congress Cataloging-in-Publication data has been applied for.

ISBN 978-0-472-07513-3 (hardcover : alk. paper)
ISBN 978-0-472-05513-5 (paper : alk. paper)
ISBN 978-0-472-90273-6 (open access ebook)

DOI: https://doi.org/10.3998/mpub.12080141

Cover illustration courtesy of Julia Matthews / www.juliamatthewsphotography.com

Meinen Eltern
Christa & Wolfgang

Contents

Acknowledgments	ix
List of Figures	xiii
List of Tables	xv
ONE The Language(s) of Politics: Multilingual Policymaking in the European Union	1
TWO Multilingualism in the EU: How It Works	26
THREE The EU's Language Regime: Institutional Stability and Change	81
FOUR Foreign Language Use and Depoliticization	113
FIVE "EU English" and Depoliticization	140
SIX Translation, Interpretation, and Depoliticization	160
SEVEN Conclusion	187
Appendix: Multilingual Lawmaking under the Ordinary Legislative Procedure	205
Notes	211
Bibliography	233
Index	257

Digital materials related to this title can be found on the Fulcrum platform via the following citable URL: https://doi.org/10.3998/mpub.12080141

Acknowledgments

This book has been long in the making, much longer than my actual work on it. I have been intrigued by the language aspect of European Union (EU) politics ever since I started studying decision making in the EU institutions. My interest only increased over time as I saw the EU actors I interviewed over the years carefully choose their words in a foreign language, or do so surprisingly casually; as a freelance translator shared with me anecdotes about the pitfalls of legal translation; as a former interpreter recalled the challenge of translating Silvio Berlusconi's slippery jokes in the European Council; as I sat on the visitors' balcony in the European Parliament listening to interpretation into two dozen languages; as I heard a Portuguese judge in Luxembourg read out loud a judgment in German; and as I shared lunch with Commission officials who effortlessly switched back and forth between English, French, German, and Dutch. Foreign language use and language services are omnipresent in EU politics, yet political scientists have scarcely considered that multilingualism may influence their outcomes of interest. This is despite the reality that, as I write in chapter 1, language is foundational to all politics in that it provides the basis for all interaction, collaboration, contestation, deliberation, persuasion, negotiation, and transaction between political actors. I hope this book will help set the stage for future research on the intersection of language and politics in the EU and inform similar research elsewhere.

I am deeply indebted to the 92 people in the European Parliament, the Commission, the Council of the EU, the Court of Justice, and in a number of Permanent Representations who allowed me to interview them for this project. Every conversation was informative, stimulating, and enriching. Thank you! I am also grateful to those in the EU institutions who otherwise helped me advance this project, especially Lyudmila Aleksieva-Stratieva, Ralph Bendrath, Jim Cloos, Ann D'haen-Bertier, Nick Gheysen, Jose Gonzalez Holguera, Ana-Iuliana Postu, Ellen Robson, Ingemar Strandvik, Patrick Twidle, Susan Wright, and several others who put time and effort into responding to my queries and requests for information or data.

Andrew Maxfield provided superb research assistance, including the careful transcription and thoughtful coding of interviews. I am also grateful to Ethan vanderWilden for writing the index. Particular thanks are due to Anna Meier for her help with the linguistic corpus analyses in chapter 5.

Kai-Uwe Schnapp hosted me during my sabbatical at the University of Hamburg. I am thankful for his hospitality, collegiality, and suggestions as I moved from data collection to analysis and writing.

I thank George Ross, Jason Koepke, Lew Friedland, and Art Goldhammer for carefully reading the manuscript and offering important substantive comments that helped me improve the book. Art was the first person with whom I discussed my initial ideas for this research, and I am grateful for his encouragement, comments, and conversations throughout. Melody Herr was also an early supporter, and I thank her for her help bringing this project to a close.

Numerous people provided input, help, and support of various sorts, all valuable and much appreciated. Many thanks to Sanja Badanjak, Rikhil Bhavnani, Mary Bresnahan, Paul Cardwell, Stephanie Cobb, Molly Costanzo, Elizabeth Covington, Chad Damro, Michele Gazzola, Mike Gleicher, Justin Gross, Roger Haydon, Florian Heimerl, Jess Howsam, Francis Jacobs, Michael Kaeding, Rita Kaushanskaya, Boaz Keysar, Helen Kinsella, Kim Lane Scheppele, Tomislav Longinović, Ewa Mahr, Melanie Manion, Julia Matthews, Karen McAuliffe, Graham Neubig, Guy Peters, Sven-Oliver Proksch, Eric Raimy, Angelika Redder, Sue Ridgely, Adriana Ripoll-Servent, Tim Rogers, Nadav Shelef, Csanad Siklos, Stefan Thierse, Yulia Tsvetkov, Jason Yackee, and Jerry Zhu.

I am grateful for comments and suggestions from participants in seminars and workshops at the University of Wisconsin-Madison (HAMLET; Europe in Translation), the University of Duisburg-Essen, the University of Pittsburgh, Heinrich-Heine University Düsseldorf, the University of Hamburg, and the University of Edinburgh, as well as from discussants and audiences at the CES International Conference of Europeanists in Madrid (2019), the General Conference of the European Consortium for

Acknowledgments

Political Research in Hamburg (2018), and the American Political Science Association in Boston (2018).

Many thanks to Elizabeth Demers and Haley Winkle at the University of Michigan Press for their support of and assistance with the manuscript. I am also grateful to Julia Matthews for creating the cover art.

I received much appreciated financial support from the University of Wisconsin-Madison Center for European Studies (a U.S. Department of Education Title VI National Resource Center and Foreign Language Area Studies Fellowships Program); my Jean Monnet Chair (2015–2021) and the UW-Madison Jean Monnet EU Center of Excellence (2015–2018, 2019–2022), with the support of the Erasmus+ Program of the European Commission; and the Center for German & European Studies at UW-Madison (a DAAD Centre of Excellence). Support for this research was also provided by the University of Wisconsin–Madison Office of the Vice Chancellor for Research and Graduate Education with funding from the Wisconsin Alumni Research Foundation.

Thanks to the staff at Colectivo Coffee on Monroe Street, where I spent countless hours writing. I very much miss both place and people while finalizing this book, at home, during the COVID-19 pandemic.

Observing and experiencing my son Max grow up bilingual has been a joy. It also helped me make deeper sense of the new intellectual territory I encountered as I ventured into the study of language and linguistic. Max's energy and enthusiasm are boundless, as is my love for him.

My wife, partner, and best friend Sarah Halpern-Meekin is a constant source of love, thought, support, and encouragement. Her contributions to this project are immeasurable, and I cannot thank her enough.

I am dedicating the book to my parents, Christa and Wolfgang Ringe, whose support and sacrifices throughout my life allowed me to pursue a personal and professional path that took me far from home. *Ich danke Euch.*

Figures

2.1 Language Use in EP Plenary: Big, Medium, and Small Languages	42
2.2 Language Use in EP Plenary: Old vs. New Member States	42
2.3 Language Use in EP Plenary: The Big Three	43
2.4 Interpretation Requests (DG LINC): Big, Medium, and Small Languages	50
2.5 Interpretation Requests (DG LINC): The Big Three	50
2.6 Interpretation Requests (DG LINC): Old vs. New Member States	51
2.7 Interpretation Days (DG SCIC): Big, Medium, and Small Languages	52
2.8 Interpretation Days (DG SCIC): The Big Four	52
2.9 Interpretation Days (DG SCIC): Old vs. New Member States	53
5.1 Ideology in EU Speeches	156

Tables

2.1	Predicting i-Slots	54
5.1	Sentences, Tokens, and Types	153
5.2	Sentences and Syllables	153
5.3	Lexical Richness	154
5.4	Adjectives and Adverbs	154
5.5	Disfluencies	155

ONE

The Language(s) of Politics
Multilingual Policymaking in the European Union

On what would be a typical day, a Member of the European Parliament (MEP) starts her morning going over the schedule with her office staff using their native language, after which she fields a call from an interest group representative in English. Next, she attends a committee meeting in which her remarks, offered in her mother tongue, are simultaneously interpreted into a dozen languages. While on break, she consults informally with other parliamentarians using French, before negotiating the content of a series of amendments in English. During lunch in the Members' restaurant, she and a group of colleagues switch off between English and French. After ordering "un big café" (one size up from "un grand café") at the cafeteria in French, she uses her little German to make small talk with an Austrian MEP in the elevator. She returns to her office and to her mother tongue in a briefing with her office staff. A party group advisor stops by, with whom she goes over a policy document in English. They carefully compare different language drafts of the same amendments in the process, before she rushes to make a short speech on the European Parliament (EP) floor. She uses her native language and is interpreted into the other 23 official languages of the European Union (EU). Before she returns to reading various English-language policy documents at the close of her day, she gives an interview to a national TV crew in her mother tongue.

Multilingualism is an ever-present feature not only in the EP, but in all EU politics. The Italian prime minister is told not to make jokes to lighten the mood in the European Council, because humor does not translate well into other languages. For the same reason, the German finance minister avoids using long, run-on sentences in meetings of the Council of the European Union. Amendments to EU legislation may be introduced in any the EU's 24 official languages. All language versions of EU legislation have equal legal force. Most interactions in the EU institutions are between nonnative speakers of a shared foreign language. Thousands of translators and interpreters process millions of pages and facilitate thousands of meetings every year.

The list goes on and is not limited to the EU. In numerous contexts, politicians and policymakers do not share a native tongue and use foreign languages to interact or rely on translators to facilitate communication. Examples range from international organizations like the United Nations, the International Monetary Fund, and the African Union to multilingual states like India, Canada, and Belgium. Despite these realities, multilingual politics and policymaking have scarcely received attention from political scientists. This is remarkable because language is fundamentally political and all politics is a function of political communication. Language is no arbitrary, neutral, or interchangeable instrument of communication (Grin 1994). It can unite and divide, mobilize and repress, empower and disenfranchise, engage and alienate, convince and dissuade, exalt and denigrate.

Language is inherently political as an *instrument of thought* (Grin 1994, 32),[1] because we view and interpret reality, in part, through our language (e.g., Anderson 1983). Language thus defines our cognition and "our ways of reasoning" concerning political matters (Gravier and Lundquist 2016, 78). Language and language choice affect people's views on politics and attitudes toward policy, how they respond to surveys, their views and evaluations of others, and how they make decisions (e.g., Pérez 2016; Pérez and Tavits 2017; Danziger and Ward 2010; Costa, Duñabeitia, and Keysar 2019).

Language is political as an *instrument of identity and solidarity* (Grin 1994, 32), as a bond that unites mankind, "perhaps the strongest and . . . most durable" (de Tocqueville 1839, 25; see also Liu and Baird 2012, 1203–4). As a marker of ethnic identity (Safran 2005), language can be an instrument used to build community (Liu 2015) and, as such, has been an important focus in studies of territoriality, nationalism, and nation building (Deutsch 1942, 1953; Rokkan and Urwin 1983; Laponce 1987).[2] But language can also be divisive and serve as a powerful contributor to conflict and war (e.g., Bormann, Cederman, and Vogt 2017).

Language is also political as an *instrument of control and domination* (Grin 1994, 32). As a social phenomenon, power is intimately related to language in all interpersonal and communicative contexts (Bánhegyi 2014). Linguistic capital thus affords its holders symbolic power (Bourdieu 1992, 50–52), but language also serves as a means of material power and as a creator of social realities (Bilaniuk 1994, 23). On the one hand, it can empower speakers of a given language by increasing their social, political, and human capital (Grin and Vaillancourt 1997, 44–45); on the other, language can be used as a tool of discrimination by excluding those who do not speak it sufficiently well or by imposing social sanctions on them (Fidrmuc 2011, 8).

Finally, language is political as an *instrument of communication* (Grin 1994, 32), in that it involves the expression and exchange of thoughts, concepts, knowledge, experience, and information (Liu 2015, 5). Simply put, language is foundational to all politics in that it provides the basis for all interaction, collaboration, contestation, deliberation, persuasion, negotiation, and transaction between political actors.

David Laitin writes that "it is difficult to conceive of what 'politics' might mean without language. I think it would be possible to understand what 'love' or 'economics' or 'religion' are without language, but not 'politics'" (Laitin 1977). This book seeks to provide the foundation for better understanding the role and impact of language choice and multilingualism on politics and policymaking. An increasingly important reality in a globalized world is that consequential political decisions are made at the international level between politicians who do not share a common native language; in this book, the EU serves as a laboratory for better understanding what is standard practice in both multilingual states and international organizations. The book also makes a contribution specifically to the study of EU politics and hopes to add languages to the list of topics scholars pay attention to when investigating different political phenomena and outcomes of interest, as either a variable previously missing from their considerations or as a factor that fundamentally shapes the nature of EU politics. Finally, the book sets out to bridge disciplinary boundaries by putting insights from a variety of academic disciplines in conversation with one another and by drawing out their implications specifically for politics and policymaking in multilingual political contexts.

This introductory chapter opens by relating multilingualism in the EU to other multilingual polities and by explaining why the EU is an instructive case for investigating multilingual politics and policymaking more broadly. It then discusses existing research on language and politics, as well as on EU multilingualism specifically, both of which would lead us to expect language heterogeneity to be a source of division and conflict. That is not, however, what this book finds. Instead, the main argument and conclusion is that both communication in nonnative languages and reliance on translators tend to *depoliticize* EU politics and policymaking: they make language a mere instrument for communication, as opposed to a political tool used in pursuit of particular political agendas; they make EU actors less distinguishable based on what they say or write, as they are compelled to depend on widely shared expressions, commonly used linguistic constructs, and a customized terminology; and they make language less indicative of EU actors' national and political backgrounds, preferences, and priorities. The very nature and flavor of politics and policymaking in the EU are thus affected by its multilingual character, in ways both subtle and profound. Finally, after describing the methods and data used, the chapter closes with a preview of the remainder of the book.

Multilingualism: A Common Feature in International Politics

The EU is one of many multilingual polities in the world today. Examples of formally multilingual states include Belgium (French, Dutch, and German); Canada (English and French); Finland (Finnish and Swedish); Switzerland (German, French, Italian, Romansh); South Africa (Afrikaans, English, Ndebele, Pedi/Northern Sotho, Southern Sotho, Swati, Tsonga, Tswana, Venda, Xhosa, Zulu); and India (with 22 official languages designated in the constitution).[3] Most international organizations are also multilingual, although the number of languages used varies. The UN, for example, has six official languages: Arabic, Chinese, English, French, Russian, and Spanish. UN documents are generally issued in all six official languages and delegates may speak in any official UN language and will be interpreted simultaneously into the other official languages.[4] French and English serve as the main administrative working languages, with English dominating in New York and French in Geneva (The Economist 2013). International organizations with a similarly high number of official languages include the African Union (Arabic, English, French, Portuguese, Spanish, Kiswahili) and the Organization for Security and Co-operation in Europe (English, French, German, Italian, Russian, and Spanish). The Council of Europe has English and French as official languages and German, Italian, and Russian as working languages.[5] The Organization of American States uses English, Spanish, French, and Portuguese as its official languages and Mercosur Spanish, Portuguese, and Guarani. Both the Economic Community of West African States and the Southern African Development Community rely on English, French, and Portuguese as their official languages, a list that also includes Spanish for the Economic Community of Central African States, while the East African Community recently added Kiswahili as its second official language next to English. The World Trade Organization's official languages are English, French, and Spanish.[6]

What sets the EU apart from other international organizations is a greater number of official languages and much more extensive language services (which primarily offer *translation* of written and *simultaneous interpretation*—or *interpreting*—of spoken language but also provide legislative drafting support, for example) (European Union 2017). But the EU is also an example—in fact, *the* quintessential example—of "deep" international cooperation and integration. Its member states have voluntarily "pooled" their sovereignty and ceded decision-making authority to independent institutions at the European level. The member states are the principal actors in EU politics, but they share power with the EU's "supranational" institutions, most importantly

- the *European Commission*, which is the EU's public administration and quasi-executive and possesses important agenda-setting powers through its exclusive right to propose legislation;
- the *European Parliament*, the EU's directly elected lower legislative chamber, which "co-decides" EU legislation together with the *Council of the European Union* (also known as the Council of Ministers), in which the EU member states are represented; and
- the *Court of Justice of the EU*, which ensures that EU legislation is interpreted and applied consistently across the EU member states and makes binding decisions on disputes over treaty provisions and secondary legislation.[7]

Most legislation today is passed using the ordinary legislative procedure,[8] in which the Council and EP are equal colegislators.[9] Once EU legislation is passed, it becomes binding on the member states, even if a member state or its delegates are outvoted in Council and Parliament. The EU's four core institutions possess genuine decision-making power across a wide range of policy areas, covering issues as diverse as the environment, consumer protection, public health, research and innovation, agriculture, transport, and even internal security and civil rights issues like immigration and asylum policy. EU politics thus involves democratically elected representatives passing legislation that EU citizens are directly subject to and that is superior to national law across a vast range of policy areas.

The EU is, in other words, an international organization composed of sovereign member states that also has some "state-like" features, which makes it a useful case for beginning to understand how reliance on nonnative shared languages and translation services affect politics and policymaking. Indeed, one reason why I consciously focus on a single case and only implicitly engage in comparison with other multilingual political entities is that the careful investigation of language and politics in this particular context provides a useful theoretical and empirical basis for comparative research in the future. A comprehensive investigation of the intersection between language and politics in the EU can inform and serve as a reference point for understanding multilingual politics in multilingual states and international organizations, because the EU shares features with both. Hence, this is a book about multilingual politics and policymaking in the EU that sets the stage and has important implications for consideration of other cases.

Language and Politics: A Story of Conflict and Division

Languages and multilingualism largely fly under the radar in accounts of international politics. In the popular sphere, they only receive attention in relation to problems and mistakes that result from misunderstandings or mistranslations. A number of well-known examples tend to be referenced in which the real or potential consequences were dire. One dates back to the days leading up to the nuclear attacks on Japan in 1945, when the Japanese prime minister's response to an Allied ultimatum was conveyed incorrectly to President Truman as "silent contempt" instead of "no comment, we need more time." Another example, from the early days of the Cold War, is Nikita Krushchev's 1956 declaration to the West that "we will outlast you," which was translated as the more belligerent "we will bury you" (Polizzotti 2018). Perhaps the most well-known example of important written documents suffering from errors in translation is Article (i) of UN Security Council Resolution 242 of November 1967. While the English version of the resolution, which was adopted after the Six Day War between Israel and Egypt, Jordan, and Syria, provided that Israeli forces should withdraw from "occupied territories," the French version referred to "the occupied territories" ("les territoires occupés"). As a result, there was ambiguity as to whether Israel was to withdraw from some or all occupied territories.[10] In a more recent example, a political crisis in Sri Lanka in late 2018 revolved around purported differences between the English and Sinhala versions of the constitutional provision giving the president the power to appoint and remove the prime minister (Jayakody 2018).[11] In the EU context, numerous mistakes and irregularities were identified in translations of the executive summary of the United Kingdom's Brexit White Paper into 22 EU languages, which the UK government published in an effort to sidestep the EU's negotiating team and appeal directly to individual member state governments (Morgan 2018).

Given the inherently political nature of language, it is striking that multilingualism tends to be discounted as a variable of interest in most research on international relations and comparative politics.[12] When it is considered, it is for the most part linked to ethnicity and ethnic relations (e.g., Laitin 1998; Laitin, Moortgat, and Robinson 2012; Posner 2005). Most research on language and politics thus treats language as an identity marker and multilingualism as a particular form of social heterogeneity.[13] As such, multilingualism is almost always considered a source of division and conflict, and it is generally taken as almost a truism that language heterogeneity is associated with a variety of negative outcomes.[14] Examples include poor economic performance (Brock and Durlauf 2001; Easterly and Levine 1997; Rodrik 1999), lower quality of government (Alesina et al. 2003), constitutional crisis (Miles 2000), lower levels of interpersonal trust and diminished interest in politics (Anderson and Paskeviciute 2006), social and political divisions (Bilaniuk 1994), and inequalities that undermine the social basis of democracy (Laitin 1977). Particularly troubling is the association between linguistic heterogeneity and violent conflict. More than half of all post-1948 civil wars revolved around language in some capacity (Liu 2011), and intrastate conflict is more likely to be associated with linguistic divisions than even with religious ones (Bormann, Cederman, and Vogt 2017).

As language divisions contribute to overall greater population heterogeneity, they help suppress economic development, undermine stable democratic rule, and breed conflict along material and identity lines (Fearon and Laitin 1996). The reality that "linguistic entrepreneurs" often try to exploit the emotiveness of language to advance their particular political goals (Miles 2000, 216) aggravates these challenges. Hence, a real or perceived "language problem" or "language question" is not easily neutralized, and important and difficult questions surround the issue of how multilingual polities should set up their language regimes to ensure efficient policymaking, the protection of minority languages, and the establishment of a social and political community (Addis 2001; Esman 1992).[15] The challenges associated with this are significant, because they relate to complex policy issues such as education, linguistic standardization, the promotion or prohibition of regional and minority languages, the political and economic impact of language policies, as well as their (actual or perceived) fairness (Fidrmuc, Ginsburgh, and Weber 2006, 6). This is further complicated by the reality that views on and attitudes toward language and language policy are shaped by a great variety of highly salient factors, such as "anticolonialist resentments, memories of past injustice, status paranoia, xenophobia, collective megalomania, religion, ideology, and the desire on the part of a group to base its collective identity on a demarcation from a real or imagined enemy" (Safran and Liu 2012, 269). The sensitivity of "the language question"—due to its symbolic importance, its potentially divisive and contentious nature, and the "unpredictable material and symbolic consequences of linguistic choices" (Fidrmuc, Ginsburgh, and Weber 2006, 7)—thus makes for a particularly intractable and challenging social and political issue (Pool 1991).

Previous research that focuses specifically on EU multilingualism would also lead us to expect linguistic heterogeneity to be associated with social and political conflict. Indeed, EU multilingualism is often viewed as inherently and necessarily problematic because of the emotiveness of language and its significance as a marker of in- and out-group. Seen as particularly challenging is that the formal equality of all 24 official languages is combined with—and allegedly undermined by—the heavy reliance on one primary working language for communication inside the institutions (today that language is English, but historically it was French). This disjuncture has led to criticism of the EU for paying mere "lip service" to multilingualism (House 2003, 561; Wright 2009, 93; Fidrmuc 2011, 13), or for offering a "costly and cumbersome illusion" of equality (House 2001) that amounts to an "alliance of pious pretence and parlous pragmatism" (Gubbins 2002, 48). The ostensible contradiction in EU multilingualism is seen by some of the primary observers as an "unresolved dilemma for the EU" (Kraus and Kazlauskaitė-Gürbüz 2014, 525–26) that bears "injustice and inequality" (Wright 2009, 111)—which ought to be a source of continuous division and contestation.[16] Another source of conflict is suggested by a third leading scholar on EU multilingualism, who writes that "as interviewers . . . we often had the impression that misunderstandings of many kinds (arising from linguistic diversity) occurred on a regular basis" (Wodak 2009, 89).[17] There is, in other words, a practical component to the difficulties associated with multilingualism, in that it leads to misunderstandings, disruptions, and uncertainties in political and policymaking processes. Yet European leaders are apparently unwilling to acknowledge and fix what is considered to be already broken or in danger of imminent collapse, especially when another round of enlargement is looming. The 2004 and 2007 EU enlargements to central and eastern Europe were seen as particularly threatening to the sustainability of the multilingual regime (Fidrmuc 2011, 4; Cogo and Jenkins 2010, 272; Gubbins 2002, 48; Kraus 2008, 132–34; Wright 2000, 174–75). Modiano (2000, 34), for example, predicted that the language services of the EU would be "overwhelmed" by enlargement, and House (2003, 561–62) warned that "the unwieldy machinery of translation . . . will probably be *de facto* impossible once there are 27 or more member states." (This would not turn out to be the case, however, as will be discussed in detail below).

In sum, popular accounts of multilingualism in international politics, existing social science research on language and politics, and previous work on multilingualism in the EU institutions would all lead us to expect multilingualism to be a disruptive and divisive force. Linguistic heterogeneity ought to make EU politics and policymaking more contested and conflictual. That is not what I find in my research, however.

The Argument: The Depoliticizing Effects of Multilingualism

The main argument and finding of this book is that multilingualism, in fact, *depoliticizes* EU politics. It does so, first, by providing an institutional framework that safeguards the formal equality of all national languages while ensuring effective communication between participants in EU policymaking and keeping costs to a level that is broadly acceptable to the member states. In other words, the language regime is designed to allow for the pragmatic use of some languages more than others, but under a "veil of formal language equality." The *de facto* "uneven multilingualism" prevalent in the EU institutions is not a flaw, but a feature that allows the EU institutions to mold their language rules and practices according to their particular needs. The "veil of formal language equality," meanwhile, defuses "the language question" in the EU as a potentially highly volatile and contested political issue. The language rules are thus an example of depoliticization by design, an area the EU excels in more broadly. Starting with the European Coal and Steel Community, the EU's first predecessor organization, what is today's EU has been set up to avoid arousing suspicion and objection in the member states. The building of the united Europe was to a substantial degree an effort at integration by stealth, often using economic logic and technocratic expertise to advance political goals.

National identities were downplayed and masked in the emerging "supranational" political and economic union in order to not only advance, but to create in the first place, a common European interest. The language regime is, in that sense, part of a broader story of deliberate depoliticization of the European project (see, especially, Ross 1995), a topic to which I will return in the conclusion chapter.

This, however, is only one part of the story this book tells, because multilingualism also depoliticizes EU politics in ways that are distinctly *unintentional*. Specifically, my analysis of how multilingualism affects politics and policymaking in practice shows that "the political" is partially suppressed by the linguistic limitations of those involved in making political decisions and by their reliance on indirect communication via interpretation and translation. Neither of these tendencies is purposely depoliticizing or a reflection of the EU's broader tendency toward depoliticization. It is partly for that reason that the definition of depoliticization I adopt eschews suggestions of intentionality and more generally focuses on *the reduction of the political nature of and the potential for contestation in policymaking*. This avoids an undue and misleading focus on depoliticization as a deliberately employed strategy aimed at stifling conflict over contested issues; denying agency and, therefore, political responsibility; and avoiding blame. My conceptualization of depoliticization thus deviates from others that revolve around the "range of tools, mechanisms and institutions" employed by politicians to diminish or deny the political nature of decision making and to insulate it from public scrutiny by denying political choice, altering the arena of decision making (for example by delegating decisions to technocratic experts), and ultimately by "[persuading] the demos that they can no longer be reasonably held responsible for a certain issue, policy field or specific decision" (Flinders and Buller 2006, 55; see also Beveridge 2017; Buller et al. 2019; Wood and Flinders 2014; Hay 2007; Standring 2018).[18] Instead, I allow for the possibility that depoliticization may be contextually driven, exogenous to human agency, or the unintended consequence of an unrelated action.

Multilingualism depoliticizes politics and policymaking in three main ways. First, it makes language used in EU policymaking more simple, utilitarian, and pragmatic; language is a mere instrument of communication rather than a political tool used to serve or signal a particular agenda. Second, it results in a standardization of language, as EU actors rely on commonly used expressions, linguistic constructs, and terminology; speakers and drafters thus become less distinguishable on the basis of what they say or write. Third, multilingualism leads participants in EU policymaking—

politicians and bureaucrats alike—to use language that tends to be neutral, decultured, and de-ideologized; language is thus less indicative of their national and political backgrounds or agendas.

These effects are unintentional in that they are driven, first, by EU actors' use of nonnative languages in the process of deliberation and negotiation, which limits their linguistic repertoires. When people use a foreign language, they generally express themselves using less complex linguistic constructions; fewer rhetorical figures and embellishments; and more commonly used and understood terms, phrases, and expressions. And while simple language is not inherently or necessarily depoliticized, in the case of the EU it robs the "language of politics" of much of its political flavor. The need for effective communication between nonnative speakers becomes pivotal, which means that language is not wielded as a tool to advance political goals in the same way as would be the case in monolingual contexts. Language is more complex and expressive in monolingual environments, involving metaphors, symbols, or allusions to convey arguments, emotions, attitudes, or ideological connotations. Words and phrases are used freely to suggest deeper meanings, by appealing to the imagination, extending the literal to include the figurative, or leaving ideas unspoken. At the extreme, a single word or utterance may (implicitly or explicitly) communicate a political point of view, persuade, or mobilize. Language thus serves a political function unlike in a multilingual environment, in which the need for efficient and effective political communication elevates its practical, communicative purpose over the political or ideological. In the context at hand, these effects are heightened by the prevalence of "EU English" as the main shared nonnative language, which is more neutral, utilitarian, standardized, pragmatic, "decultured," and de-ideologized than 'standard' English.[19]

Those listening to a speech in a foreign language or reading a nonnative drafter's text, meanwhile, are acutely aware of potential language handicaps and adjust their expectations accordingly, which involves greater perspective taking, tolerance, and empathy toward others. It also compels even native speakers and capable linguists to use language that is easily understood, thus diminishing the "linguistic advantage" they enjoy. Moreover, anticipation and tolerance of linguistic shortcomings leads EU actors to disregard expressions of political differences when they do occur, because they cannot be sure that nonnative speakers really meant what they said or wrote. For example, the use of ideologically charged terms like "austerity" or "illegal immigrant" does not lead to political flare-ups, because they may not have been used with intent by nonnative speakers and are therefore discounted. Multilingualism thus requires that people put a particular focus on "getting their message across," seek to understand what their counterparts are trying to say, and give others the benefit of the doubt.

The second way in which multilingualism depoliticizes EU politics and policymaking is through the translation of written texts and the simultaneous interpretation of oral "interventions" (which is EU-speak for speech, remark, or address), as they inevitably constrict, condense, and transform what is being transmitted. The processes of translation and interpretation not only take intensity out of political debate by making communication less direct, they are so innately complex and challenging that even the very best translators and interpreters necessarily alter what is written or said in the source language, sometimes in obvious but often in subtle ways. They, for example, express complex messages in more straightforward fashion, rely on standard terminology, fall back on common phrases and expressions, and tend to avoid or downplay politically or emotionally charged language. Nuances in meaning are subdued as a result and recipients are left unsure about the original speaker's true intentions. The outcome is, once again, that language is utilitarian and standardized; that speakers are given the benefit of the doubt; and that political differences are muted.

Reliance on language services also has other, less direct effects on political communication in the EU. One is that policymakers are well aware of the "distorting prism" of translation and interpretation and change the way they speak and write in anticipation thereof: they "write for translation" and "speak for interpretation" by using simple, straightforward language that lends itself to transmission in another language. Hence, even those capable of using sophisticated, complex linguistic constructions tend to avoid them in order to be more easily understood by policymakers and language service providers alike. Another effect of the provision of language services is that language service providers serve as de facto foreign language teachers to nonnative speakers and as their primary linguistic reference points. As such, they define and prescribe acceptable terminology and ways of expression to EU policymakers. They also force terminological precision and constrain politicians' ability to use vague or ambiguous language to overcome disagreement or contestation. Hence, EU actors are necessarily "loose" with their language in the multilingual deliberation process, but they are forced to be precise and unambiguous when drafting and finalizing legislation.

All this means neither that all problems are rendered apolitical, nor that all contestation is neutralized or eliminated. Rather, multilingualism entails that choices are considered, deliberated, negotiated, and agreed using overall less political and contested language; to an extent, language becomes defanged. Multilingualism thus depoliticizes the language(s) of politics in EU politics and policymaking by diminishing the expression of political differences, such that conflicts generated by language are not amplified, but subdued. This has potentially consequential effects on perceptions of political and policy differences, polarization of opinion, levels of contestation, intensity of debate, and the resonance of arguments. Put differently, multilingualism depoliticizes the *language of politics*, which in turn depoliticizes *political communication* and thus *politics and policymaking*. That the political tone or character of interaction and communication is tempered also has important implications for the EU's political culture, broadly speaking, in that the depoliticizing effects of multilingualism contribute to what has been described by some as a "consensus norm" inside the EU institutions. Finally, the EU's language of politics helps prescribe what is considered persuasive, in particular by prioritizing substance over style and rhetoric. Perhaps most important, in this regard, is that the depoliticized language used inside EU institutions has potentially beneficial repercussions for the process and quality of policymaking, which becomes more deliberate and rationalized. There is a distinct downside, however, in that genuinely divisive political problems may become unduly depoliticized simply because they are debated in a multilingual environment. An overly rationalized language of politics is also problematic for the EU as a polity and as a political project. After all, a language of politics that is functional, technocratic, and depoliticized will likely be perceived by the general public as bland, abstract, and distant. This undermines the quality of representation and contributes to the gap between the EU and the citizens whose interests it is expected to serve.

This book makes a contribution to a research agenda that looks at language as more than "just" an identity marker. One prominent example is David Laitin's book on "Politics, Language, and Thought" in Somalia, which concludes that "the language you speak influences the way you act in the world" (Laitin 1977, 222), including the ways you think and act politically. Another is Benedict Anderson's work on the mediating effect of language on power and culture in Indonesia (Anderson 1990). Such studies of the "deeper" implications of languages and language choice on politics provide important theoretical and empirical grounding for increasingly popular analyses of text-as-data in political science and other disciplines (e.g., Klüver 2009; Grimmer and Stewart 2013; Proksch and Slapin 2015; Catalinac 2016). The same is true for recent research in political psychology. Daniel Hopkins' work, for example, demonstrates that language skill and nonnative language use affect attitudes toward immigrants and immigration (Hopkins 2014, 2015),[20] while Efrén Pérez and others show that language can affect people's views on politics, as public opinion varies by interview language (e.g., Pérez 2016; Adida et al. 2016; Wong et al. 2011; Lee and Pérez 2014; Lien, Conway, and Wong 2004).[21] For instance, Latinos interviewed in English report nearly 10 percent more knowledge of U.S. politics that those interviewed in Spanish, and they are less likely to refuse and quicker in answering knowledge items; respondents also express higher opinion levels on constructs that "match" the interview language (Pérez 2016). Pérez (2016) proposes that such effects relate to the language in which a political construct is learned, or encoded, and then retrieved from memory: different concepts are associated more or less strongly with different languages, and the degree of correspondence between the two affects the ease with which a concept is retrieved. This has implications for which concepts are evoked in a given political context, as well as their meaning. Together with Margit Tavits, Pérez also finds that language can affect the way people perceive time, with important consequences for attitudes toward future-oriented policies, and how they think about gender equality. They show that speakers of languages that do not have a future tense, like Estonian, are more supportive of future-oriented policies than speakers of languages with a future tense, like Russian, because they view the future as temporally closer to the present (Pérez and Tavits 2017). Similarly, speakers of a gender-less language have more progressive views on gender equality than those of languages that assign a gender to objects (Pérez and Tavits 2019).

This research in political science relates to a broader set of findings by cognitive psychologists, which confirm that language choice reliably influences human thinking (e.g., Boroditsky 2001; Boroditsky, Schmidt, and Phillips 2003; Fuhrman et al. 2011; Slobin 1996). The language we speak can affect, for example, whether we interpret events as accidents or foul play (Fausey and Boroditsky 2011), whether we save money and exercise (Chen 2013), conceptions of time (Boroditsky 2001; Fuhrman et al. 2011), risk aversion (Bernhofer, Constantini, and Kovacic 2015), and individualism (Meyer-Schwarzenberger 2015; Kashima and Kashima 2003; Fausey et al. 2010). Language can also affect how people think of others. Danziger and Ward (2010), for example, show that bilingual respondents associate Arab names more easily with positive characteristics when asked in Arabic than when asked in Hebrew. A particularly interesting body of research in cognitive psychology considers the impact of foreign language use on decision making and finds that people make systematically different decisions in a foreign compared to their native language (see Costa, Duñabei-tia, and Keysar 2019). Foreign language use affects, for example, how people deal with risks, make inferences, and approach moral dilemmas, thus making decision making overall more rational, deliberate, and utilitarian. This research has important potential consequences in political contexts where decision makers engage with one another in foreign languages (and is reviewed in detail in chapter 4).

Another contribution of this book is to our understanding of EU politics, of which multilingualism is an integral yet understudied part. Many EU scholars appreciate that multilingualism is ever-present in EU policymaking and recognize its potential for influencing political processes and outcomes, yet most tend to take multilingualism as a given and fail to explicitly take into account its effects and consequences. By describing and analyzing the EU's multilingual regime and different aspects of how it works in practice, I provide a foundation for consideration of multilingualism as a factor with the potential to systematically impact a wide variety of outcomes of interest to political scientist and scholars. The book also offers a basis for additional research specifically on the topic of language and politics, in the EU and beyond, which more political scientists ought to take seriously and focus their research efforts on. Potential topics abound, including the study of language effects on political attitudes and behavior, language and representation, language and identity, language and conflict, language and development, language and nationalism, or language and decision making. While such topics have received some attention, a great deal more is to be learned.

The argument that multilingualism depoliticizes politics and policymaking has the potential to travel well beyond the EU, in the first place to a variety of other international organizations. In an ever more economically, socially, and politically interconnected world, consequential political decisions are increasingly negotiated between political actors who do not share a common native language. As in the EU, decision makers in those contexts make use of interpreters and translators, or they rely on shared foreign languages to communicate and negotiate, English first among them. International and internationalized politics thus require an understanding of multilingualism and its dynamics, which this book begins to provide. At the same time, it is important to consider and take seriously that the EU is, in many ways, not a typical international organization, but the leading example of "deep" economic and political integration. The decisions made at the EU level relate to a greater number of policy areas, are more consequential because they become binding on the member states, and for that reason closely relate to the EU's legal order. In part because of those realities, the EU recognizes a greater number of official languages than is the case elsewhere, expends a great many resources on language services, and offers the highest quality translation and interpretation in the world. In that sense, the EU is both an example of "normal" politics at the international level and closest to an "ideal type" of multilingual politics, and thus a useful starting point for investigating the language(s) of politics in multilingual settings.

Future comparison to other multilingual international organizations promises to provide important insights into an increasingly common feature of politics today. The same is true of comparison to politics in multilingual states, as opposed to multilingual international organizations. In some respects, the EU case may be more similar to the former given its "state-like" features, although the EU has a much larger number of official languages than multilingual states like South Africa, Canada, or Belgium. The "language question," however, is of crucial political importance in many, if not all, multilingual states, as is the case in the EU. Investigating multilingual policymaking, as well as the institutional setup of the EU's language regime, thus adds to our knowledge of comparative federalism and comparative nationalism. A particularly important contribution, in that regard, is offered in chapter 3, which explains how the EU's language rules successfully depoliticize language itself as an issue of contestation. EU multilingualism as a political institution thus neutralizes one key avenue for political mobilization and the expression of nationalist sentiment, with potential lessons for other multilingual political contexts.

Methods and Data

This book is both motivated and informed by insights and experiences of almost two decades of research on EU politics and policymaking, for which I have spent extended periods of time observing operations inside the institutions and conducted large numbers of detailed interviews with EU politicians and officials for this and other research projects. It builds on a mixed-methods empirical approach that combines the analysis of qualitative, quantitative, and linguistic data.

In-depth interviews with 92 respondents in Brussels and Luxembourg, which on average lasted 45 minutes, constitute the book's empirical backbone. Of those interviews, 39 were with language service providers, among them interpreters, translators, lawyer-linguists (whose general responsibility is to ensure that EU law is drafted and translated so that it has equivalent effect across all member states, although their exact roles vary across the institutions), and officials who coordinate language services. I also interviewed 53 policymakers and officials involved in the policymaking process: 21 in the EP (including MEPs, MEP assistants, political group advisors, and members of the EP secretariat), 20 national counselors in the Permanent Representations of the EU member states (including 3 Antici and 5 Mertens counselors),[22] 5 members of the Council secretariat, 6 officials in the Commission, and one former Advocate General of the Court of Justice. Twelve of my respondents were from the British Isles, 12 from the Nordic countries, 24 from eastern Europe, 20 from western Europe, and 24 from Mediterranean countries. I pursued interviews until a "point of saturation" was reached, meaning I was generally not learning new information from additional respondents. Most interviews took place in 2015 and 2016; afterwards, I only conducted interviews with a select group of respondents that promised particularly valuable insights (the last one in January 2019).[23]

The interview data were analyzed based on careful coding using the qualitative data analysis software NVivo. A research assistant and I first separately open-coded three randomly selected interviews to create lists of themes (or "nodes" in NVivo) covered in the interviews. The resulting themes were consolidated into a single set of nodes, which the research assistant used to code the remaining interviews. About 10 percent of the interviews were randomly selected for coding comparison and independently coded by both the research assistant and me. The comparisons revealed high levels of coding consistency: the average level of agreement was 96.24 percent for nodes that were selected at least once by at least one coder. For only 7 of 158 nodes (4.4 percent) was agreement lower than 90 percent, and it was less than 87 percent for only one single node.[24]

I also examine quantitative, longitudinal data in chapter 2 on speaking time for different languages in the EP plenary, interpretation requests in the EP, and the proportion of "interpreter days" devoted to each official language by the Commission's Directorate-General (DG) for Interpretation (which serves the Commission, the Council of Ministers, the European Council, and other EU institutions and agencies). Most of the data are descriptive, but I conduct statistical analyses to establish which factors determine the proportion of interpretation into different languages offered by DG Interpretation. Furthermore, chapter 5 includes a linguistic corpus analysis aimed at identifying features of "EU English."

Last but not least, the book draws extensively from existing multidisciplinary research on EU multilingualism, especially those studies that built on a clear empirical foundation. In fact, among its main ambitions is to have insights from research outside political science help shed light on multilingual politics and policymaking, and to put those insights in conversation with one another. Indeed, while Robert Phillipson's observation from almost two decades ago still holds today, that most books and articles on EU politics make no reference to language and multilingualism (Phillipson 2003), much existing research that is not explicitly about politics in fact tells us a lot about language and politics in the EU.[25]

Most existing research and commentary on EU multilingualism, not surprisingly, comes from scholars in linguistics, sociolinguistics, and language or translation studies (e.g., Ammon 2006, 2010; Balič 2016a, 2016b; Labrie 1992; Phillipson 2003; Pym 2000, 2014; Pym et al. 2013; Schlossmacher 1994; Tosi 2005, 2013; Trebits 2008, 2009a, 2009b; Truchot 1994; van Els 2001, 2005; Wodak and Krzyżanowski 2011; Wodak, Krzyżanowski, and Forchtner 2012). There is also an extensive body of work in legal studies, some of which focuses explicitly on institutional multilingualism in the Court of Justice of the EU (e.g., Baaij 2012a, 2012b, 2018; Creech 2005; McAuliffe 2009, 2011, 2012, 2015; Paunio 2013; Šarčević 2012a, 2013, 2015; Van der Jeught 2015). Another substantial portion of contributions consists of scholarly accounts from practitioners, such as translators, interpreters, and lawyer-linguists (e.g., Cosmidou 2011; Duflou 2016; Guggeis 2014; Koskinen 2008; Robertson 2010a, 2010b, 2011, 2012a, 2012b; Robinson 2014a, 2014b; Strandvik 2014, 2018; Wagner, Bech, and Martínez 2014; Szabó 2020). There is also some work by economists (e.g., Fidrmuc 2011; Fidrmuc and Ginsburgh 2007; Fidrmuc, Ginsburgh, and Weber 2006, 2009), anthropologists (e.g., Abélès 1999; Bellier 1997, 2002), sociologists (e.g., De Swaan 2001, 2007; Barbier 2015), and public policy scholars (e.g., Ban 2013; Gazzola 2006, 2016a, 2016b).

Only a small number of political scientists have looked at language and politics in the EU.[26] Pool (1996) points to the tension between the formal equality of all official languages and cost reduction and emphasizes the deep normative commitments involved in language policy. Laitin (1997) relates multilingualism to EU "state building" and compares the European Union to other multilingual contexts, especially India. He takes note of the tension between the rise of English as Europe's "lingua franca," the persistence of national languages, and the EU's institutional support for regional languages, but maintains that this tension is unlikely to be "resolved" through an explicit political bargain. A more likely outcome is a steadfastly multilingual Europe that combines an international lingua franca with continued reliance on and support for national and regional languages. Kraus (2008) also thinks broadly about EU multilingualism, including its societal and institutional dimensions. He ties the language question to the quality of democracy in the EU, questions of identity, and the development of a transnational European demos. The political space he considers is thus much broader than mine, but part of his book deals explicitly with multilingualism inside the EU institutions, which Mamadouh (1999, 2002) also homes in on. Her 1999 article relates institutional multilingualism to the nature of the EU's supranational political system and examines how different "visions of Europe" shed different lights on the EU's "language question" in terms of communication, identity, and power. In 2002, she looked at the growing dominance of English in the EU institutions, which is also considered by others; Longman (2007), for example, asks how the rise of English privileges native or near-native English speakers inside the EU institutions. Mamadouh reflects on the impact of linguistic homogenization but emphasizes that politicians carefully avoid the issue because there is "no possible compromise between improving EU-wide communication and respecting national linguistic identities" (Mamadouh 2002, 327), although I will argue in chapter 3 that the current EU language regime is, in fact, such a viable compromise. The most extensive research agenda on institutional multilingualism in the EU is Sue Wright's (2007, 2009, 2013), which is based on interviews with legislators, assistants, and interns in the EP. Her 2007 article, in particular, offers valuable insights into language practices in the EP, some of which confirm or complement my own empirical findings, as will become apparent throughout the book. Some of our views on multilingualism in the EU are also at odds, however, with important implications for our respective empirical foci and the conclusions we draw. In particular, Wright's focus on EU multilingualism as a "problem" detracts from her otherwise substantial contributions to our understanding of language use inside the EU institutions. It leads her to concentrate on apparent solutions (e.g., Wright 2009, 2013), rather than further drawing out the consequences of foreign language use and reliance on language services for EU politics.

To a substantial degree, the process of researching and writing this book was an exercise in "soaking and poking" (Fenno 1978), and I hope to see its argument and conclusions scrutinized and subjected to new evidence in the future. For the time being, I seek to establish when and how multilingualism comes into play in EU politics; to identify where, when, and how multilingualism matters; and to draw out some of its implications. In this effort, I aim to add substance to what for many EU scholars is a lurking feeling that

A Note on Terminology

there is something important and consequential about multilingualism; to speak to political scientists as well as a multidisciplinary audience; and to both raise new questions and provide a basis for future research.

A Note on Terminology

The terminology used in the context of language use in the EU can be vague and unclear due to reliance on the same or similar terms to describe different things. "Multilingualism," for example, may refer to the language repertoires of individuals or groups of people, but also to language use in whole societies or inside organizations. Sometimes, a distinction is made between an individual's "plurilingualism" (also referred to as "personal multilingualism") and the multilingualism of institutions on the one hand, and groups of people on the other (also referred to as "social multilingualism") (Berthoud, Grin, and Lüdi 2013, 433; Krzyżanowski and Wodak 2010, 125). It is telling that the Commission itself uses the term "multilingualism" to variously describe, in the same document titled "The New Framework Strategy for Multilingualism," a person's ability to use several languages, the coexistence of different language communities in one geographical area, and the Commission's policy aimed at promoting a climate that is conducive to the full expression, teaching, and learning of languages (European Commission 2005). I use the term multilingualism in reference to two realities of EU politics: that most interactions are between native speakers of different languages who either (1) use a shared nonnative language to communicate or (2) rely on translation or interpretation.[27]

De Swaan (2001) differentiates between four levels of communication in the European Union: domestic communication within each member state; transnational communication between EU citizens; formal, public communication of the EU institutions with the member states, national institutions, and member state citizens; and, finally, internal communication within the EU institutions. This book is concerned with the latter, and thus with what is also known as "institutional multilingualism" (Mamadouh 1999; 2002; Phillipson 2003). Institutional multilingualism in the EU is defined by the EU's *language regime*, or its formal and informal language rules; this language regime establishes "a set of official and working languages along with rules concerning their use for the communication within and outside the organisation, and the extent of translation and interpreting to be provided in such languages" (Gazzola 2016b, 549). While the main focus of this book is on language use inside the institutions, it is difficult to entirely separate this internal multilingualism from communications with outside actors; the language choices of elected politicians inside the Council and EP, for example, are in part driven by their desire to communicate their views and decisions to constituencies in the member states. Hence, while the external communication of EU institutions is not the primary subject of my research, I consider when and how it relates to or affects the language use of participants in EU policymaking.

At the core of the EU's language regime are the 24 *official languages*. Those are not only the *authentic languages* of the EU Treaties, but also the languages in which all EU legislation is equally authentic. The *principle of equal authenticity* means that all language versions are equally "legally valid" (Wagner, Bech, and Martínez 2014, 8) and requires that EU legislation must be drafted and translated so that it is interpreted and applied consistently across the member states.

The primary language rules do not make a distinction between official languages and *(internal) working languages*, but the latter are often referred to as those languages used for communication within and among EU institutions, while the official languages are used for legislation and for external communication (European Commission 2010a, 15–16; Gazzola 2006, 396; Wagner, Bech, and Martínez 2014, 10–11). Ammon, for example, explains that the subset of languages used regularly inside the institutions "have come to be referred to, informally, as the EU working languages"; "in some cases preference for these languages has been declared (e.g. for the Commission), and in other cases their preferred use is based on convention (i.e. based on function)" (Ammon 2006, 321). To further narrow it down, some observers refer to English and French as the EU's "procedural" or "administrative" languages (Phillipson 2003, 120), but the term "procedural language" is also used inside the Commission to refer to English, French, and German, as "those languages in which documents have to be provided before they can be adopted at a meeting of the Commission ('non-procedural' language versions must still be produced, but for a later deadline); the concept of procedural languages has no legal basis in legislation or the rules of procedure, however" (Wagner, Bech, and Martínez 2014, 10–11).

Finally, English is often referred to as the lingua franca of EU politics, because it is the most commonly used language between speakers of different tongues. I refrain from using this term, however, because it implies a flexibility and ad hoc quality that is not reflected in the use of English inside the EU institutions. To preview a point elaborated in chapter 5, the "EU English" that prevails inside the institutions is quite structured and predictable, meaning that lingua-cultural norms are not spontaneously negotiated between people within each particular interaction, as would be the case with a true lingua franca (Seidlhofer 2011, 18). Moreover, the objective is not just basic intelligibility and communication, but also integration and membership into a community of speakers of a shared "type" of English. For these reasons, I refer to English as the EU's primary *vehicular language* or *shared language* (i.e., the main language for communication inside the EU's institutions).

Plan of the Book

The book proceeds as follows. Chapter 2 offers a wealth of descriptive information on EU multilingualism, including details on language use in the EU institutions; the make-up, responsibilities, and costs of the EU's language services; and the incidence of mistakes and other difficulties caused by multilingualism. The chapter also highlights that EU multilingualism works quite well in practice and explains why problems are not nearly as frequent and disruptive as one might expect in a polity featuring 24 official languages.

Next, four substantive chapters make that case that multilingualism depoliticizes EU politics. Chapter 3 looks at the origins of the EU's language regime and its development over time. It conceptualizes EU multilingualism as an *institution*, or the *rules of the game* pertaining to language use in the EU, which are made up of both formal rules and informal norms, conventions, and practices. Those rules of the game, it is argued, carefully and successfully balance four distinct "dimensions" of language: a *symbolic* dimension that preserves the formal equality of all member state languages; a *representational* dimension that provides the basis for popular participation in EU politics; a *legal* dimension that ensures the uniform application of EU law; and a *functional* dimension that aids communication inside the EU institutions by providing for a degree of flexibility in the relative use of official languages. This functional dimension explicitly allows for reliance on some languages more than others, while the other three dimensions safeguard the principle that no one language is formally superior. It is in this sense that the EU language regime provides for *uneven multilingualism* under a *veil of formal language equality*. The member states have accepted this reality since the very early days of the European integration process in the 1950s, because uneven multilingualism—and in particular the reliance on a primary shared language (historically French, nowadays English)— helps ensure effective communication between EU actors inside the institutions and keeps the already substantial costs of multilingualism in check. A firm, continuous commitment to formal language equality is of crucial symbolic importance, however: it is only because all national languages are formally equal that the member states consent to uneven language use in practice. This arrangement constitutes a strong institutional equilibrium that the member states have little incentive to change; as a result, the EU language regime successfully depoliticizes "the language question" in EU politics and defuses a potentially highly conflictual issue in a union of sovereign member states engaged in "deep" international cooperation.

Chapters 4 through 6 consider how multilingualism (unintentionally) depoliticizes EU policymaking by examining two distinct aspects of EU multilingualism: the reality that most interactions between individuals inside the EU institutions take place in a shared foreign language on the one hand, and EU actors' communication via translation and interpretation on the other. Chapters 4 and 5 focus on nonnative language use among EU actors, with a particular focus on English as their main shared language. Chapter 4 considers, in general terms, how nonnative language use affects the nature of communication between EU actors. This, in turn, has important implications for the nature of policymaking in the EU, since interpersonal communication provides the basis for all policy-relevant interactions, collaborations, deliberations, negotiations, and transactions inside the institutions. It argues that nonnative language use depoliticizes decision making by simplifying, standardizing, and neutralizing both written and spoken language. Given that most EU actors are unable to express themselves with the same ease and proficiency in a foreign language as they would in their mother tongue, they tend to speak and write in simple, utilitarian terms. Their primary goal is, quite basically, to make themselves understood and to understand what others are trying to convey. Language thus serves as a mere communicative tool, rather than an instrument used to advance particular political agendas. Notably, even those who are native or highly proficient nonnative speakers tend use less complex language, because they have to make themselves understood by those with lower foreign language competencies. There is also greater reliance on commonly used words and phrases by both native and nonnative speakers, meaning that language becomes standardized and its users less distinguishable from one another based on their speeches and written texts alone. The simplification and standardization of language thus undercuts the expression of political differences between EU actors from different member states and political or ideological backgrounds. This also occurs because foreign language use leads EU actors to disregard politically charged language, because they cannot be sure that the use of a particular term or phrase is intentional or simply a function of their counterparts' limited foreign language proficiencies. Multilingualism thus neutralizes political terminology. Finally, chapter 4 suggests that foreign language use may increase empathy between political adversaries through enhanced perspective taking and more conscious efforts at understanding others' communicative intent.

While focused on foreign language use in general terms, much of chapter 4 effectively considers the use of English as the primary shared language inside the EU institutions. Chapter 5 thus constitutes an extension of chapter 4 that focuses specifically on the type of English used inside EU institutions. It considers the proposition that there is a particular kind of "EU English" that is distinguishable from standard English and provides a common basis for political interactions between EU actors. The chapter examines the use and features of EU English, which is described by my respondents as a standardized, shared language characterized by a simple, neutral, and utilitarian nature and a technical vocabulary that serves the particular, specialized needs of its users. EU actors—including native English speakers—adopt EU English upon their arrival in Brussels, which is partly created and disseminated by language service providers, such as translators and interpreters. The chapter not only relies on qualitative evidence from my interviews to investigate the nature of EU English, it also analyzes English-language oral negotiations between a group of MEPs concerning a particular legislative proposal. This first-ever analysis of spontaneous, natural speech in one of the EU institutions reveals that these particular EU actors use shorter words and sentences than their counterparts in two native-English legislatures, that their speech is lexically less rich and complex, and that they tend to use ideologically neutral language. EU English is simple, utilitarian, standardized, and neutral, and—as such—depoliticizing.

Chapter 6 shifts focus toward the second way in which EU actors interact and communicate with each other, namely using their mother tongues while relying on translation and interpretation services. It demonstrates that translation and interpretation processes lead to a simplification, standardization, and neutralization of the target (or output) language, and the anticipation thereof to a simplification, standardization, and neutralization of the source (or input) language. The chapter offers a detailed overview of the manifold challenges involved in translation and interpretation. Translators of legal and legislative texts are especially constrained by the need for legal equivalence of all language versions, which guarantees the uniform application of EU law across the member state. To ensure this equivalence, they rely heavily on existing documents, shared terminology databases, and commonly accepted and widely used phrases and formulations; language is thus standardized. Moreover, the need for equivalence limits the ability of policymakers to rely on vague or ambiguous language to gloss over disagreements or contentious issues, because ambiguity in the source language tends to be identified and rectified before or during the translation process. Interpreters of oral interventions in EU politics, meanwhile, face the challenge of having to convey—accurately and on the spot—not only the substance of a given utterance, but also the speaker's intention, culture, and personality. This already exceedingly difficult task is further complicated by often rapid speech, the wide range of highly technical issues covered in EU institutions, and the use of idioms, humor, and the occasional insult. As a result of these difficulties, the output of simultaneous interpretation tends to be more functional, simple, and standardized than the input language. EU actors are, moreover, aware of the distorting effects of translation and interpretation and adjust the way they speak and write to ensure that their messages and intentions are conveyed accurately. Translation and interpretation thus simplify, standardize, and neutralize the target language directly and the source language indirectly.

Chapter 7 concludes the book. It briefly reviews the argument and evidence and explicitly considers areas for improvement of the EU's language regime, while recognizing that EU multilingualism works (perhaps surprisingly) well overall. The chapter's main focus, however, is on the implications, contributions, and possible extensions of this research. Multilingualism thus matters for institutional, political, and social hierarchies inside EU institutions, some of which it reinforces and some of which it undermines. Moreover, the depoliticizing effects of multilingualism affect the EU's political culture, and they help determine what is considered valid and persuasive in EU politics. Multilingualism may also benefit the quality of EU policymaking by "rationalizing" the language(s) of politics, yet this reality is potentially detrimental to the link between the EU and its citizens—an alarming prospect for the EU's quest for political and democratic legitimacy. Finally, the concluding chapter considers which insights from the EU case might "travel" to other cases, as well as the factors that likely affect the extent to which they do.

Multilingualism is a feature, not a bug, of EU politics. As an essential and inherent part of politics and policymaking in EU institutions, it is deserving of a great deal more attention from political scientists than has been the case to date. This book hopes to help set the stage for greater consideration of language and politics in the EU and beyond.

TWO

Multilingualism in the EU

How It Works

There are two aspects of multilingualism in the European Union (EU). One is that EU actors communicate with each other in shared nonnative languages, the other that they rely on the EU's extensive language services for the translation of written documents and the simultaneous translation of spoken language. After highlighting the most important reasons why the EU operates as a multilingual political system in the first place, part 1 of this chapter provides detailed information on those two features of EU multilingualism. It discusses foreign language use in general, followed by specifics from the EU's four core institutions: the Commission (the EU's executive and public administration), the Council of the European Union (also known as the Council of Ministers, which has some executive functions but is primarily the EU's "upper" legislative chamber, in which the member state governments are represented), the European Parliament (EP, the EU's "lower house," composed of directly elected representatives of the European people), and the Court of Justice of the EU (the EU's highest court, which has the power of judicial review concerning matters of EU law). Next, it describes the EU's language services, in particular the simultaneous interpretation of oral proceedings, the translation of written documents, and the work of lawyer-linguists, whose responsibility is to ensure the equivalence of all language versions of EU law. This section includes some descriptive quantitative data on interpretation requests for different languages, as well as a statistical analysis of interpretation services rendered for various languages by the Commission Directorate-General (DG) Interpretation, which covers both Commission and Council.

Part 2 considers how well the language regime works in practice. It starts by laying out three common lines of criticism leveled against EU multilingualism: its costs, the disconnect between formal language equality and the privileging of some languages in practice, and an apparently high incidence of mistakes and misunderstandings. My own evaluation does not discount or negate all concerns, but nonetheless concludes that for those working inside the EU institutions, the language regime actually works well. There surely are examples of mistakes, misunderstandings, and uncertainties—indeed, those are all but inevitable in any multilingual context—but considering the large number of official languages and the complexities of EU policymaking, it is remarkable how positively multilingualism is evaluated by my interview respondents. Most also consider it possible for EU actors with "language handicaps" to be politically influential, although the overall consensus is that it is certainly easier to wield power with good foreign language skills. Those are relative advantages, however, not a requirement for influence. The chapter closes by briefly outlining the explanations offered by my respondents for why EU multilingualism works as well as it does.

Part 1: Language Use and Language Services

There are three main reasons why the EU operates as a multilingual political community. First, multilingualism is indispensable in the EU as an "inter-national" entity, as it allows individual languages to retain their position as markers of national identity while providing the basis for building a common political community. EU multilingualism is consciously built on the recognition that languages are a means of social, cultural, and political identification and differentiation, and also of power and control. This makes the elevation of one or some languages over others fundamentally problematic in a political system that has to continuously strike the delicate balance between assuring the national sovereignty of its member states—no matter how small—while constructing a political union. Multilingualism is a key instrument in building a European community that is "united in diversity."

Second, multilingualism is crucial to the functioning of democracy in the EU and by extension for the EU's democratic legitimacy (Mamadouh 1999), because "speaking the language of the state is often the critical condition enabling the citizen to participate in the political arena of that state," as Laitin put it succinctly (Laitin 1977, 3). Offering EU citizens access to information in an official language of their choice is thus vitally important in that it helps ensure the right and capacity of citizens to participate in EU politics by having access to the information they need to understand how decisions are deliberated, negotiated, and finalized; to learn about the content and consequences of laws and regulations they are subject to; and to evaluate the performance of the representatives they elect. Even if citizens do not actively take advantage of those opportunities, EU multilingualism is critical for democratic accountability, because elected representatives are only responsible to their voters if those voters are able to get the information they need to decide if an incumbent should continue to serve in office or be replaced by somebody else. It is also essential for the legitimacy of the EU's institutions and the decisions that are made therein. A language regime centered on a small number of official languages would make EU citizens feel even more disconnected from EU institutions than many already do and undermine the extent to which they view those institutions as rightfully making decisions that affect the individual lives of EU citizens in countless ways.

It is not only the represented who rely on a functioning multilingual regime, however, but also their representatives. As the EP put it its resolution of January 1995, "the right of an elected person to express himself and to work in his own language is an indissociable part of democratic rights and of his mandate" (cited in Athanassiou 2006, 17). Here one must make a clear distinction between EU civil servants and politicians who are either elected to represent the European people in the European Parliament, or who represent the elected national governments of the EU member states in the Council of Ministers. EU civil servants can be (and are) required to master multiple languages,[1] but such a requirement would be "plainly incompatible with the workings of a democratic system" if placed on elected representatives (Gazzola and Grin 2013, 105). This may seem obvious, but a number of commentators have raised the possibility of a language requirement, noting that it would not be much different from expecting elected representatives to be literate (e.g., van Els 2001, 2005; Wright 2007). It is not, however, actually a requirement for elected representatives to be able to read or write (as far as I am aware), and such a requirement would be very different from the expectation or preference that they are. While it is perhaps unlikely that an illiterate person would seek elected office, be nominated, and ultimately elected, it would be hugely problematic to implement a rule barring this possibility.

Not making language services available to the elected representatives of EU citizens would also undermine people's equality of rights and, given current levels of language proficiency and the distribution of language skills across societal groups, come at the expense of the less educated and socio-economically disadvantaged (Gazzola 2016b). Citizens would be prevented from selecting candidates, independent of their language proficiency, who they feel would best represent their interest, and they themselves might be prevented from pursuing one of the most important democratic rights: to seek elected office. The quality of democracy would also suffer in the absence of language services, because lower-quality candidates with foreign language skills would crowd out more qualified competitors, and because only experts with sufficient foreign language proficiency would be able to bring their knowledge to bear on policy decisions in EU meetings and hearings.

It is possible that, over time, foreign language competence among Europeans improves such that the capacity to operate in multiple languages comes to be an expectation or that parties only nominate candidates with sufficient language proficiency to operate effectively in what would be an increasingly monolingual environment (centered, in all likelihood on English) (De Swaan 2007, 17; see also chapter 3). If this occurred organically, it might still entail some de facto exclusion, but this exclusion would not be discrimination rooted in formal rules or the absence of language services—a crucial difference indeed.

The third major reason for EU multilingualism is the principle of equal authenticity of language versions of EU law, meaning that all language versions of EU legislation are equally "legally valid" (Wagner, Bech, and Martínez 2014, 8).[2] Put differently, there is no "original" version of legislative text that prevails when two or more versions are incompatible or in conflict with each other.[3] This principle dates all the way back to the European Coal and Steel Community in the early 1950s, when France argued that, for the sake of legal coherence, there ought to be a single reference language and that this one authentic language should be French.[4] This was rejected in favor of the position advocated by Germany, which maintained that legal certainty could only be assured if legal acts were authentic in all official languages (Van der Jeught 2015, 57).

The principle of equal authenticity means that it is of crucial importance that all language versions of EU legislation are drafted so that they have equivalent effect across all member states. It also means that—formally—there are no "translations" of EU legal acts, because an equally authentic language version cannot be a translation of an original text. Paradoxically, this is the case even if one or more language versions of a legal act were, in fact, prepared by translation (Pym 2000; Doczekalska 2009; Gibová 2009; Kjær 2015). This is apparently contradictory, but it legally precludes the possibility of distinguishing between an original source text and a translated target text (Doczekalska 2009), because once a legal document has been finalized, whatever version served as the "original" throughout the drafting process ceases to exist as such (Gibová 2009). And so the EU features a law-making process that fundamentally depends on legal translation, but whose results cannot be called or treated as translations (Doczekalska 2009, 132). The principle of equivalence, Anthony Pym writes, is thus "is a legal fiction necessary for multilingual EU legislation to work" (Pym 2000, 6).

The reasons why it would be problematic to have an authentic text in only one or some official languages are the two most important doctrines of EU law, those of supremacy and direct effect. The principle of the supremacy of EU law establishes that EU law prevails over national law if the two conflict, while the principle of direct effect bestows rights upon EU citizens based on the EU's treaties and secondary law, which can be invoked by EU citizens in their own language before their national and EU courts. These two core provisions of EU law, however, which are among the most important features differentiating the EU from other international organizations, could not operate effectively if all language versions of EU legislation were not equally authentic. Multilingualism is thus a necessary corollary of the two most important provisions of EU law (Athanassiou 2006, 6), because its equal application would be violated if citizens were prevented from understanding and thus invoking the rights conferred upon them through EU law (Šarčević 2013, 4; Paunio 2007, 396). It would be similarly problematic if EU legislation were only authentic in some language(s), and thus foreign and potentially incomprehensible to some EU citizens, since it prevails over national law. Finally, it is imperative that the member state institutions charged with transposing (i.e., writing into national legal code), implementing, and adjudicating EU legislation— namely national legislatures, executives, and judiciaries—be able read and understand them in their own languages. This is essential for the sake of the stated EU objective of harmonizing laws and to ensure that EU legislation confers the same rights to EU citizens across the member states in practice. It is thus no overstatement that multilingualism ensures the equality of all EU citizens before the law (Biel 2007, 145; McAuliffe 2012, 201), and thus the rule of law itself (Athanassiou 2006, 7).

In order for this to be true, however, language versions cannot be divergent, because the equally authentic language versions of EU legislation must be uniformly interpreted and applied in the member states (Baaij 2012a).

This is an important and difficult challenge and one that, if not met, has the potential to undermine the very principle it is supposed to safeguard. It is also an ideal that can be approximated at best, as "both lawyers and linguists are quick to concede that it is impossible to produce parallel texts of a single instrument which have the same meaning" (Šarčević 2013, 8); legal translation is a necessarily imperfect process (Šarčević 2012a; van Calster 1997). The system of equally authentic language versions thus relies on the inherently imperfect instrument of legal translation, which inevitably involves some "slippage" in the uniform application of EU law and thus the equality of all EU citizens before the law. Since the alternative would be a system of only one or some authentic language versions, however, and thus a system that would be fundamentally flawed with regard to that equality, the status quo is preferable as long as the equally authentic language versions are sufficiently similar so that major and consequential discrepancies are the exception rather than the rule, which is the case nowadays.

It is, of course, a reality that a term may be interpreted differently in various member states, either because of ambiguities across language versions or because legal concepts have divergent meanings in different national legal systems (De Groot and Laer 2006).[5] It is also the case that some, perhaps even many, such discrepancies have the potential to be of consequence but simply go unnoticed (Ginsburgh and Weber 2011, 175). But the emphasis on divergences that are actually consequential is important here because, as Robertson explains, it may well be that the precise formulations in different language versions differ in the abstract but result in the same application in practice (Robertson 2012b). For this reason, and also because every legal system involves some degree of uncertainty and potential for legal action that is not actually pursued, equating evidence of imperfection with evidence of dysfunction would be misguided.

When ambiguity or uncertainty do become consequential, the Court of Justice may be asked to interpret the law. One well-known example is the case of *Stauder v City of Ulm* (1969), in which the German pensioner Erich Stauder objected to his name being revealed to merchants on coupons for cheap butter that were to be distributed as welfare benefits to poor citizens. The distribution of the butter was part of an effort by the Commission to help reduce surplus stocks that had accumulated as a side effect of the Common Agricultural Policy, and butter was to be sold at lower prices to the needy through normal retail outlets (Brown 1981). To avoid abuse, however, eligibility was limited to recipients of certain welfare payments in each member state. The Commission's decision was issued in the (then four) official languages and provided, in the German and Dutch versions, that butter was to be made available in exchange for a coupon "issued in their names" (German: "auf ihren Namen ausgestellten Gutschein"; Dutch: "op naam gestelde bon"), while the French and Italian versions merely required an individualized coupon (French: "bon individualisé"; Italian: "buono individualizzato") (Van der Jeught 2015, 127–28). Mr. Stauder felt that his dignity was violated by his identification, by name, as somebody eligible for the benefit. The Court decided that the intention of the rule could not have been to impose a stricter obligation on one member state than on another, and that the French and Italian versions should therefore prevail (for more details, see Brown 1981; Van der Jeught 2015).[6]

Language-related cases before the Court illustrate, on the one hand, that the existence of different language version of legislation can result in uncertainty as to its intent; in the absence of an "original" text, it is difficult to establish the "will or intention of the legislator" (Bengoetxea 2016, 104). On the other hand, as Solan argues, the different language versions can assist in the interpretation of the law, because their comparison can help identify a law's likely intent (although it is not clear that the Court in fact does this consistently). The "proliferation of language versions," he writes, "appears to add to the likelihood that the court will get a case right, where getting it right means issuing a judgment that is more likely to further the purpose behind the law, and which is consistent with the intent of the enacting legislature" (Solan 2009, 52; see also Piris 2005).

In sum, EU multilingualism exists for important symbolic, political, and legal reasons. It aids the maintenance and building of a political community while safeguarding cultural, social, and political diversity; it helps ensure democratic representation; and it constitutes a cornerstone of the EU's legal order.

Foreign Language Use in the EU Institutions

English is by far the most dominant language used inside the EU institutions today, with the exception of the Court of Justice, which continues to rely primarily on French. Deliberation and negotiation, both formal and informal, most commonly take place in English, whether in the preparatory phrases of the legislative process, in intra-institutional bargaining, or in trilogue meetings involving representatives from the Council, the EP, and the Commission.[7] English is also the most frequently written language in the EU institutions. Draft legislation is usually written in English, which puts the rest of the policymaking process on a mostly English track, even if translations are available. Most amendments are tabled (i.e., introduced) in English and, as is the case with other policy-relevant documents, most quickly translated into English if they are not. Legislation is almost always finalized in English, both inside the institutions and interinstitutionally. One EP official estimates that "95 percent of the time, it is the English version that is approved" (#4).

Since English is the language most commonly spoken and written by participants in EU policymaking, the focus of this book is disproportionately on the role of English. The dominance and increasing role of English over time do not mean, however, that other languages are irrelevant for communication inside the EU institutions. French, in particular, continues to be an important and frequently used language. It may have lost its status as the primary vehicular language in the EU, and French politicians and officials may be forced to rely on English more than before, but having French as a native or foreign language continues to be of value. There are a number of reasons for this:

- meetings, especially in the Commission (#55), often rely on a mix of English and French (#11, 55);
- French remains a language of administration inside the institutions (#38), again especially in the Commission (#55);
- native French speakers tend to be less willing or able than speakers of other languages to use English (#20);
- many emails directed at EU officials are in French (#12);
- French terms have been incorporated into EU jargon, so even when somebody speaks English it may be "tricky to understand if you don't know any French" (#61);
- French continues to be a language that many EU actors have in common, so numerous direct interactions inside the EU institutions still take place in French.

French is also the second most frequently used drafting language for written documents, even if it trails far behind English. This can be a challenge for EU actors who do not have a strong command of the language (#59), the number of whom has increased following the eastward enlargement of the EU. The same is true when, for example, a country holding the rotating Council presidency insists on operating in French, as was the case for Luxembourg during the second half of 2015 (#20). Because of the difficulties this may cause, some member states have a strong preference for English; one even has an informal guideline in place to promote the use of English over French inside the EU institutions.[8]

While less common today than it used to be (#47, 67), many EU actors capably mix English and French, especially in the Commission (Ban 2013). At the extreme, such "code switching" results in "Franglais," as one Member of the EP (MEP) recalled; people "say things like 'so, I saw this document, je dois dire que je ne comprends pas le premier paragraphe, but I agree with the purpose of the document. Mais le titre, il faut changer'" (#47).[9] Alternatively, an English speaker may address a French speaker in English and receive a reply in French. Code switching happens for a variety of reasons and is ultimately dependent on the speakers' language competence and the ability of others to understand them (Wodak, Krzyzanowski, and Forchtner 2012, 162). My respondents described a variety of reasons for why and when it occurs, including when actors use somebody else's language as a courtesy (#3, 55, 56), when something is better said in another language (#14, 70), when responding to a question asked in another language (#3, 14), or because a speaker who said something important in her mother tongue repeats it in English to ensure everyone understood (#13, 70, 72, 73). Code switching may also occur when a general discussion gives way to the consideration of particular amendments that are only available in another language (#65), or when technical discussions involve particular terminology in English, for example (#70). Finally, code switching may simply reflect a speaker's mood. One long-term EP official recalled that when his German superior "was in a good mood he spoke to me in English, and when he was in a bad mood he shouted at me in German" (#79).

Because of the continued importance of French, member states today still have an incentive to send representatives to Brussels "who at least have enough knowledge of French to be able to understand it . . . [even if] they will not be able to express themselves in French" (#20). Yet French is still losing ground overall, even in the Commission, as a high-ranking official in that institution whose native language is French acknowledges. He described that in one recurring high-level meeting, "I'm the only one who speaks French from time to time. The only one. And if I speak French [some of the other high-ranking officials] will reply to me in English, although they speak perfect French. . . . Yesterday [we had] the first meeting without the [British], and still we all speak English" (#55).

German, in contrast to English and French, does not play a major role as a vehicular language, although it is recognized across all institutions as the EU's "third language." It derives this status, first, from Germany's position as Europe's political and economic powerhouse; second, the size of the German-speaking population in the EU (in Germany and beyond); and, third, the resulting size of German-speaking delegations, especially in the

Council and the EP. Moreover, German serves as the language of procedure in the Court of Justice particularly often, which makes it "an extremely important language" in the Court (#24) and when dealing with legal texts more generally (#56). Nevertheless, German is not frequently spoken in meetings in the EU institutions, except by some German speakers when interpretation is available, and it does not come even close to rivaling English or French as a shared language between EU actors (#11, 12).

The use of other languages inside the institutions largely depends on the size of national delegations representing various language communities. The size (and also the power) of the member states thus matters in determining the relative importance of a national language, but it does not translate one-to-one. One EP staffer, for example, suggests that "Slovakia is less important than Luxembourg because [Luxembourgers] speak German, English, and French."[10] The other main factor that determines the use of languages other than English, French, and German is the particular configuration of participants in a given meeting or interaction. One Council official, for example, emphasized that "a lot of people speak Italian, you'd be surprised" (#58). Another one described in more detail how

> we participated in drafting sessions during the Italian Presidency. . . . And it happened, it just happened this way, that the Commission representatives, four of them, were all Italians. And of course the Italian representatives, also three or four. . . . [And the representative from the] Council Secretariat, she was French, but she understands Italian, so she replied in French but she assumed all the information in Italian. . . . So 70 percent of the drafting session was Italian, while the text was in English on the screen. (#61)

In an attempt to generalize, one official described the use of languages in the Council as "the big three plus an opportunity language," by which she meant a fourth language that is the national language of the Council presidency or a function of the policy area under consideration: "it may be that in Fisheries sometimes Spanish is an easy language between various people, there are Spanish people in the Commission, Spanish people here, and so on. . . . That would be a matter of context" (#58).

There is some pushback against the dominance of English inside the institutions, but it is rare. The EP's former Secretary General, Klaus Welle, attempted "an intensive push" for greater use of German, according to one EP official; this proved futile, however, because "you cannot add a third [vehicular language] and you will not replace English or French, that's not realistic" (#12). Individual actors might also attempt to counteract the prevailing use of English. One German MEP thus insists on "speaking in German 90 percent of the time, consciously so, because I want to force the Brits to put on their headsets" (#45).

But the issue seems to have become less contested over time, at least according to one high-level Council official who has been serving in the institutions for several decades, who said that

> from time to time the Spaniards are sort of getting a bit upset about it, because after all Spanish is a world language. But . . . within Europe it's smaller. . . . It's a status issue, it's an issue of pride. . . . [But] we used to have very different debates about language, it has calmed down, more people are a bit more relaxed about it. (#52)

The main focus and concern for member states when it comes to the status of their language in the EU seems to be relative to "peer" languages. Sweden, for example, does not try to have Swedish rival English, French, or German, but merely wants to ensure that their language is "not discriminated against in relation to other comparable languages such as Danish, Finnish, Greek, and Portuguese" (#74).

Some EU institutions are, at times, described as more or less multilingual than others. Van der Jeught (2015), for example, maintains that the EP and the Court of Justice are the most multilingual institutions. This is certainly correct when we consider the extent to which the language regimes of the institutions are (formally or informally) more or less restricted, since the representational and legal dimensions of language (which, respectively, provide the basis for popular participation in EU politics and ensure the uniform application of EU law) are of greater importance in the EP and the Court of Justice and tilt their language regimes in favor of greater equality between languages. As a result, it is also correct that the EP and the Court of Justice are more multilingual in the extent to which different languages are used regularly in these institution. The EP, in particular, sees much greater language variation than the other institutions in its day-to-day operations. This, however, masks the extent to which individuals inside the different institutions rely on multiple languages in their day-to-day work (Wodak 2014, 141). By that measure, the Commission is more multilingual than the EP because Commission officials more frequently rely on multiple languages in their work and use them with greater facility. This is in part because foreign language proficiency is not a formal job requirement for lawmakers and turnover is much greater than it is for officials working in the Commission, but also because the representational role played by the directly elected delegates of the European people entails strong incentives to use native languages when communication is directed at national constituencies. In what follows, I briefly outline specific patterns in language use in each of the EU's main institutions, to qualify or add nuance to the general tendencies in language use just described.[11]

The Commission

The Commission's procedural languages are English, French, and German, as the institution indicated in proceedings before the EU Ombudsman in 2007. This was a rare formal acknowledgment of its internal language practices, which are not spelled out in the institution's Rules of Procedure (Van der Jeught 2015, 136–7). The main languages used in the College of Commissioners are English and French, as Kruse and Ammon found in their investigation of 996 oral contributions by all 27 EU commissioners over the course of one year: 55.92 percent of interventions were in English and 16.67 percent were in French. Some commissioners consistently spoke only their native language, however, which explains fairly high proportions in the use of Italian (6.1), Czech (5.7), Greek (5.5), German (5.22), and Spanish (4.58) (Kruse and Ammon 2013, 167).

Languages other than the procedural ones are only used when it is legally required, which are instances when all languages are equally authentic (i.e., legal texts or instruments of general application), when the addressee of a communication is entitled to it in another language, or on formal occasions and in public meetings with participants from the member states (Athanassiou 2006, 20). Overall, English has established itself as the main procedural language in the Commission, a status that used to be held by French. The use of German lags far behind both English and French; it is used when a sufficient number of participants in a given conversation share the language, which is also the case (on occasion) for some other languages like Spanish or Polish (Krzyżanowski 2014, 112). The fact that Commission officials speak multiple languages allows for such flexibility in language choice and the efficiency gains that come with it; as one Council official observed, the reality in the Commission is that the officials "always speak in languages other than their own" (#76). Commission officials are de facto multilingual, as both their recruitment and promotion in the institution depend in part on their language repertoires (Wodak 2013, 96).

The tide turned decisively against French as the main internal language of the Commission after the 2004 eastward enlargement, when few of the new officials that entered the institution spoke French, even though their language repertoires on average exceeded those of their colleagues from the old member states (Ban 2009). Today, one can still reasonably assume that everyone in the Commission has at least passive knowledge of both French and English and that most can comfortably speak either (Ban 2009). Moreover, some enclaves remain where French plays a more active role, such as the Commission's Legal Service and Secretariat-General (Van der Jeught 2015, 138). French also still dominates in a small number of Directorates-General (DGs), such as DG Human Resources and Security (Gravier and Lundquist 2016, 80).[12] The EU's quintessential supranational institution has thus adopted a rather restricted language regime, which reflects the Commission's "composition and operational requirements" and is "dictated by the imperatives of speed and efficiency" (Athanassiou 2006, 20). At the same time, however, new requirements that Commission staff members must master a third language prior to their first promotion also signal the institution's continued commitment to linguistic diversity (Ban 2013, 224).

The Council of the EU (Council of Ministers)

The Council's language regime is, on the surface, centered on the principle of the equality of all official languages, which stands to reason given that it is the institution in which the member states and their interests are represented and which adopts legislation, jointly with the EP, that is equally authentic in all language versions (Athanassiou 2006, 18). In practice, however, the Council of the EU relies on a full language regime only in its formal meetings and in a very limited number of preparatory meetings financed entirely from the Council budget.[13]

Language services are critical at this level because national politicians who come to Brussels to take final decisions on legislative matters often do not possess the foreign language skills to negotiate complex legislation (#16, 72); moreover, as delegates of their member states, they have an incentive to use their national language because they often address a national constituency, especially in meetings that are broadcast (Van der Jeught 2015, 135). Many of the detailed discussions, however, have already happened at the working group or Coreper (Committee of Permanent Representatives) levels, meaning that "language capacity and interpretation do not matter that much" because "in meetings with ministers in the Council there usually isn't much left to decide" (#59).

Meetings of Coreper, the Council's most important preparatory body, take place in English, French, and German. English still dominates, however, and even the French and Germans speakers understand English well enough that they probably do not actually need interpretation (#59). In meetings of attachés from the Permanent Representations "you mostly speak English, everybody does" (#68), and as you go down to the working group level, at least passive knowledge of English becomes more important (#58, 65). Preparatory meetings rely on restricted regimes or entirely on English; at the technical level "we are de facto just about monolingual" (#59), unless working groups are staffed by people from member state capitals or invited experts (#59, 65). In general, the more technical the level the more English is used, and "the higher the level, the more use of national languages" (#65).

Hence, English is very much the dominant language in the Council (#20, 58, 59, 60, 65, 68, 70, 71, 72), both among officials in the Council's administration and staff of the Permanent Representations. "I haven't come across anybody who didn't speak English in such a way that I couldn't understand," one Mertens counselor emphasized (#71). Only representatives from francophone countries will tend to intervene in French, and Germans and Austrians in German (#20, 58, 59, 72, 73), but "just about everyone else will in principle speak English, unless they are trying to show off their language or unless they are trying to pass a particular message" (#58). French is used to a much lesser extent in the Council than in the Commission, and the language of the rotating Council presidency may also gain temporary prominence but is usually not widely shared and thus of limited practical use. Even when a francophone member state held the Presidency, one respondent recalled, "we chaired in French . . . but we concluded meetings in English to be sure that everyone was involved."[14] Such limits on multilingualism are, according to the Council, "dictated by both practical considerations and budgetary constraints, in the interests of keeping operating expenditure down" (as quoted in Van der Jeught 2015, 135). Interpretation can be requested by member states and will be covered out of the Council's budget up to a certain amount,[15] beyond which the member state has to pick up the tab. Which working groups will be staffed with interpreters is thus largely decided by the Permanent Representations (#1).

Translation into all official languages is required for certain documents in the legislative process, of course, and when the Council is approached by and responds directly to EU citizens. Article 14 of the institutions' Rules of Procedure further provides that members of the Council "may oppose discussion if the texts of any proposed amendments are not drawn up in [one of the official language] as he or she may specify." The article also stipulates that legislation and other documents of general application cannot be adopted if they have not been drafted in all official languages, unless the member states unanimously agree to waive that requirement "on grounds of urgency."[16]

The European Parliament

The EP, one of my respondents claimed, "is the only real multilingual institution" (#83), because the representational dimension of language plays a particularly important role in an institution whose members are directly elected by EU citizens. On the one hand, MEPs cannot be required to possess foreign language skills in order to stand for election. On the other, in order to fulfill their representational mandates, MEPs must be able to effectively communicate with their constituents, which includes the option of speaking their own languages in EP meetings. There is, as a result, greater language variety in the everyday operations of the EP than in the other institutions and greater variation in "what people speak and what they understand" (#70; also 76).

Key provisions of the EP's Rules of Procedure (Rule 158) are that the EP draws up "all documents" in the official languages; that all members have the right to speak in Parliament in the official language of their choice; that speeches delivered in an official language shall be simultaneously interpreted into the other official languages; that interpretation shall be provided in committee and delegation meetings from and into the official languages used and requested by the members; and that "after the result of a vote has been announced, the [EP] President shall rule on any requests concerning alleged discrepancies between the different language versions." In practice, as spelled out by the EP's Code of Conduct on Multilingualism, the EP's "controlled" or "resource-efficient full" multilingualism approach means that there are varying "degrees" of multilingualism in EP meetings, depending on "real needs" of the particular MEPs taking part in a meeting (European Parliament 2014). Deviations from the language regime are also permissible if and to the extent that interpreters or translators for an official language are not available in sufficient numbers, "despite adequate precautions" (Van der Jeught 2015, 134), but such situations are rare. Meanwhile, informal and preparatory meetings take place primarily in English these days, and MEPs often (have to) rely on English-language documents when deliberating and negotiating, for example when their own language versions become available too late for those purposes. EP, party, and personal staff primarily use English and to a lesser extent French, but the use of French has declined markedly in the past two decades. One party official highlighted that his party group still expects advisors and other staff "to have really good English and more than good

French, because we consider both to be the official languages within our secretariat; [but] French is losing traction as we speak" (#39). Even a southern European MEP acknowledged that "the real important language here to communicate is English, not even French" (#44), even though southern Europeans in particular historically used to be francophone.

The EP plenary is the place in which one is most likely to hear many of the official languages, because MEPs choose to exercise their right to use their native language when speaking on the EP floor; Kruse and Ammon thus found that 88.4 percent of the EP speeches they considered were delivered in the speaker's native language (Kruse and Ammon 2013, 166). One southern European MEP described that, in committee, she uses one of three foreign languages she speaks (including English and French), depending on who is chairing the meeting and whom she is addressing. In plenary, however, she speaks her native language because she is addressing the public and media at home (#44). Notably, using even a "small" native language at this point in time does not impede MEPs' political effectiveness, one party group advisor explained, because "the plenary part in particular doesn't really have a role in the votes, because you've had another debate already that went on for several months in committee; it all has been kind of teased out" (#39).

The EP keeps track of the languages spoken in plenary and made those data available for the 2008–2014 period, which I used to calculate the percentage of each language spoken relative to the total speaking time for each year. Figure 2.1 shows EP plenary speaking time for big (more than 10 percent of speakers as a percentage of the total EU population: English, German, French, Italian), medium (3–9 percent of speakers: Spanish, Polish, Romanian, Dutch, Hungarian), and small languages (2 percent or less: all others).[17]

The figure shows a slight decrease in the use of big and small languages between 2008 and 2010, offset by an increase in the use of medium-sized languages. Between 2010 and 2012, big languages were used more, while the use of medium-sized languages declined and small-language use remained stable. From 2012 to 2014, big-language use again declined somewhat, while small-language use increased and medium-size-language use remained steady. Overall, there is no clearly identifiable pattern toward or away from languages of particular sizes. The same is true for the official languages of old (pre-2004) and new (post-2004) member states (fig. 2.2): the starting and end points in 2008 and 2014 are almost identical, with some ups and downs in between.

Figure 2.3, however, shows some notable trends in the use of the three

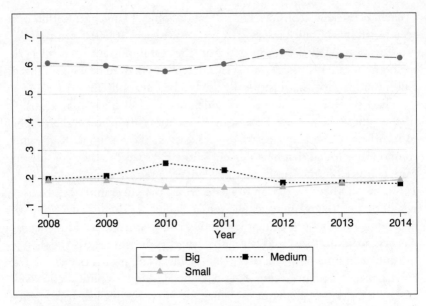

Fig. 2.1. Language Use in EP Plenary: Big, Medium, and Small Languages
(*Source:* Plenary Records Unit, European Parliament)

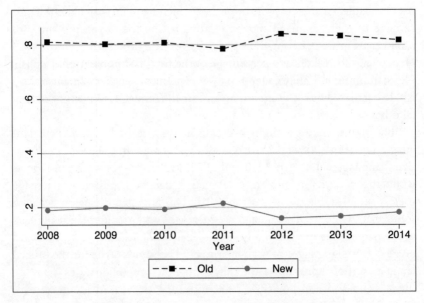

Fig. 2.2. Language Use in EP Plenary: Old vs. New Member States
(*Source:* Plenary Records Unit, European Parliament)

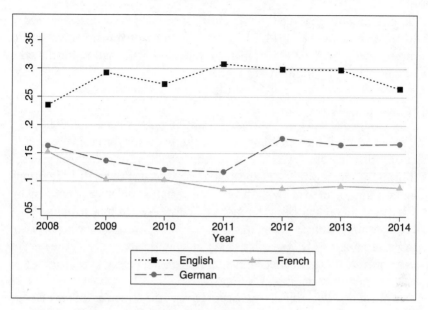

Fig. 2.3. Language Use in EP Plenary: The Big Three
(*Source:* Plenary Records Unit, European Parliament)

biggest languages: English, French, and German. There was greater reliance on English and German in 2014 than there was in 2008, but with different pattern in between: the use of English increased until about the middle of the EP's 2009–14 term (hitting a high point of 30.8 percent in 2011), and then declined. The use of German decreased from 2008 to 2011, then hit a high of 17.7 percent in 2012, and declined slightly thereafter. Most remarkable, however, is the decline of French as a language spoken in the EP plenary, from 15.2 percent of the time in 2008 to only about 9 percent after 2011.

The comparatively greater reliance on national languages in the EP relative to the other EU institutions is not, however, indicative of "language nationalism" (Forchtner 2014), nor is it suggestive of a "key ideology in the EP" that revolves around the "expression of national standpoints" (Wodak 2014, 131). These interpretations not only broadly misrepresent the nature of politics inside the EP, which revolves around left/right and pro-/anti-EU ideologies and is structured around competition between party groups (see especially Hix, Noury, and Roland 2007), they also confuse incentives that follow from the representational role of MEPs with their role as lawmakers. It is, in fact, only in the representational context that MEPs are "largely monolingual" and "tend to use just one language in their everyday work" (Krzyżanowski 2014, 115). In their substantive (legislative) work, most (have to) rely on other languages, in particular English, for the sake of internal communicative efficiency.

The Court of Justice of the EU

The Court of Justice is "inevitably" multilingual (Athanassiou 2006, 21), because it needs to communicate with the parties involved in a case and ensure that its case law is disseminated throughout the member states.[18] This is a prerequisite for giving equal access to justice to all EU citizens and to allow them to enjoy the protection of rights conferred upon them by EU law. The preliminary reference procedure—whereby a national court requests a preliminary ruling from the Court of Justice on the appropriate interpretation of EU law—plays a key role, in this regard, and the system can only function as intended if national judges and the affected parties can rely on their own languages.

One of the EU's official languages serves as the "language of the case" or the "language of procedure." It is chosen by the applicant in direct actions before the Court or, when the defendant is a member state or a natural or legal person holding its nationality, it is the official language of that country. In the case of preliminary rulings, the language of procedure is that of the national court that made the request, but the request is translated into all languages and forwarded to the member states (Wagner, Bech, and Martínez 2014, 55). The language of procedure is used in written and oral proceedings, including correspondences with the parties of the case (McAuliffe 2008, 808), although witnesses and experts can use their own languages before the Court and be interpreted (Kraus 2008, 117). Member states are also entitled to use their own language in their written or oral submissions (McAuliffe 2012, 203). One implication of having a language of procedure—and something that sets the Court apart from the other institutions—is that much work in the Court is actually conducted in the small official languages (#33). In that (narrow) sense, it is true that in the Court, "all languages are equally important from a legal point of view" and taken "equally seriously" (#21).

While English has come to dominate proceedings in the other institutions, the internal and administrative language of the Court is French. This makes French "a bit special, but it does not mean the French version is more important, it has simply a different status in the production line" (#21, also 33). The Court relies on French-language texts (either drafts or translations) for its day-to-day operations, and deliberations between the judges occur mostly in French (and also, at times, in English)[19] and always without interpretation. Texts are authentic only in the language of procedure (McAuliffe 2008, 808), but judgments are drafted in French and then translated into the language of the case and into all official languages.

Horspool (2006) traces the dominance of French back to the origins of the Court in the 1950s, when the founding treaties of the early European Communities were closely aligned with the rules of French administrative law, when most legal texts intended for an international audience were written in French, and when French was the language used in communications between international legal experts (including jurists in the member states). In the absence of the UK, French was thus a natural and acceptable choice for the six original member states as the Communities' legal language. It has persisted as the working language of the Court for a number of mutually reinforcing reasons. One is the insulation of the Court in Luxembourg from the day-to-day politics of the EU and the interactions of the other institutions therein. Simply put, the rise of English in one institution affects language use in other institutions if interactions between their members are commonplace, as is the case for the Commission, the EP, and the Council. Contacts between Court officials and their counterparts in the other institutions are more limited, which is further reinforced by their geographic isolation in Luxembourg. Another important reason lies in the longer and overlapping tenures of judges, who are individually recruited into a French-speaking group of peers that is quite stable over time. There are only one or very few newcomers at any one moment in time, and those newcomers are selected in part because of their ability to operate and deliberate in French; it is thus unlikely that their inclusion in the Court would change its linguistic culture (#21). This was true even at the time of the 2004 "big bang" enlargement, when the Court incorporated a large group of new members, all of whom were chosen in part in consideration of their French language skills. In other words, while the other institutions experienced an influx of new people, many of whom did not speak French, newcomers at the Court necessarily had some French.[20]

The judges are, in effect, only expected to know French, and even though judges and Advocates General are entitled to use any language (Athanassiou 2006, 22), they have effectively waived that right (McAuliffe 2008, 808). Since 2004, some the Advocates General no longer use their mother tongues to draft their opinions but one of the "pivot languages" of the Court (English, French, German, Spanish, Italian, and Polish, which serve as "bridges" for translation between lesser-used languages) (McAuliffe 2012, 208). All this means that

> The Court preserves multilingualism as an institution but becomes a monolingual decision-maker. . . . A common working language is superimposed on a multilingual institution where the language of the procedure, the languages of the intervening governments, the language in which the AG [Advocate General] delivers the opinion and the working language of the formation (always French) will usually always differ. (Bengoetxea 2016, 106)

And while English has found its way into the Court and is increasingly used "in staff training seminars; on the Court's intranet site; for communications from the administration; in corridors and canteens" (McAuliffe 2008, 816), French remains the dominant language.

Language Services in the EU Institutions

The language services of the EU are the largest in the world not just in terms of size, but also in terms of the variety of languages and subject areas covered.[21] The main language services provided are the interpretation of oral proceedings and the translation of texts to and from all official languages and, if needed, into a variety of others (for example when a foreign dignitary visits the institutions), as well as the efforts by lawyer-linguists to ensure the legal equivalence of all language version of EU legislation.[22] Translators and interpreters make up a substantial proportion of total staff in the four main institutions, namely about 7.5 percent in the Commission, about 20 percent in the Council, about 13 percent in the EP, and about 30 percent in the Court of Justice.[23]

Interpretation

Simultaneous interpretation of oral proceedings is offered by specialized units housed in the Commission, the EP, and the Court of Justice. DG Interpretation is the unit in the Commission that provides interpretation services for the Commission, the Council of the European Union (Council of Ministers), and the European Council (the meeting of the heads of state and government of the member states). It also helps cover the Committee of the Regions, the European Economic and Social Committee, the European Investment Bank, and agencies and offices in EU member states. Part of its responsibilities are the allocation of Commission meeting rooms for meetings and conferences. In 2016, its total staff was 760, of which 529 were interpreters who could interpret from an average of 4 foreign languages into their mother tongue (European Commission 2016a, 3).[24]

Seventy percent of interpreters were women. In addition to staff interpreters, the DG relied on 3,000 accredited freelancers who worked at least ten days in 2016. DG Interpretation assigns 600 to 800 people daily to 40 to 60 meetings (#10) and provides about 100,000 "interpreter days" (one full work day of one interpreter) per year, of which about half are covered by freelancers.[25] Most interpretation services are provided to the Council and the Commission (which has meetings in both Brussels and Luxembourg), who together used 89 percent of the total services offered in 2016 (the Council 60 percent, the Commission 29 percent) (European Commission 2016a, 29). Sixty-three percent of meetings in the Commission that year had interpretation, of which 47 percent had interpretation for 2–6 languages, 9 percent for 7–11 languages, and 4 percent each for 12–17 languages and 18–23 languages. Of the meetings with interpretation, 98 percent had interpretation into English, 74 percent into French, 59 percent into German, 51 percent into Spanish, and 49 percent into Italian. The languages with the least interpretation were Finnish (offered in 9 percent of meetings), Estonian (9 percent), and Danish (7 percent) (European Commission 2016a, 110). The number of interpreters in meetings exceeds 70 for meetings with a full language regime.[26] The languages with the greatest number of interpreters in 2019 were English (51), German (48), and French (46), and those with the fewest are Maltese (7) and Croatian (5).[27] The DG gives as the total interpretation cost 119.5 million euros in 2016 (or 0.24 euros per citizen), for a total of 0.08 percent of the EU budget.

In the EP, interpretation is provided by DG Interpretation and Conferences, which employed 275 staff interpreters in early 2019.[28] Of the about 110,000 interpreter days provided per year, half are again covered by freelancers. The Court of Justice and the General Court of the EU also have their own Interpretation Directorate. The 70 or so staff interpreters must not only have the relevant linguistic capacities for their jobs, but also knowledge of the law and the specialized vocabulary that comes with it, both in the EU legal system and their national contexts. Since French is the main working language of the Court, knowledge of that language is of particular importance, for example to study case documents that may not be available in other languages. These special requirements entail that only about 23 percent of the roughly 12,000 interpreter days per year are covered by freelancers.

Assigning interpreters to meetings is a complex process of balancing supply and demand. Demand is driven by the language needs of participants in various meetings, the number of meetings scheduled at a given time, and the relative importance of those meetings. Supply is a function of the availability of interpreters (which depends in part on rules about working time and conditions), meeting rooms (since only some rooms can accommodate meetings with large numbers of interpreters), and efforts to contain the costs of multilingualism. The process of assigning interpretation in the European Parliament illustrates the complicated nature of the exercise (as described by #3, 8, 10, 11), which is governed by the EP's Code of Conduct on Multilingualism. The Code of Conduct specifies, first, the order of priority for interpretation (Article 2). The greatest priority is thus the EP's plenary sitting, followed by so-called "priority political meetings," such as meetings of the President, the EP's governing bodies, and Conciliation Committees (in the context of the ordinary legislative procedure). Beyond these general meetings, priority is given based on the EP's calendar, which dedicates certain weeks to committee work and others to the work of the political (party) groups. During committee periods, priority is given to meetings of parliamentary committees, delegations, and trilogues; during political group periods, meetings organized by the political groups take priority.[29] The Code of Conduct (Article 7) also imposes an upper limit of 16 per day on the number of parallel meetings with interpretation (except during plenary week and "subject to the availability of Human Resources"), of which at most 5 may have coverage of up to 23 languages, at most 4 of up to 16 languages, at most 5 of up to 12 languages, and at most 2 of up to 6 languages. These rules, combined with regulations governing the working conditions for interpreters and the practical availability of meeting rooms, mean that there is not actually much leeway in the assignment of interpretation. The assignment process is thus fairly technical, as one respondent emphasized: "To be honest, we don't even check who is asking for interpretation because we have so many requests" (#11). In contradiction to such assurances, at least one observer suspects that political considerations do come into play, at least at times. She suggests that "if [name of prominent MEP] asks to have interpretation, no one dares to say no" and that "if, for example, the head of European Central Bank was coming and . . . from one day to another you need 15 teams of interpreters, you will have these 15 teams. So all the rules could be bent, could be broken, if it was really in the interest of Parliament" (#12).

When a request for interpretation comes in that complies with the rules laid out in the Code of Conduct on Multilingualism, it is fed into the responsible unit's IT system. Once all meeting request for a given week are in, the pool of staff interpreters available is determined along with the necessary number of freelancers to cover all meetings and language combinations. When the right number of freelancers has been recruited, both staff interpreters and freelancers are assigned to the meetings in part in anticipation of how much each language will be spoken by meeting participants (i.e., a greater number of interpreters may be assigned if a particular language will be spoken a lot). If covering a certain language is a problem because of limited staff,[30] the planning unit may contact the requester to inquire if that language must absolutely be present, and it may be dropped from the request. If this is not possible, the meeting may have to be postponed.[31]

The interpretation needs of some meetings are fairly predictable because of stable membership (e.g., committee meetings), but others are more difficult to plan ahead for. The group of participants in rapporteur–shadow rapporteur meetings[32] or trilogues, for example, may be established ad hoc (#10), and adjustments have to be made on relatively short notice. This has been a challenge given the proliferation of trilogue meetings brought about by the greater incidence of early agreements (Reh et al. 2013), and the need for flexibility clashes with the requirement that requests be made at least three weeks in advance (Conduct of Conduct on Multilingualism, Article 8.1. [European Parliament 2014]).

Data on interpretation requests in the EP between 2004 and 2014 allow us to discern some basic patterns over time; unfortunately, earlier data are not available, which means that a comparison to the pre-2004 enlargement situation is not possible. I calculated the proportion of requests for each language relative to the total number of requests for each year.[33] Figure 2.4 shows EP interpretation requests for the same big, medium-sized, and small languages as above (see fig. 2.1). It shows little variance for medium-sized languages, while there are some ups and downs for big and small languages. The bands in variance, however, are fairly narrow (2.7 percent for big and 3.4 percent for small languages), and there is no clear trend toward or away from languages of different sizes.

There is, however, a slight trend toward more requests for English, as figure 2.5 indicates: the percentage of requests increases from 9.5 percent in 2004 to 12.1 percent in 2013 before it drops down to 11.2 percent in 2014. Another—and more obvious—trend is apparent in figure 2.6, which shows a decrease in interpretation requests for languages of the pre-2004 member states (from a high of 75.7 percent in 2005 to 66.3 percent in 2014) and an increase of interpretation requests for new member state languages (from a low of 25.9 percent to 32.9 percent in 2014).[34]

The data I received from the Commission's DG Interpretation are slightly different from the information on interpretation requests in the EP. It shows the number of "interpreter days" from January 1, 2000, to

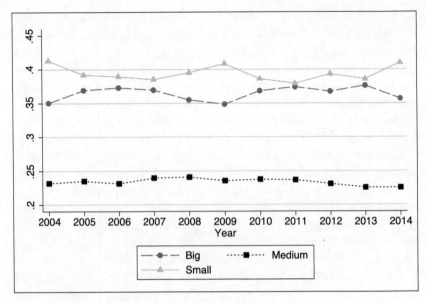

Fig. 2.4. Interpretation Requests (DG LINC): Big, Medium, and Small Languages
(*Source:* DG Interpretation and Conferences, European Parliament)

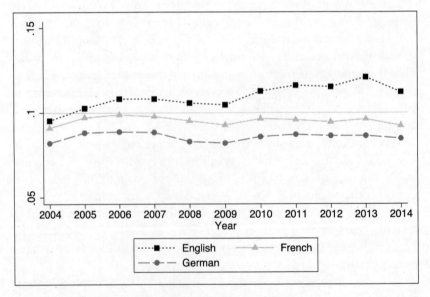

Fig. 2.5. Interpretation Requests (DG LINC): The Big Three
(*Source:* DG Interpretation and Conferences, European Parliament)

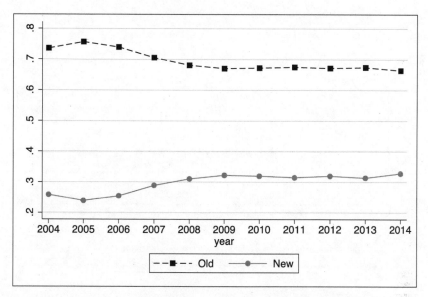

Fig. 2.6. Interpretation Requests (DG LINC): Old vs. New Member States
(*Source:* DG Interpretation and Conferences, European Parliament)

October 30, 2016, covering interpretation services provided in the Commission, the Council, the Committee of the Regions, the European Economic and Social Committee, the European Investment Bank, and the agencies and offices in the member states. An "interpreter day" includes not only the time spent in the interpretation booth, but also preparation time, time spent traveling to an assignment, "stand-by" times, and the like.

Figure 2.7 shows the proportion of interpreter days over time for big, medium-sized, and small languages. There is an overall decline over time in the proportion of interpreter days of the four big languages, from 59 percent in 2000 to 40 percent in 2016. This decline is fairly comparable for all four languages, as figure 2.8 demonstrates. The proportion of small language interpreter days increases (from 20 percent in 2000 to 36 percent in 2016), while the proportion of medium languages remains fairly steady.

Since these data go back to 2000, we can see that changes over time are driven to a substantial degree by the eastward enlargement of the EU, as illustrated in figure 2.9: the proportion of interpreter days for the languages of the old EU-15 member states decreases after 2004 (from 98 percent in 2003 to 67 percent in 2016), while the share of interpreter days for the new, post-2004 member state languages increases (from just over 1 percent in 2003 to 10 percent in 2004 to 32 percent in 2016).[35] Since about

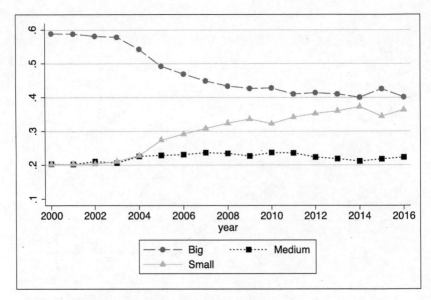

Fig. 2.7. Interpretation Days (DG SCIC): Big, Medium, and Small Languages
(*Source:* DG Interpretation, European Commission)

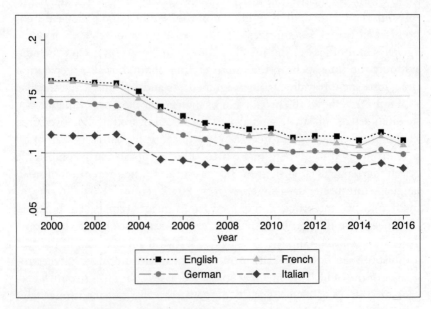

Fig. 2.8. Interpretation Days (DG SCIC): The Big Four
(*Source:* DG Interpretation, European Commission)

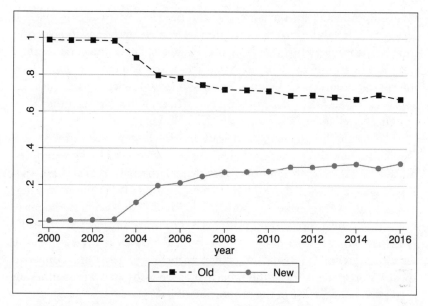

Fig. 2.9. Interpretation Days (DG SCIC): Old vs. New Member States
(*Source:* DG Interpretation, European Commission)

2011, the numbers have held fairly steady, however, suggesting that a new equilibrium may have been reached.

DG Interpretation also provided data on so-called "interpretation slots" (or "i-slots"), which are based on the unit's invoicing system: it identifies charges by DG Interpretation for services rendered (i.e., for the provision of interpretation into different languages) in both the Commission and the Council, by month and by language, for the time period from January 1, 2007, to November 30, 2016. An i-slot corresponds to roughly half a day of interpretation. For each month and language, the proportion of i-slots covered by staff interpreters and freelance interpreters was calculated, respectively, relative to the total number of staff and freelance i-slots; for example, one observation is that 4.1 percent of the staff i-slots in January 2007 covered Danish. A third variable aggregates the staff and freelancer i-slots.

These proportions are the outcome variables in a series of linear regression analyses with language fixed effects. The predictors are the percentage of native speakers of each official language and the percentage of nonnative speakers (in the EU as a whole),[36] as well as dichotomous variables capturing whether a member state associated with a language held the

Council presidency at a given moment in time and whether the language serves as a "relay language" (interpreting from relay means interpreting indirectly through a pivot, or bridging, language; for example, rather than interpreting from Slovenian into Swedish, a Slovenian intervention will be interpreted into French by one person and from French into Swedish by another).[37] The final predictor variable is the number of years that have passed since a language became an official EU language.

The results for the combined staff and freelancer i-slots in table 2.1 (Model 1) show that newer official languages are covered by a greater proportion of i-slots; each additional year that a language has been an official EU language is associated with a 0.7 percent decrease in the proportion of i-slots. Moreover, when a country associated with an official language holds the Council presidency, it is covered by a greater number of i-slots (+0.7 percent), as is the case when the language serves as a relay language for interpretation (+7.3 percent). The percentages of native and nonnative speakers of a language, on the other hand, are associated with neither an increase nor a decrease in the proportion of i-slots.

Looking separately at staff (Model 2) and freelancer i-slots (Model 3) reveals that the length of time since a language became an official EU language is not associated with the proportion of staff interpreter i-slots, but

TABLE 2.1. Predicting i-Slots

	Model 1: Staff & Freelancers	Model 2: Staff	Model 3: Freelancers
% Native speakers	−.2634	.0073	−.2055
	(.4327)	(.1735)	(.3133)
% Nonnative speakers	−.0437	.1073	−.1784
	(.1993)	(.0799)	(.1443)
# of years official language	−.0072***	−.0003	−.0049***
	(.0019)	(.0008)	(.0014)
Presidency	.0074*	.0044***	−.0006
	(.0034)	(.0014)	(.0025)
Relay language	.0725***	.0256***	.019***
	(.0031)	(.0013)	(.0024)
Freelancer slots		.1893***	
		(.0071)	
Staff slots			.6174***
			(.0232)
Constant	.0839***	.0123***	.0455***
	(.0084)	(.0034)	(.0061)
R^2	.6682	.8001	.4884
Adj R^2	.6592	.7954	.4743
N	5,498	5,498	5,498

Data source: DG Interpretation, European Commission.
Note: ***$p < 0.001$, **$p < 0.01$, *$p < 0.05$

that older official languages are less likely to be covered by freelancers (–0.5 percent for each additional year a language has been an official EU language). Languages associated with the Council presidency are covered by a greater number of staff interpreter i-slots (+0.4), while the predictor is not statistically significant for freelancer i-slots. This suggests that the assignment of i-slots seeks to ensure high-quality translation for the language of the Presidency through greater reliance on staff interpreters. Relay languages are covered by greater proportions of both staff (+2.6 percent) and freelancer i-slots (+1.9),[38] and there is a positive and statistically significant relationship between the proportion of staff and freelancer i-slots.

In sum, the results show that

- Newer languages get more total i-slots, but those slots are more likely to be covered by freelancers.
- The language of the Presidency is covered by more total i-slots and is more likely to be covered by staff interpreters.
- Relay languages are covered by more total slots, more staff slots, and more freelancer slots.
- The numbers of native or foreign speakers of a language are unrelated to the assignment of interpreters.[39]

Translation

The four main institution each have their own translation service, with 1,600 translators working in the Commission's, 660 in the EP's, 688 in the Council's (which also covers the European Council), and more than 600 in the Court's in 2016.[40] In the Commission, the languages with the greatest number of designated translators are—as in the case of interpreters—English, German, and French; Irish has the fewest.[41] Relatively smaller translation units also exist in the Court of Auditors, the European Central Bank, the European Investment Bank, and one for the Committee of the Regions and the European Economic and Social Committee. Finally, the Translation Centre for the Bodies of the European Union in Luxembourg offers translation services to 61 EU agencies and other bodies.

While Wagner, Bech, and Martínez (2014, 67) suggest that "in the EU institutions, the majority of translators spend most of their time translating outgoing documents," a great many—and the most important—documents translated in the Commission, the EP, and the Council relate to the legislative process. They include proposed legislative acts, final texts, and documents that are needed for informed decision making along the way. Aside from making legislative proposals available in all official languages, the translation services variously cover policy documents, reports, and statements; background papers; international agreements; reports to and communications with other EU institutions; speeches; minutes of meetings; press releases; information brochures and promotional materials; and webpages. Translators in the Commission, in particular, are also busy dealing with correspondence with citizens, stakeholders, and member state authorities. The Commission's service translated 2.2 million pages in 2016 (one page is about 1,500 typed characters without spaces) (European Commission 2016b); approximately one-quarter of translations are handled by freelancers. In 2012, the Council's translation service processed 13,000 documents, for a total of about 1 million pages.[42] In the Court of Justice, 1.1 million pages were translated each year between 2014 and 2016, of which between 26 percent and 36 percent were covered by external translators.[43] The Court is out of the ordinary when it comes to translation in that the translators employed by the Court have relevant legal qualifications in addition to being trained as translators.

Translators across institutions must be able to cover many different types of documents across a wide range of policy areas (Robinson 2014b, 200). Most have also developed considerable expertise in legislative matters and are intimately familiar with EU institutions, procedures, and terminology (Robinson 2014a). There are some efforts made, for example in the Commission (#15), to allow translators to specialize in particular policy areas so that they become familiar with the subject, existing rules, and relevant specialized terminology (Robinson 2014a), but most translators have to be policy generalists.

Lawyer-Linguists

A special role in the translation process is fulfilled by so-called lawyer-linguists, whose responsibility is to ensure the linguistic and legal equivalence of all language versions of EU legislation so they produce the same legal effect. Lawyer-linguists are thus "professionals with a rare blend of skills: capable lawyers with outstanding abilities in several languages and an innate flair for discerning precisely what EU legislation and complicated court decisions are intended to convey" (Šarčević and Robertson 2013, 201). In the words of one lawyer-linguists in the Court of Justice, their job involves "walking a tightrope, continuously trying to balance their responsibilities as linguists with their responsibilities as lawyers" (as quoted in McAuliffe 2010, 243).[44]

Lawyer-linguists play a critical role in the EU's legislative process, when the texts are not yet fixed and language versions can be compared and adjusted. The profession dates back to the late 1960s or early 1970s (Šarčević and Robertson 2013), but lawyer-linguists used to be involved only at the final stage of the legislative process in the past, when the final text was more or less fixed. Today, they are more and more involved in earlier stages to offer guidance on drafting matters and to identify possible problems and ambiguities before texts are finalized. In other words, the focus of their work has shifted from ensuring the correspondence of the different language versions toward improving the drafting of original texts (Robinson 2014a; Šarčević 2013). Indeed, the role of lawyer-linguists now extends into the realm of negotiation, as they are "increasingly becoming involved at earlier stages when they offer advice on drafting and legislative matters generally" (Robinson 2012, 13). In the words of one lawyer-linguist:

> We can only advise, but we can't ultimately take any decisions. When an MEP introduces an amendment, negotiations are taking place in trilogues, the Council makes a proposal, the EP reacts, at that point the lawyer-linguist would become involved and say, "listen, that for-mulation is ambiguous, this is stated too open-ended, it is not clear enough." That's ultimately our role. (#9)

Lawyer-linguists are thus not policymakers, with their role narrowly focused on the language of legislation, but their involvement linguistically circum-scribes the deliberations, negotiations, and decisions of policymakers.

Lawyer-linguists are employed by all four core institutions of the EU, where they play slightly different roles depending on the institution's role in the creation or adjudication of EU law. The work of the 60 or so lawyer-linguists in the Commission, who are referred to as *legal revisers*, consists principally of the legal-linguistic revision of draft EU legislative texts. This includes not only revision of the target texts to eliminate inconsistencies and errors, but also the simultaneous legal and linguistic revision of all language versions, including the base text. Lawyer-linguists are part of the Quality of Legislation teams in the Commission and key actors in the internal consultation stage that precedes the translation of proposed legis-lation into all official languages and its submission to the Council and the Parliament (Šarčević and Robertson 2013).

The about 90 lawyer-linguists each in the Council (aka *jurist-linguists* or *legal-linguistic experts*) and the EP (aka *reviser lawyer-linguists*) become involved only after the draft legislation has been received by their insti-tutions, but their work also consists for the most part of linguistic revi-sion, along with involvement at the working party stage to provide drafting advice "because a lot of the text are drafted by nonnative speakers, so it is good if we can clean it up a little bit" (#5). In the Council, four lawyer-linguists per language form the "Quality of Legislation" Directorate, which is part of the Council's Legal Service. In the EP, three or four lawyer-linguists per language (with a few more in English, given the dominance of the language in legislative drafting) work in the Legislative Quality Units within the Legislative Acts Directorate in the Directorate-General for the Presidency of the Parliament (Šarčević and Robertson 2013).

EP lawyer-linguists in the past were "checking everything that members produced," but today they focus entirely on legislative documents and "providing drafting advice," which they do as part of policy teams of between two and eight lawyer-linguists who support committee work (depending on the legislative work load of the committee and, to a lesser extent, its linguistic makeup) (#4). This puts them in a position to raise a red flag early on when potentially problematic language is included in a draft text (#9). Lawyer-linguists in the EP have also been playing an increasingly active role in the amendment process, in that they help rapporteurs, committees, and individual members draft high-quality amendments that will translate well into the other official languages (#4, 9, 19). In 2014, the EP introduced a new process for this purpose, whereby MEPs can get help from lawyer-linguists when introducing an amendment by using specialized software (#4, 19), in whatever language they choose (#19). Lawyer-linguists also check amendments that are submitted, as well as other texts that are relevant to the legislative process, and drafters may well "get a phone call after a couple of days from them saying 'what exactly did you mean by this, this isn't really particularly well written'" (#39). Lawyer-linguists have also become more involved at the stage of the legislative process when compromise amendments are prepared and introduced, which usually involves nonnative speakers "negotiating a deeply internal political compromise very quickly" and can result in "compromise amendments which are very, very unclear and there is little you can do afterwards" (#4).

Aside from providing drafting advice, the core responsibility of lawyer-linguists in the EP and the Council is to compare different language versions of a text to ensure their consistency,[45] a task led by the "file coordinator" in the EP and the "quality advisor" in the Council, who are appointed once a proposal under the ordinary legislative procedure arrives from the Commission (Guggeis and Robinson 2012, 68). One EP lawyer-linguist describes how "we receive the text and look through it, literally word for word, to make sure it matches the draft language version. We check if legal terms have been used correctly, since it has to be legal language, not just some translation" (#9). This often requires difficult and highly consequential decisions, as the example offered by a respondent in the Council illustrates: if the English version of a text referred to "nationals" of a given country, it would not be obvious if the term included so-called "noncitizens" in Latvia (former citizens of the Soviet Union who reside in Latvia but do not possess Latvian citizenship). The lawyer-linguist comparing the English and Latvian versions of the text would then have to determine if the intent of the legislator was to focus narrowly on *citizens* of a country or if the term ought to be translated in a more inclusive fashion (#2). Discussions about terminology are often quite complex as a result. An EP official recalled the following illustrative episode:

> When I came to Parliament as a trainee . . . I went with one of my supervisors to a meeting with lawyer-linguists about a piece of legislation. And they really spent 40 minutes discussing, "well, in my language I can't say that, so I'll say that instead." I think there were six nationalities, and six of them came up with different problems for the same word. (#12)

Lawyer-linguists in the EP and the Council cooperate throughout the lawmaking process to avoid such ambiguities or, at the least, to ensure that the two institutions are on the same page, by "sending the text back and forth" (#9) in a process called legal-linguistic revision. The final step, designed to ensure smooth transposition into national legal code (#9), involves lawyer-linguists from both institutions jointly finalizing all the language versions of legislation that has been agreed upon, to iron out any formal problems in the draft language version of the legislation and to ensure that all translations produce the same legal effect (Robinson 2014b, 201). Also involved at this "legal-linguistic verification" or "legal-linguistic finalization" stage are representatives of the member states, the Council Secretariat, and the Commission (usually the person who drafted the original proposal), as well as lawyer-linguists from the EP and the Council (Guggeis and Robinson 2012, 69).[46] Notably, legal-linguistic verification may even include revisions of the base text, as long as no substantive changes are made, to eliminate inconsistencies and improve precision through what is called "retroaction" (Robinson 2014b, 201–2; see also Šarčević 2013).

The role of lawyer-linguists in the Court of Justice differs from those in the other institutions in that the focus of their work is not the revision of (draft) texts, but the translation of court documents and judgments. The other difference between the Court and the other institutions is the sheer number of lawyer-linguists, as the Court employs six hundred of them;[47] in fact, all of its translators have the legal training necessary to process documents required for the Court's judicial proceedings and to make the Court's decisions available in all official languages. Lawyer-linguists in the Court work in language units within the Directorate for Translation; those working in the Court's pivot languages are particularly important for the functioning of legal translation, and some are charged with providing linguistic assistance in the drafting process (McAuliffe 2010, 254).

Across the institutions, the job of lawyer-linguists is highly complex. It requires them, first, to possess comprehensive knowledge of the EU's legal system, the legal system of their member state, the legal systems of other member states, and how they relate to each other (McAuliffe 2009, 103). Second, they need to balance their roles as lawyers and linguists, which are often and perhaps inherently at odds with one another. In this regard, McAuliffe's observation about lawyer-linguists in the Court also applies to their counterparts in the other institutions:

> On the one hand, lawyers are defined relative to the definite and determinate concept of "the law"; on the other, translators' role definitions are based on the acceptance of the indeterminate nature of language and translation. The two professions, in their respective professional norms, appear to be incompatible; yet, in the context of the lawyer-linguists at the Court of Justice of the European Communities, they are brought together. (McAuliffe 2010, 241)

Third, it is not enough for lawyer-linguists to be competent lawyers with expertise across legal system and skilled linguists capable of navigating the vagaries and ambiguities of legal translation, they also need to possess the negotiating skills necessary to convince legislators of the merits of their suggestions, because their modifications are not mandatory and may be challenged by policymakers (Guggeis 2014). A point to which we will return in more detail in chapter 6 is that this is often far from an easy task, when the very ambiguities the lawyer-linguist seeks to eliminate may facilitate compromise and prove politically expedient.

While the different language services operate separately, they collaborate across institutions when it comes to terminological issues, in particular using terminology databases and glossaries such as Euramis, an interinstitutional system to store and retrieve translation memories. Perhaps most important is IATE (Inter-Active Terminology for Europe), an interinstitutional database for EU-related terminology covering more than eight million terms in the 24 official languages. IATE is the largest terminology database in the world and in 2016 received 36.5 million queries in its public version and 18.5 million queries in its internal institutional version (Translation Centre for the Bodies of the European Union 2017). Language service providers working on the same legislative proposals will also check in with each other on an ad hoc basis to confer on proper terminology and conduct quality checks along the way. Beyond that, some interpreters, translators, and lawyer-linguists of the same "language community" have their own formal meetings or informal shared meals or get-togethers for the sake of exchanging information, discussing difficult terms they have encountered in their work, sharing best practices, or building language-specific glossaries. Such channels appear more common and important for the smaller-language communities, but there are also regular meetings, for example, between French interpreters in the Commission and the EP (#24). There is also variation between different types of service providers, with lawyer-linguists apparently most likely to cooperate across institutional borders (see also Guggeis 2014). Finally, there are exchange programs between interpretation services, where interpreters from one institution spend several weeks or months in another institution, for example.

Part 2: Does It Work?

Having described language use and language services in detail, in Part 2 this chapter relies on the interview data to establish how the EU's language regime works in practice. My findings and evaluation do not discount the validity of some of the criticisms that are commonly leveled against EU multilingualism, but they are overall more positive than previous commentary. The bottom line is that in the opinion of those working inside the institutions, the EU language regime works quite well. My respondents offer four main explanations for this reality: the high quality of the language services offered; sufficient opportunities to catch and correct potential problems at various stages of the EU's policymaking process; EU actors' tolerance of other people's language handicaps; and reliance on "EU English" as a shared working language.

The primary criterion I apply in my evaluation of the EU's language regime is whether it meets the needs of those "participating" in institutional multilingualism in their own minds. This reflects the main focus of this book: the impact of multilingualism on politics and policymaking in the EU. For that reason, I am mostly concerned with the third criticism of EU multilingualism discussed below: that multilingualism so commonly leads to mistakes, misunderstandings, and uncertainties that EU policymaking is seriously hampered. Before assessing this critique, however, I will consider two other common criticisms, which relate to the monetary costs of multilingualism and to concerns about language equality and the "right" number of languages. Evaluating those critiques is complicated, however, by their fundamentally normative nature. After all, whether the EU expends too much money on language services depends entirely on one's preconception of how much it *should* be spending; there is no objective measure of what is too much. Similarly, what constitutes the "right" number of official or procedural languages reflects different normative concerns and, as a result, different criteria for evaluation; moreover, each proposed solution entails problems of its own. It is for those reasons, among others outlined below, that I avoid treating EU multilingualism as a "problem" to be "solved." Instead, I briefly and critically discuss proposed solutions before considering whether the EU's language regime is perceived to be working for and by those inside the institutions (in the remainder of this chapter) and how it affects EU politics and policymaking in practice (in the remainder of the book).

Critique 1: The Costs of Multilingualism

The substantial costs of maintaining a multilingual regime involving 24 official languages is one important point of critique of EU language policy that is especially prevalent in journalistic coverage of the topic.[48] Calculating the exact costs of multilingualism in the EU is far from easy, however. The most straightforward way to go about it is to focus on the amount of money the EU spends on its language services. A Commission press release from September 2013 offers such a calculus:

> The total cost of translation and interpretation in all the EU institutions (including the European Commission, European Parliament, the Council, Court of Justice of the European Union, European Court of Auditors, European Economic and Social Committee, Committee of Regions) is around €1 billion per year. This represents less than 1 percent of the EU budget or just over €2 per citizen.[49]

Today's expenditures on language services remain at a similar level. The total costs covering the language services for all institutions are estimated to be about €1.1 billion, which is about 0.8 percent of the 2018 EU budget.[50]

The problem with such numbers is that they can variously, and reasonably, be presented as either very large or rather minor. It is certainly true that total expenditures of €1 billion mean that a large amount of money is spent on language services and that they really do make up a large portion of the EU institution's budgets; Clark and Priestley (2012, 164) identify languages as the single biggest cost factor in the EP, making up about one-third of the EP's budget. But it has—also reasonably—been pointed out that just because a service is expensive "does not mean that it is *ipso facto* too expensive" (Gazzola 2006, 400, citing Grin 1997, 4). Moreover, the expenditures really are small as a percentage of the EU's total budget, never mind as a proportion of the member states' overall economic prosperity: the monetary cost of multilingualism amounted to 0.0085 percent of EU's GDP in 2012 (Gazzola 2016b). And indeed, maintaining multilingualism at a cost equivalent to the (often cited) "one cup of coffee per citizen" does not seem overly burdensome (especially when considering that the budget allocated to language services has not increased proportionally to increases in the number of official languages over time). There is, in other words, room for cherry picking when it comes to either decrying or justifying the costs of multilingualism, and perceptions of whether the services are too expensive ultimately depend on the subjective value an observer places on them (Gazzola 2006).[51] Those perceptions are also not necessarily coherent, as the results of a recent Eurobarometer survey suggest. In it, 53 percent of respondents "totally" or "tended to" agree that the European institutions should adopt one single language to communicate with European citizens, yet 81 percent also totally or tended to agree that all languages spoken in the EU should be treated equally.[52] A substantial proportion of those surveyed, in other words, wanted all languages to be equal yet one to serve as the EU's main language of communication with its citizens. A similar disconnect can be observed among some member states who "want to reduce the EU budget, but at the same time they want us to translate more documents," as the Commission spokesman for education, culture, and multilingualism once put it (Simon 2012).

A number of observers have also argued that focusing only on the direct monetary costs of multilingualism is problematic in the first place. Several point to indirect costs in the form of administrative inconveniences, delays in the availability of documents, and the postponement of meetings when interpretation it not available (Fidrmuc 2011; Fidrmuc and Ginsburgh 2007; Kraus 2008; Ginsburgh and Weber 2011; van Els 2001). Or they highlight the costs of errors and misunderstandings and the legal uncertainty that may follow from ambiguities or discrepancies in different language versions (Fidrmuc 2011; Ginsburgh and Weber 2011). The argument is that once those additional costs are factored in, multilingualism is much more expensive than that one cup of coffee per citizen. Such accounts are themselves problematic, however, because they tend not to take into account the counterfactual. As Pool emphasizes, "it is wrong to claim (as is often done) that having many official languages is necessarily inefficient" (Pool 1991, 503). In the end, we simply do not know if administrative inconveniences, errors, or misunderstandings would be more or less frequent if the EU only relied on one or a small number of procedural languages. There could be many more such problems given that nonnative speakers would be forced to use shared foreign languages to communicate with others without being able to fall back on their mother tongues. The availability of translation, interpretation, language editing, and legal-linguistic services may, in fact, lead to fewer problems than there otherwise would be.

In addition to the problem of accounting for the counterfactual, Gazzola (2016b) emphasizes that a proper evaluation of the costs of multilingualism requires consideration of implicit costs, meaning the costs private citizens would incur, for example through the need for private translations or the need to learn a new language, if a more restricted language regime were put in place that included a language they do not speak or understand (see also Gazzola and Grin 2013). Implicit costs thus relate to the relative "linguistic disenfranchisement" that different potential language regimes entail, which have been calculated in several studies (e.g., Fidrmuc and Ginsburgh 2007; Gazzola 2006, 2016b; Ginsburgh and Weber 2011; Gazzola and Grin 2013). Gazzola argues that given current language skills among EU citizens, "reducing the direct costs of the EU language regime would essentially amount to shifting the costs of non-multilingualism onto Europeans who do not know the official languages well enough, and in particular onto those who are less educated and belong to the lowest deciles of the income distribution" (Gazzola 2016b, 563). It is for these reasons that Gazzola maintains that the current, full multilingual regime is actually more efficient than more restrictive alternatives and will remain so for the foreseeable future. And, in the end, there is much to Longman's conclusion that "democracies do not baulk at the cost of elections, so why should they resist paying for the equally democratic rights associated with deliberation, participation, and access to information?" Expenses, Mamadouh (Mamadouh 2002, 331) maintains for the same reason, "are rather irrelevant in such a matter of principle."

Critique 2: The Number of Languages

Another point of criticism of EU multilingualism revolves around different ideas about what constitutes the "right" number of languages. Most critics fall into three categories identified by Mamadouh (1999): those who consider EU multilingualism to be not inclusive enough of lesser-used languages, in particular minority languages inside the member states;[53] those who want to limit the number of official or working languages; and those, previously referenced in chapter 1, who want greater equality in the use of the EU's current official languages. The solutions proposed by each group of critics is thus a function of the different problems each sees with the EU's language regime: it is not inclusive enough and needs more languages; it is not efficient enough and needs fewer languages; or it is not equal enough and needs less English. What constitutes the "right" number of languages is thus subject to much debate but ultimately a function of one's normative preconceptions.

One popular idea focuses on the three "biggest" languages, English, French, and German (Ginsburgh and Weber 2005; Ginsburgh, Ortuno-Ortin, and Weber 2005; Kraus 2008; van Els 2001), or those three plus Spanish and Italian (Ammon 2006), plus Polish (Fidrmuc, Ginsburgh, and Weber 2009; Ginsburgh and Weber 2011). Particularly radical are proposals to introduce a single official or working language to enhance the quality of communication in the EU, to support the development of a shared European identity, or to enhance the EU's internal cohesion. While exotic candidates for such a single working language are sometimes proposed, like Latin (see Gubbins 2002, 54; van Els 2001, 343), sign language (see Gubbins 2002, 54), or Esperanto (see Christiansen 2006; Gobbo 2005; Phillipson 2003, 184), the focus is usually on English (e.g., van Els 2005; House 2001; Archibugi 2005; Cogo and Jenkins 2010; De Swaan 2001; Rose 2008; Van Parijs 2011).

In recognition of (some of) the downsides and complications of a limited language regime, different concurrent or compensating actions have also been proposed to alleviate the consequences of any such change. One suggestion is to put in place a limited regime of, for example, English and French, but to require nonnative speakers not to use their mother tongue; this would force everyone to speak in a second language, which would level the linguistic playing field (van Els 2005, 276). Such an arrangement was proposed by Denmark when it was first negotiating accession to the European Community; it was not acceptable to the member states at the time, however (Wright 2000, 175), and there is no reason to believe that it would be today. Moreover, the proposal only addresses one particular issue associated with a limited language regime while ignoring others. Most importantly, large segments of the EU's population would face linguistic disenfranchisement, and it would be problematic to institute a foreign language requirement for elected representatives of the European people. Another popular suggestion is to adopt English as the main working language while boosting language teaching of English in the member states (e.g., De Swaan 2001; Van Parijs 2011; House 2003). The EU has a limited capacity to help realize this objective, however, because of its narrow competences in the realm of education. Moreover, the average level of competence achieved by students remains limited despite greater foreign language learning of younger generations (Gazzola 2016b, 564). In light of the linguistic disenfranchisement of large parts of the EU's population were English adopted as the primary language in the EU, De Swaan (1999, 19) suggests a model that limits languages for informal and administrative purposes inside the institutions but maintains multilingualism for public debate. This, however, would again amount to a language requirement for elected officials. Moreover, the choice of which languages should be used in what forums would remain highly contested. To address this reality, Fidrmuc and Ginsburgh (2007) and Ginsburgh and Weber (2011) suggest that the provision of language services could be decentralized, so that individual countries pay for interpretation and translation as they see fit, or that countries be compensated for not receiving certain language services. It would thus be left to the member states to determine the value they place on having their languages represented and used at the EU level, and a reduction in the number of languages would result from the choice of member states to forgo linguistic services. Fidrmuc, Ginsburgh, and Weber (2006) make a similar suggestion for the EP, that MEPs arrange language services at their own expense. Wright also raises the possibility of MEPs covering the costs of multilingualism by having their language repertoires reflected in their salaries, as a way to "prod" them "towards more complex language repertoires" (Wright 2007, 163). Yet it is fundamentally problematic from the perspective of democratic representation to charge elected representatives for the opportunity to represent their constituents and to participate in collective decision making. Salary discrimination based on language proficiency is similarly difficult to justify for elected popular representatives.

In the end, there are a number of reasons why this book does not seek to offer any "solutions" to the perceived "problem" of multilingualism in the EU, especially when it comes to identifying the "right" number of languages. First, any given solution is reflective of particular normative concerns, which is not what is driving my own research. Second, it is not at all clear that a language regime involving a different number of languages would be more efficient or otherwise appropriate than the status quo. Third, any proposal to change the number of official languages would be highly unlikely to pass, because the EU's language regime constitutes a powerful equilibrium the member states have no incentive to deviate from (as chapter 3 discusses in detail). Fourth, proposals for changing the number of languages tend to disregard the cost of politicizing "the language question" in the EU.[54] Fifth, there is a similar tendency among scholars outside of legal studies to ignore that elevating one or more language(s) over others would introduce a linguistic hierarchy and thus "destabilize the entire [EU legal] system" (Šarčević 2013, 20) by undermining the equality of EU citizens before the law (e.g., Biel 2007; McAuliffe 2012). Finally, treating EU multilingualism as a problem to be solved detracts from focusing on the nature and consequences of multilingual policymaking and thus from the main contribution this book seeks to make.

Critique 3: Mistakes, Misunderstandings, and Uncertainty

The third reason why EU multilingualism is subjected to criticism is because of what are perceived to be frequent instances of confusion or flat-out mistakes. Examples are quickly picked up in the popular press, such as when the Irish translation of the treaty establishing the European Stability Mechanism included as many as 17 grammatical errors and typos (Reilly 2012), and especially when they involve "a rich schoolboy seam of Brussels lore on how 'frozen semen' in an agricultural working group emerged in French as 'matelot congelé' (frozen seaman)" (Black 2004).

Examples of mistakes brought about by EU multilingualism ought not be minimized or ignored, but nonetheless should be treated with some caution, because not all mistakes are created equal. In fact, mistakes due to EU multilingualism can be categorized into those that directly affect EU law, and thus the *outcomes* of EU policymaking; mistakes without legal consequences that lead to sufficient confusion or misunderstandings to disrupt policymaking *processes*; and mistakes that simply occur without consequence. These different types of mistakes should not be conflated, but they often are by critics of EU multilingualism who consider every mistake to be indicative of systemic dysfunction. This is problematic because some inaccuracies in translation and interpretation are inevitable in a multilingual context, so simply pointing to their existence does not mean that EU multilingualism is flawed or unsustainable.

Treating all mistakes as equal is also problematic because not every apparent mistake is, in fact, a mistake. As discussed in detail in chapter 6, there generally is not one single way of translating a text, because translation in the EU involves a great many choices with regard to technical vocabulary, legal concepts, and other terminology. Therefore, a choice of words that is perceived as awkward or incorrect may actually be the result of careful consideration of a variety of terminological options and, ultimately, help ensure the functional equivalence of all language versions.[55] One respondent in the Court of Justice, for example, described how sometimes "people write in from outside, academics for example, to say that there is an error in the translation, paragraph X of such and such judgment or point Y of such and such opinion"; and while "sometimes they're right, more often they're wrong" (#29).

According to Susan Šarčević, "most lawyers regard divergences in meaning between the various language versions as an inevitable fact of EU multilingual lawmaking" and—more importantly—"many divergences are not harmful" (Šarčević 2013, 10). This crucial observation was also offered by some of my respondents (e.g., #84): even if there technically is an error, it may not have any tangible legal or political consequences. For example, in what might be seen as an ironic twist, the very foundation of the EU's language regime, Council Regulation No. 1, suffers from inconsistent wording between language versions. Wright (2000, 177–78) highlights that the French version of Article 6 provides that the institutions of the Community "may stipulate in their internal rules of procedure the way in which these rules on languages are to be applied" ("Les institutions peuvent déterminer les modalités d'application de ce régime dans leurs reglements intérieurs"), while the English version entitles the institutions to "stipulate in their rules of procedure which of the languages are to be used in specific cases." Similarly, Robertson (2012b) points out that Article 7 of Regulation No. 1 refers to "régime linguistique" (linguistic regime) in French, "languages to be used" in English, and "Sprachenfrage" (language question) in German, all of which are slightly different from each other. But he also emphasizes that "within the context of the article it looks as if they are all pointing toward the same thing"; hence, "in the abstract the precise formulations differ, but the results seem to be the same in practice" (Robertson 2012b, 12). And so, this "notorious" example of mistranslation (Wright 2000, 177) is not actually of tangible consequence.

With regard to language-related mistakes that affect EU case law, Baaij (2012a) identified a total of 170 judgments by the Court of Justice from 1960 to 2010 in which it observed divergences between different language versions of EU legal provisions, an average of 3.4 cases per year. Given that the total number of judgments issued by the Court of Justice over that same time period was 8,334,[56] this number (equivalent to 2 percent of all judgments) is hardly overwhelming. The number is also dwarfed by the total volume of EU legislation: 5,732 legislative acts were passed in just the last 20 years of the 50-year period considered by Baaij, not counting amending acts.[57] In relation to the huge amount of legislation passed by the EU and the large number of judgments handed down by the Court of Justice, 170 cases represents a very small proportion indeed. It becomes even smaller if we take into account that each legislative act is translated into the other official languages, which means that each involves a number of language pairs with the potential for discrepancy that ranges from six in 1960, when there were four languages, to several hundred after the EU's eastward enlargement. And the proportion is smaller still if we consider that each legislative act includes a multitude of legal provisions, each with the potential for divergence. And so the number of actually observed discrepancies between language versions is minuscule relative to the number of *potential* instances of divergence.

A critique of these numbers might be that the 170 cases identified by Baaij are only those when a divergence was both detected and adjudicated, which likely masks a larger number of cases in which there are divergences that have not been identified or brought before the Court (McAuliffe 2013b, 881). This is, however, inherently true of *all* law, because all law is ambiguous and thus potentially subject to interpretation and adjudication. Hence, there is *always* a higher number of potential cases than actual cases of adjudication. Moreover, it is again important to emphasize that not all divergences matter from a legal perspective: just because a discrepancy exists does not mean that it impacts the uniform application of the law. Indeed, even if there were a much larger number of actual divergences than those observed by the Court, the fact that they apparently did not warrant adjudication suggests that they have not been of legal consequence, at least not yet. Šarčević (2013, 16) foresees the possibility that "victims of multilingualism" may take their cases to court in the future, which would have the potential to shake the foundations of EU multilingualism, but it is not clear if and why this would start happening more often than it has in the past.[58]

Hence, institutional multilingualism in the EU does not produce mistakes that are numerous or serious enough to systematically affect political and legal outcomes. They are also not numerous or serious enough to impede or undermine political processes. Indeed, it was notable that none of my respondents suggested that mistakes, misunderstandings, or uncertainties were all that frequent. Some were not able to come up with any examples when multilingualism led to tangible problems (e.g., #2, 53, 60, 61, 64, 66, 81), although a few also suggested that mistakes may simply go undetected or unreported (#34, 36, 46). Others recalled particular episodes that happened long ago or did not have any notable consequences (e.g., #4, 14, 15, 16, 19, 22, 24, 29, 41, 42, 47, 52, 56, 57, 59, 61, 67, 68, 70, 71, 72, 73, 74, 75, 79). One respondent concluded that mistakes do happen, but her "45 years of experience say that arithmetically it's insignificant" (#83), while another suggested that the low incidence of mistakes is "really surprising. . . . There should be more!" (#12). My respondents thus bluntly contradict Wright's conclusion that EU multilingualism is beset by "problems of communication" impacting "every state of the process" (Wright 2000, 120).

When a mistake appears to have happened, the situation is carefully investigated (#8, 13, 18), but this happens infrequently; one respondent in a position to know estimated that it happened "only five times [in the] last three years" (#14). Sanctions include reprimands of language service providers or requirements for further training; in extreme cases, they may have a language "taken away" (#18), be excluded from high-level assignments, be put on administrative duty, or even have their formal accreditations withdrawn (Duflou 2016, 121). If a mistake is found in a legislative text that has already been published, it can be fixed using a so-called *corrigendum*. While some corrigenda affect policy substance or legal meanings, most simply correct typos, omissions, or minor mistakes (Bobek 2009).[59]

The most common examples of mistakes and misunderstandings offered by my respondents were those describing "small problems" (#67) that did not end up "stopping anything" (#60), while "real mistakes don't normally happen" (#34). Indeed, it was unusual for respondents to suggest that mistakes are commonplace, as was the case for two respondents in the Council who suggested, respectively, that language-related misunderstandings happen "quite regularly" (#71) and that she could "probably think of a dozen examples" (#58). It was more typical for respondents to have to think for a bit before specific examples came to mind. Moreover, the particular instances my respondents did recall were seen as isolated incidents rather than systemic failure; even the more critical among my respondents suggested as much.

One interpreter, for example, described her own contribution to a misunderstanding early in her career when she caused a stir by using the equivalent of "impose" or "force upon" in reference to negotiations between employers and employees; a Commission official present in the meeting suspected that a possible misunderstanding had occurred and helped resolve the situation (#35). Several respondents also recalled particular situations when an interpreter translated a statement to mean the opposite of what the speaker had said (e.g., #16, 58, 75), and one national counselor described an episode when she was speaking in her mother tongue in a Council meeting and much of the room suddenly burst out laughing. Her remarks had not been humorous in the least, however, and the mistake was quickly discovered because only those who had listened to the English interpretation had found it funny (#74).[60] But in all those instances, the mistake was immediately caught and corrected. This seems to be what usually happens, for two main reasons. First, there often are people in the room with the language skills to understand both the original statement and the interpretation thereof and who will indicate right away if the two conflict (#16). Second, the general policy positions of speakers are usually known in advance, so sudden, radical deviations are noticed and trigger requests for clarification (#22, 58, 75). For example, one Council official recalled a situation when a former Austrian chancellor's statement on nuclear energy was misinterpreted to mean the opposite of what he said, but since "everybody kind of knows Austrian positions on nuclear energy . . . we all knew that [he] could not have said that, he had to have said the opposite. So that was not a major problem" (#58).

There were very few examples I learned about in which interpretation mistakes had any kind of notable consequence. One Permanent Representation counselor remembered an incident when the prime minister of his member state was misinterpreted toward the end of a European Council meeting, "late at night" when "the people who were around didn't pay that much attention." What followed was "a huge blow up" in the national media the next morning that had to be addressed and corrected (#75). A second example came from the EP, where the assistant of one MEP described how her boss's being misinterpreted from French caused a fuss in her national capital and required a public clarification (#54). Finally, a former official in the EP's Directorate for Interpretation recounted how a parliamentary vote had to be repeated because an interpretation error had previously occurred and might have caused confusion. The same respondent also explained, however, that this was unlikely to have affected the outcome of the vote, because MEPs do not make up their minds on the spot, but cast their votes based on voting lists supplied by their political groups (#83).[61]

Some of my respondents also offered examples of mistakes in the written translations of EU texts and their repercussions. Two anecdotes from the EP describe misunderstandings caused by incorrect translations that were quickly resolved. First, an MEP recalled an episode when the translation of a Spanish-language amendment led to confusion: it mixed up the European Union and the United States, because the Spanish "Estados Unidos" had been abbreviated as "EU" and then translated accordingly. The confusion was quickly resolved, however, because reference to the EU "was nonsense" in the given context, while reference to the United States was not (#47). Second, a former EP official conveyed a situation in the 1980s when the German word "Tarif" was translated into English as "tariff," when in the relevant context it should have been "wages" or "pay scale." This resulted

> in a ten or fifteen minute hodge podge between the rapporteur, other members, and the British members who were complaining. And then someone went to have a look at the German original. . . . So we had a pointless ten or fifteen minute political debate because of the mistranslation. . . . We lost fifteen minutes, there was nothing more fundamental or serious. (#79)

A few examples in which the fallout from mistranslation was more serious also came up. A Court translator recalled a mistranslation between the French and German versions of a draft judgment, a "serious mistake," but the kind of thing that "doesn't happen often" (#32). Another respondent described how controversy erupted in the EP when a translated text used the term "holocaust" in reference to the Armenian genocide (#4). In the Commission, one respondent recalled a Green Paper being drafted that involved "pretty awkward" wording; this led to confusion in the translation process when "several languages had got it wrong" (#15). Finally, a high-ranking Commission official remembered an incident when a policy recommendation issued by the Commission was interpreted as "a sort of legal obligation" in the affected member state because of how the English original had been translated. Since the policy area in question was politically sensitive, the apparent attempt by Brussels to "dictate" national policy caused a stir and was strongly rejected by that member state's head of government (#55). These episodes, however, were the only examples of notable controversy I learned about from my respondents; otherwise, it is "very rare to have a major blow up" (#58). On the whole, mistranslations and incorrect interpretation are not frequent or serious enough to disrupt policymaking in the EU institutions. "Funnily enough," they are "not such a big deal," according to a high-ranking Council official with a long and storied career in the EU institutions (#52).

Multilingualism Is Working (Reasonably) Well

Despite readily identifiable shortcomings in EU multilingualism, the frequent knee-jerk reaction of associating EU multilingualism with the biblical myth of the Tower of Babel is often misguided and misleading. The story is generally understood to be about pride and punishment (Runions 2014) and, as such, its reference puts a negative spin on EU multilingualism. The invocation of Babel has thus been "highly detrimental to multilingualism" (Mamadouh 1999, 135), even though the story can also be read more positively as being about the divine legitimation of diversity and pluralism (Strawn 2011; see also Hiebert 2007, 30–31).

In the end, those working inside the institutions generally evaluate the functioning of the EU's language regime quite positively,[62] despite situational frustration that arises when negotiators present their ideas, arguments, or proposals in subpar English (#59); when meetings are chaired by politicians with limited foreign language skills (#20, 58, 71); when the language handicaps of others have to be accommodated (#44); or when the scarcity of rooms with a sufficient number of interpretation booths or the limited availability of interpreters for a given language lead to the postponement of meetings (#46). Most of my respondents share the impression of one MEP, however, that such difficulties make policymaking "more cumbersome" at times, but they are "not insurmountable" (#44). What is more, my respondents consider it possible for those with limited language skills to participate and wield influence in EU policymaking.

Whether or not a political actor with a substantial "foreign language handicap" can operate successfully and be influential in the EU institution is difficult to establish in the absence of obvious and unambiguous indicators, and since individual-level data on foreign language skills are unavailable.[63] My strategy was to ask my interview respondents to apply a rather strict criterion when considering the disadvantages that come with limited foreign language skills in EU politics. Specifically, I asked them whether or not somebody with a foreign language handicap can be a political "heavyhitter" or "heavyweight" in EU politics. This question still leaves room for ambiguity, of course, in that it does not specify what constitutes a policy heavyweight. But it prompts respondents to apply a high standard in their evaluation, which minimizes some of the ambiguity that comes with asking about the relative influence of political actors and ensures that respondents are not too forgiving in their assessments of the negative consequences of a foreign language handicap. The disadvantage of asking this question, however, is that the standard it applies may be inappropriately high. After all, we might falsely conclude that the EU's language regime is too restrictive if we observe that actors with foreign language deficits are unable to become "heavy-hitters," when in fact they are able to operate reasonably effectively, if not at the level of their colleagues with better language skills. In that sense, the question is likely to produce a conservative estimate, and my respondents concluded by a two-to-one margin that it is in fact possible for a linguistically handicapped politician to be a political heavyweight in the EU's institutions: of the respondents who offered an unambiguous answer to the question, 25 said that it is possible and twelve said that it is not.[64] This suggests that EU multilingualism may put those with limited foreign language skills at a relative disadvantage, which stands to reason; but it also indicates that the EU's language regime is not inherently or necessarily exclusionary. A respondent in the EP, for example, explained that "I've asked myself the same question as well, whether speaking multiple languages really is an asset. And I like to be convinced that it is, but on the other hand I don't see it putting any barriers to people" (#49). Another similarly recalled having seen MEPs "struggling in English a little bit, but that doesn't mean to say that they can't be more successful in the end as to what amendments get adopted" (#78). Ultimately, one long-term observer maintains, language is "never really an obstacle for any member who really wants to be understood and to be heard. . . . For me the problem is more the drive of the member and the message that he has to pass, his conviction, his passion, and his willingness to pass it; then he will make it happen. . . . If you want to be influential, you will find a way to be influential" (#82).

This, however, presupposes being a "pragmatic monolinguist" rather than "militant monolinguist," a useful distinction Wright makes between those who are able and willing to make language choices aimed at furthering a mutual understanding and those who are not (Wright 2007, 154–56). Moreover, EU actors without sufficient foreign language skills have to work harder to make up for their handicaps, as several respondents emphasized. One former high-ranking official in the EP Secretariat, for example, readily acknowledged that "you will be a more efficient, a more influential MEP if you do speak English, but it's not that if you don't, you don't exist. I mean, it's a relative advantage" (#81, also #38, 41, 47). You may not be "the first choice to become the Parliament's negotiator," for example in interinstitutional legislative bargaining with the Council, but nonetheless "you can be a politically important MEP" (#19). My interviewees also suggested that EU policymakers can make up for their own limited language repertoires with the support of their staff (e.g., #38, 41, 43, 48, 60, 70, 79, 82). One respondent made this point based on his experience in the Council, where "you will have your assistant with you and your assistant at least will speak English. . . . That works pretty well" (#71). So it is possible to "compensate, but it's not exactly easy," according to an EP official with a long career in that institution; "you can do it if you are well equipped in terms of your entourage, your assistants, if you have good staff around you" (#82, also 39).

But this cannot fully make up for a lack of language skills, of course, and it is in informal or social situations that this problem is particularly pronounced (#13, 16, 21, 38, 39, 43, 45, 49, 52, 54, 55, 59, 63, 65, 70, 71, 83; see also Wright 2007, 151), as well as on those rare occasions when staffers are not allowed to participate in meetings (#38, 54). Difficulties thus arise when

> wielding your influence . . . is done through speaking to your colleague on the way to the bathroom break, or speaking to your colleague on the way to the family photo.[65] Here, you speak to one or two colleagues simply walking on a corridor, and putting a position together. If you cannot speak to them directly and you need an interpreter with you, you lose a lot of opportunities of communication. (#58)

As a result, "your network is very limited, and your capacity to interact in a conversation, to jump on what has been said, to be a lively interlocutor is very limited" (#55); "you really miss something there, you miss bonds, you miss personal relationships with your colleagues, with staffers, with lobbyists, with the whole world" (#82).

When thinking about political heavy hitters with limited language skills, several respondents confirmed in general terms that there are examples (#16, 47, 49, 75, 78), while others were more specific and pointed to particular individuals (#64, 82). For example, one MEP recalled that

> between 1999 and 2004, in the social affairs committee there was a Danish socialist, speaking only Danish. . . . He was a former worker in a metal company, even not finalized his secondary school. But he was brilliant on social affairs because he had a trade union background. And although his language capacities were very minor, he managed to become on certain issues with his background and with

his sense of negotiating, although he had not the capacity of speaking English fluently, he was important. . . . [He] left a trace here in legislative work. (#40)

One name that came up repeatedly was Guido Sacconi, a former Italian MEP who is most well-known for serving as rapporteur for the REACH chemicals legislation, one of the most important and high-profile pieces of EU legislation of the past decades. Sacconi "did a really magnificent job with that file, even though he was, shall we say, linguistically challenged" (#39, also 78, 79).

In the end, the language services offered in the EU allow those with limited foreign language skills to operate in the multilingual environment by letting them use their native languages as needed (#49, 52). Indeed, one of the EU officials I interviewed conveyed a story that described the extent to which monolinguals are accommodated. She recalled going on a mission to a non-EU member state with a delegation of MEPs, one of whom spoke only his mother tongue. "We had seven members and then six interpreters for [him]," she remembered, each paid "1,700 euros per day" (#12). As a result of such extensive efforts, one MEP I interviewed highlighted, "I can speak [my native language] everywhere, if I want to. . . . It's not so efficient, but I can work like that. So the system works" (#47). Even a respondent who described her frustration with the inefficiencies and difficulties that multilingualism entails, and who emphasized the desirability of being "very proficient in the language in which you legislate," ultimately concluded that "nevertheless, that's what experts, translators, interpreters, legal experts are for. And that can be sorted out" (#44).

One interview was particularly telling in establishing that it is possible for actors with foreign language handicaps to operate and wield influence in the EU institutions, even if they are at a relative disadvantage. It was with the assistant of an MEP who has limited English skills, which was one reason why I explicitly sought it out, as it would allow me to better understand the difficulties foreign language handicaps cause for active participants in EU policymaking. What the respondent described is in line with the above: that it is more difficult and at times frustrating for an MEP to have limited foreign language skills, but that the system does in the end offer sufficient accommodation for participation. This is particularly the case for official meetings, when interpretation is generally provided, if at times only after someone insists on it. The respondent described three instances when her MEP was supposed to attend meetings without interpretation from and to her mother tongue. One was a rapporteur–shadow rapporteur meeting, the second a political meeting in the EP in which personal assistants were not allowed, and the third a meeting in the Commission in which she was also not supposed to be present. In all three cases, the MEP and her staff had to push back against the lack of interpretation and insist that she be accommodated, which took effort and was cause for frustration; in all cases, however, interpretation was ultimately provided (#54). The language problem is more pronounced in informal situations, but she still manages most of the time:

> [My MEP] understands [English] pretty well. Understanding is not a problem when people address her in the corridor, so she knows what they are telling her. But the problem is if she wants to make her point, sometimes it's not easy for her. . . . When we have meetings in the office it's fine, I translate, my colleague, or whatever. Also, at the end some people speak French. We manage. But there are MEPs who only speak English, they don't speak French at all, and if they ask for something it's complicated. . . . She needs that I'm with her, or to pass the message to the others . . . And I know that even if my English is not well enough, I can make myself understood. This I know, I never had problems with that. Because I know the texts, I know the ways, I know the subject very well. So even if my verb is not correct, they know what I mean at the end. (#54)

In sum, the MEP faces particular difficulties and has to invest additional effort and resources, but she is able to actively participate in EU lawmaking, as her legislative record also demonstrates: during each of the last two EP terms she served more than a dozen times as rapporteur or shadow rapporteur on reports or opinions. She is not, in other words, somebody who is unable to take part in EP politics due to her language handicap.

Also instructive were the answers I received to one of my last questions, which asked respondents to assess how close or far today's EU is from the ideal of a linguistic "level playing field" that allows everybody to participate equally, independent of foreign language skills. A greater number of respondents considered the EU to be close to the ideal of a level playing field than did not. Among the policymakers, who have less of an incentive than language service providers to view the language services offered as sufficient in addressing linguistic imbalances, those who gave an unambiguous answer who viewed the EU as close (18 respondents) outweighed those who said otherwise (9 respondents) by a two-to-one margin. Among those who thought the EU was far away from the ideal was one Mertens counselor, who maintained that "it would not be possible to participate in the European process knowing only your native language, that's for sure. . . . To be a real participant, a real actor here, you have to have at least English, but the more languages you have the better" (#65, also 44, 49, 50, 54, 56, 62, 64, 72). Yet twice the number of policymakers considered the EU to be "not far" from the ideal of a level playing field; it is "always useful when you speak English or French, or also German, . . . but not necessarily imperative," as a respondent in the EP put it (#42, also 38, 43, 46, 47, 63, 67, 70, 71, 72, 74, 75, 77, 80, 81, 82, 83). A national counselor similarly suggested that

> I think we are close to that ideal. . . . I have never experienced in my environment that somebody did not reach somebody else for linguistic reasons. . . . I think everyone can make himself understood and everybody is listened to. In meetings, everybody can speak. . . . I don't see any disadvantages because of linguistic limitations. (#66)

Four reasons were most frequently offered by my respondents as explanations for why EU multilingualism works reasonably well. The first was the quality of language services, which not only language service providers, but also many policymakers (#20, 37, 42, 45, 51, 52, 53, 56, 58, 63, 71, 72, 79, 81, 82, 83) emphasized as one reason for the smooth functioning of multilingual politics in the EU. This is, in part, notable because I did not explicitly ask for an assessment of the quality of EU language services in my interviews; their positive evaluations came up organically in conversation, describing various language services as "really amazing" (#37), "great" (#42), "quite amazing" (#52), "very good" (#56), "excellent" (#63, 82), "fantastic" (#72), and "outstandingly good . . . really extraordinarily good" (#79). One respondent in the Council paid the language service providers what they might consider to be the ultimate compliment: they are so "obviously doing a good job" that "we don't even stop to think about it" (#20).

The second reason—highlighted especially by many policymakers—is that the EU policymaking process involves a great many opportunities for catching possible mistakes or miscommunications. There generally is not one moment in time when a mistake would derail policymaking and there would be no opportunity for correction or revision. "It is not like you come together for an hour and say, this is now the regulation, and then you part ways," one respondent explained; "you talk for weeks, months, maybe even years about each directive, and during such a long timeframe every decision is chewed over" (#66). Decision making also happens in multiple arenas and at multiple levels, so there are numerous (both formal and informal) "checks and cross-checks and double-checks," as one counselor put it (#64, also 26, 33, 35, 58, 61, 62, 63, 64, 66, 67, 73, 77, 78, 80, 82). A lengthy quote from a respondent in the EP illustrates this point:

> In committee, suddenly somebody will think "well, that's not what it says in my version." And then people realize, oh, there's a problem. So then you send it back to the lawyer linguists and say "I'm sorry, can you please verify all of the linguistic versions to make sure they are saying the same thing." So that already happens at a committee level. . . . When a text is adopted in the plenary, . . . before it physically leaves the Parliament to go to the Commission and the Council, lawyer-linguists check it, and you sometimes, as a policy advisor, get a phone call after a couple of days from them saying "what exactly did you mean by this, this isn't really particularly well written." . . . So there is another verification that is done afterwards. . . . And there's a lot of people like me—MEPs much more importantly— who are reading in their language and might call their colleague from Finland and say, "I can't believe you tabled this," and the Finn will say, "well, that's not what I wrote." . . . And that's just us! We're not the final drafters of the final legislation as it will appear in the Official Journal. . . . It goes to the Council. They have experts as well. So there's so many stages in it. (#39; also #65 in the Council)

The policymaking process, in other words, is "so repetitive, everything is so repetitive. So many levels, so many levels things are discussed, so that at a certain level there is normally someone who spots the problem" (#63). And in this process, most problems are identified and corrected on the spot, or quickly after a problem might have occurred (#18, 24, 41, 42, 50, 58, 64, 66, 67, 68 70, 71, 74, 82). In the words of one respondent, linguistic uncertainty "does not lead to misunderstandings, it just leads to one question being asked: 'did I understand this correctly?'" (#24).

The third reason offered by respondents for why EU multilingualism works is that EU actors are used to and tolerant of the language handicaps of others and the imperfections inherent in the multilingual system. As is discussed in more detail in chapter 4, people are flexible in their use of language and tolerant of others being similarly flexible (#42), and they are used to making policy under the particular multilingual circumstances in the EU, so they can anticipate and be proactive about potential problems (#70). They are, as one counselor in a member state Permanent Representation explained, "very careful" about avoiding misunderstandings (#75, also #25), and their understanding and dealing with EU multilingualism is "very pragmatic," according to another national counselor (#71). People's focus is on making themselves understood and getting their main message across (#9, 12, 14, 21, 25, 37, 42, 71). The system works, in this sense, because the main objective is to convey the core message, according to one respondent, even if there are minor misunderstandings and delays along the way (#9).

The final reason highlighted by my respondents for why the potential for problems one might expect in a multilingual system is not realized in the EU is the widespread reliance on a shared working language (#22, 27, 38, 42, 46, 49, 56, 60, 61, 72, 74). "In the end," one EP official explains, "the important actors quite often have a language in common" (#12), and they can fall back on interpretation and translation if need be (#51). This combination of relying on shared languages plus language services is the "normal communication" in the EU institutions, and people make it work (#13, also 21, 27, 70, 76). A particularly important role, in this regard, is played by the particular "EU English" that dominates communication inside the EU institutions, which is the topic of chapter 5.

Conclusion

EU multilingualism works well, perhaps surprisingly well considering the great potential for mistakes, miscommunications, and other such problems. The system is not perfect—indeed, I will highlight where there is room for improvement in the final chapter—but it is seen in a positive light by most of my respondents. That participants in EU policymaking generally consider the EU's language regime to be working for them is an important finding, considering that EU multilingualism is the target of frequent criticism.

Chapters 4 and 5 revisit two of the reasons my respondents offered for why EU multilingualism "works." One aspect of EU multilingualism highlighted in chapter 4, which deals with foreign language use inside the EU institutions, is that operating in a multilingual environment involves a high degree of tolerance of other people's limited foreign language abilities and the deeper empathetic effects this may entail. Chapter 5 then focuses in on "EU English" as the main shared working language inside the EU institutions. But first, I examine the origins and evolution of the EU's language regime over time.

THREE

The EU's Language Regime
Institutional Stability and Change

This chapter discusses the origins of European Union (EU) multilingualism and analyzes how it has evolved over time.[1] It conceives of the EU's language regime as an *institution*, or the *rules of the game* when it comes to language use inside the EU institutions, and argues that those rules carefully and successfully balance four distinct "dimensions" of language: a *symbolic* dimension that safeguards the formal equality of all member state languages; a *representational* dimension that ensures a common basis for popular participation; a *legal* dimension focused on the equal authenticity of EU law; and a *functional* dimension that provides for flexibility in the use of languages inside the EU institutions. The first three dimensions affirm the principle that no one national language is formally superior to the others, which to the EU member states is of critical importance because of the symbolic power associated with language equality. The functional dimension, in contrast, explicitly provides for the possibility that one or more languages may, in practice, be favored inside the EU institutions. This not only facilitates communication between EU actors, it also ensures that the costs of multilingualism are kept in check. Both considerations matter to the member states, which is why they accept this loophole, as long as situations in which multilingualism is limited occur under a "veil of formal language equality." It is by providing the basis for effective communication under this veil of language equality that the EU language regime successfully depoliticizes the "language question" in EU politics, thereby defusing a potentially highly volatile issue.[2]

This arrangement provides for an equilibrium that the member states have little incentive to try to change;[3] we will see, in fact, that in those relatively few instances of contestation over language rules, it resulted in the existing rules being affirmed rather than undermined. In that sense, the EU's language regime has been remarkably stable: the language rules put in place in the 1950s have remained in force until today. Those rules are enshrined in Council Regulation No. 1 (1958), which I will refer to as the EU's *primary* language rules (in reference to the distinction between primary and secondary law). The EU's *secondary* language rules are the ones that govern the functioning of multilingualism in practice, but within the overall parameters set by Regulation No. 1, such as the EU institution's Rules of Procedure and relevant interinstitutional agreements (e.g., the "Joint Practical Guide" for persons involved in drafting legislation).[4] But some rules are also informal, including norms, conventions, and practices relating to language use in the institutions. For example, it was not formally decreed that English would replace French as the main procedural language inside the EU institutions, that it is acceptable to switch between languages in the same conversation, that terminology from one language may be used when conversing in another, or that EU English develop as a means of communication that differs from standard English.

While the EU's primary language rules have been stable for more than six decades, there has been a great deal of change in the EU's secondary language rules and its multilingual practices. I rely on insights from theories of institutional change to investigate this dynamic between continuity and transformation, or between stability and change, which are mutually reinforcing rather than opposing forces (see Thelen 1994, 2004). This chapter argues that the stability of the primary language rules is due to EU multilingualism functioning "properly" even in the face of far-reaching structural changes that individually or collectively would have the potential to undermine their viability; by functioning properly, I mean that the language rules successfully safeguard the symbolic, representational, legal, and functional dimensions of language and the balance between them. This proper functioning is not coincidental, however, but due to the continuous adjustment of both the EU's secondary language rules and its multilingual practices in response to or in anticipation of major changes in the EU's political system. Most important, in this regard, are changes that occurred or were consciously enacted in response to the EU's growing competences over time, the empowerment of the EU's supranational institutions, and various rounds of EU enlargement, which together entailed an increasing demand for language services covering

- more languages used by a greater number of actors with policy-making authority,
- increasingly consequential oral proceedings and written documents,
- a wider range of substantive policy areas, and
- greater variation in national legal systems.

The adjustments of the EU's secondary language rules that were made in response to these developments ensured the continued viability of the EU's primary language rules and their core objectives, but they were in turn only made possible by those primary language rules being sufficiently permissive to allow for changes to be made in the first place. Critical, in this regard, is Article 6 of Regulation No. 1, which allows the EU institutions to specify which languages "are to be used in specific cases." It is this particular provision that offered the flexibility necessary to address the consequences of fundamental changes in the EU's political system over time.

While this chapter highlights the interplay of continuity and change in reinforcing the EU's language regime, it does not necessarily predict future institutional stability. There are, in fact, a number of potential sources of institutional change, including Brexit, the politicization of the EU's language rules, improved foreign language skills of both EU actors and EU citizens, advances in machine translation and interpretation, institutional dysfunction, and changes in legal multilingualism. Those will be briefly discussed before the chapter comes to a close. For the time being and looking into the foreseeable future, however, the EU's language regime has proven durable even when confronted with dramatic contextual change. This is of crucial importance for the EU's political system, as it enables effective communication inside the EU institutions, provides the basis for the representation and participation of EU citizens, and serves as a backbone for the EU's legal system. Last but not least, the EU's language regime successfully depoliticizes language as a potentially highly contested issue.

The Origins and Evolution of the EU's Language Regime

The EU's language regime dates back to the very origins of the European integration process, to the EU's first predecessor organization, the European Coal and Steel Community (ECSC), even though the Treaty of Paris (which established the ECSC) did not contain any reference to language or establish a formal language regime for the ECSC's institutions.[5] The treaty itself was considered authentic only in French, the single language in which it was drawn up, but Germany in particular was adamant that German be equal to French as a working language of the ECSC (Van der Jeught 2015). A language regime centered on the languages of the two big member states, however, raised concerns about language equality *within* Belgium, since it would have covered two of Belgium's language communities while leaving out the Flemish (Horspool 2006). Belgium thus lobbied for Dutch, which meant that Italian also had to be included. An Interim Committee of Lawyers was established to consider the language issue and recommended the policy that would ultimately be adopted: that all four languages become official languages of the ECSC and be granted equal recognition (Mac Giolla Chriost and Bonotti 2018, 11).[6] These realities meant that the ECSC institutions required language services from the start. Those were, of course, much smaller than the relevant units today: a High Authority document from 1953 refers to 25 translators and 10 revisers, divided into language sections. Notably, in addition to the official languages, English was present from the start, because it was used most widely internationally by heavy industry, in the coal and steel trade, in relevant scientific and technical literatures, and of course by the British and American trading partners of the ECSC member states (European Commission 2010b, 12). The selection of Luxembourg as the seat of the organization prompted the imminent dominance of French, however, as did the design of the early communities' political and administrative structures after the French organizational model (Kraus 2008, 120; Phillipson 2003, 125–26). French was also the official language of three of six member states (France, Luxembourg, Belgium), served as an international and diplomatic language, and established itself early on as the main drafting language (Van der Jeught 2015).

The ECSC Language Protocol was never published, exists only in French, and lays out "considerations" rather than explicit language rules (Van der Jeught 2015). In contrast, its successor organization, the European Economic Community (EEC), established a set of explicit, formal language rules. It did so in the very first regulation ever adopted by the Council of the EEC, the organization's primary lawmaking body. "Regulation No 1 determining the languages to be used by the European Economic Community" (April 15, 1958) specifies that the "official languages and the working languages of the institutions of the Community shall be Dutch, French, German, and Italian" (Article 1). This list was expanded to include English and Danish (1973); Greek (1981); Portuguese and Spanish

(1986); Finnish and Swedish (1995); Czech, Estonian, Hungarian, Latvian, Lithuanian, Maltese, Polish, Slovak, and Slovenian (2004); Bulgarian and Romanian (2007); and Croatian (2013).[7] Irish also became an official language in 2007 but, given the difficulties of recruiting sufficient numbers of Irish-language service providers, EU institutions are exempt from drafting all acts and publishing them in the Official Journal in Irish, based on an agreement of the member states that is reconsidered every five years (Van der Jeught 2015, 64–65). Today, the EU has 24 official languages.[8]

Aside from identifying the official languages, Council Regulation No. 1 stipulates that "regulations and other documents of general application shall be drafted in the four official languages" (Article 4) and that "the Official Journal of the Community shall be published in the four official languages" (Article 5). It further states that "documents which a Member State or a person subject to the jurisdiction of a Member State sends to institutions of the Community may be drafted in any one of the official languages selected by the sender," that "the reply shall be drafted in the same language" (Article 2), and that "documents which an institution of the Community sends to a Member State or to a person subject to the jurisdiction of a Member State shall be drafted in the language of such State" (Article 3).[9] Finally, Article 7 stipulates that the languages to be used in the proceedings of the Court of Justice shall be laid down in its rules of procedure, and Article 8 that if a Member State has more than one official language, the language to be used shall, at the request of such State, be governed by the general rules of its law.

The "considerations" laid out in the ECSC Language Protocol provided the basis for the main provisions of Regulation No. 1 (Van der Jeught 2015, 61–62), with one important exception: Article 6 allows the institutions to "stipulate in their rules of procedure which of the languages are to be used in specific cases," which is of significance because the implication of this rule is that the languages are not, and never have been, fully equal in how they are used inside the institutions (Longman 2007, 192).[10] It also only regulates written languages, not oral communication (Athanassiou 2006, 10). Indeed, within the institutions, and in particular in preparatory meetings and documents, a subset of languages dominates, especially English and French. The choice of these languages is not, however, prescribed by Article 6, but is a matter of practice. French was firmly entrenched as the main language of the institutions until the 1973 enlargement (Phillipson 2003, 125), when English was first introduced as an official language with the accession of the UK, Ireland, and Denmark. But English would not seriously challenge French until the 1990s, when French was still used for spoken and written communication in the Council, the Commission, and the European Parliament (EP) about 60 percent of the time (Schlossmacher 1994). English started becoming more dominant among Members of the EP (MEPs) first, Schlössmacher found, but a generational change in the other institutions was also becoming apparent. One survey of trainees in the Commission, for example, found that majorities of these future officials spoke and wrote more English than French, with the exception of trainees from francophone countries and southern Europe (Quell 1997, 63, 66). Similarly, Haselhuber (1991) found that interns in the European Commission used English and French equally often in 1989–1990 already, when French was still dominant among officials in that institution.

The trend toward a greater use of English, which started slowly with the accession of the UK, Ireland, and Denmark in 1973 (Kraus 2008), has thus accelerated in the past 20 years. The Swedes and Finns who entered the institutions in the 1990s generally favored English over French, and that same preference among officials from the central and eastern European member states turned the tide for good after the 2004 enlargement (Ban 2013). After this enlargement round, English has established itself as the main vehicular language inside the institutions for most formal and informal meetings, as well as for most day-to-day interactions (with the exception of the Court of Justice, where French remains the working language).

Four Dimensions of Language

Two opposing forces, therefore, coexist at the heart of the EU multilingual regime: language equality and limited multilingualism. The tension between the formal status of all languages as equal and the reality that, in practice, some languages have always been more important than others is key to understanding how EU multilingualism has evolved over time and how it operates today.

Going all the way back to Regulation No. 1, the EU's primary language rules have recognized and incorporated four distinct "dimensions" of language:[11]

- *Symbolic:* all official languages are equal, Article 1; ensures language equality.
- *Representational:* citizens have the right to information in their official language of choice, Articles 2 and 3; ensures possibility of democratic participation.

- *Legal:* all language versions are equally authentic, Articles 4 and 5; ensures the equality of all EU citizens before EU law.
- *Functional:* some languages may be favored in practice, Article 6; ensures effective communication inside the institutions, keeps cost of multilingualism in check.

The symbolic, representational, and legal dimensions of language together affirm the principle of language equality, since all three presuppose that no one national language ought to be formally favored relative to the others. These dimensions are, therefore, crucially important to the member states, all of which equate the use of their language with national power and the protection of national interest (Ban 2013). Language in the EU institutions is thus not only a "neutral medium of communication"; it relates to both national and social identity, and it engenders linguistic capital that affords symbolic power (Bourdieu 1992, 50–52; Loos 2000, 44). Indeed, it is generally about *relative* symbolic power, such that member states are mostly concerned about their languages being devalued in comparison to other languages of a similar "size" and stature. Warning bells thus start ringing at the mere suggestion that the use of a given (set of) language(s) be restricted.

Concerns, in this regard, are particularly pronounced among speakers of languages with a "great tradition," such as French or German (Bourdieu 1992). The French are especially concerned about the status of their language in EU politics, for several reasons. First, the French language, even more than in other European countries, is "inextricably linked so a sense of national identity and to pride in French culture" because it "replaced the king as the symbol of national unity" after the French Revolution (Ban 2013, 205–6). As French president Emmanuel Macron put it, "France was made through its language" (Zaretsky 2017). Second, it follows that the French are particularly concerned about the diminishing status of their language globally, especially as this diminution is driven by the rise of English. This concern, finally, is particularly acute in the EU context, in which the French have been trying to defend the historically privileged position of their language against the increasing dominance of English. It bears some irony that this guarding of French privilege has, after decades of primacy in EU politics, come via a rhetorical endorsement of multilingualism (Phillipson 2003, 133; Wright 2007, 154) and the establishment of a defensive alliance with the Germans, who also have raised concern at times about the German language being disadvantaged in the EU.[12] In 2000, France and Germany thus signed "an agreement of linguistic cooperation . . . which states that both countries support each other whenever the working status or function of their languages is unduly disregarded" (Ammon 2006, 331).[13]

The functional dimension of language, in contrast, provides for the possibility that to facilitate direct communication inside the EU's institutions, not all languages must be used equally; reliance on a shared procedural language is explicitly permitted for practical purposes. It also provides a means for ensuring that the costs of multilingualism do not skyrocket, since true and complete equal use of all languages inside the institutions would require a financial investment none of the member states are prepared to make. It is the one deviation from language equality the member states are willing to accept, likely in part because it has the least potential to be noticed and questioned by their general publics. At least some EU citizens would take note and mostly disapprove if they requested information from an EU institution and received a response in a foreign language, after all, or if a case before a national court was adjudicated based on a provision that was only available in another language. In contrast, they are unlikely to notice or care that some meetings inside the institutions involve a limited language regime, especially since language services are generally available when necessary. Moreover, situations when the language regime is limited occur under a "veil of formal language equality," which secures the relative symbolic power the member states are mostly concerned about.

This "veil of formal language equality" is, in fact, of great importance for the functioning of the language regime: member states are generally willing to accept that "their" languages will be underrepresented, as long as it is in situations when language services are not formally required, when their exclusion is not widely publicized, or when it threatens to set a precedent that may undermine formal language equality in the future.

Theorizing Institutional Change

The primary language rules established in Regulation No. 1 have proven to be remarkably stable: they have not been substantively changed since 1958. Yet we can observe a great deal of change in EU multilingualism over time. Most obvious and important are the increase in the number of official languages from 4 to 24 and the resulting increase in the language diversity of participants in EU policymaking and the number of unique language combinations, as well as the switch from French to English as the main shared language inside the institutions. There have also been notable shifts in the practical operation of the language services—discussed in more detail below—such as changes in the types of documents that get translated, the provision of interpretation based on the "real needs" of participants, the introduction of pivot languages for translation and interpretation, and the changing role of lawyer-linguists in policymaking. The costs of EU multilingualism have also increased over time, although not relative to the increase in the number of languages or possible language combinations.

An institutionalist approach lends itself to considerations of such stability and change in EU multilingualism, as one of the primary questions advanced by the "new institutionalism" relates to the sources of institutional continuity and change. It is, however, institutional stability—or the absence of institutional change—that institutionalists are good at explaining, while accounting for institutional change has been one of their primary challenges. Rational choice institutionalists, for example, view institutions as equilibrium outcomes that are not easily disturbed because no one has an incentive to alter them; historical institutionalists emphasize that institutions are path-dependent and become entrenched once put into place; and sociological institutionalists suggest that institutions reflect what is considered appropriate, or even conceivable, in a given situation, which insulates them against change (Peters 2005). So the question is what explains institutional change, and the easiest answer is that institutions change in response to "exogenous shocks," factors or events that are external to the institution itself. Exogenous shocks disturb the inherent stability of the institution and may lead to or facilitate institutional change.

It is, however, more difficult to explain endogenous institutional change, or change that originates from within or is at least in part a function of the institution itself. Greif and Laitin (2004) offer one such explanation, which is rooted in rational choice institutionalism and thus conceives of institutions as self-enforcing equilibria. These equilibria are dependent on the parameters of the underlying game, such as "the payoffs from various actions, time discount factors, risk preferences, wealth, and the number of players" (Greif and Laitin 2004, 634). Those parameters are stable in the short term—they do not change the behavior or expected behavior associated with an institution—but they may in fact slowly and marginally change over time. In the long term, therefore, they are endogenously determined, and thus variable. Indeed, the institution itself may change its own parameters over time.

According to Greif and Laitin, these slowly and marginally changing aspects should therefore be considered "quasi-parameters" that support the observed equilibrium in the short run but may lead to change in the long run (Greif and Laitin 2004, 634). Parametric change does not change behavior in the short term because, for example, scarcity of attention may let it go unnoticed, because individuals do not have sufficient knowledge and information to adjust their behavior to marginally changing circumstances, or because following past patterns of behavior is an easy solution to coordination problems triggered by parametric change. Put differently, marginal changes in quasi-parameters and their consequences do not change behavior in the short term because they are not "ex ante recognized, anticipated, directly observed, appropriately understood, or paid attention to" (Greif and Laitin 2004, 639). Over longer periods of time, however, parametric changes may lead to changes in behavior that are either intentional (individuals recognize changes in quasi-parameters and purposefully adjust their behavior) or unconscious (when changes in quasi-parameters are unobservable or uncertain and individual behavior changes in more "experimental" ways). These behavioral changes may have the effect of reinforcing the institution, meaning that "more individuals in more situations would find it best to adhere to the behavior associated with it," but they may also undermine the institution, when the opposite is the case and fewer individuals in fewer situations do so (Greif and Laitin 2004, 634). Endogenous institutional change thus occurs when this self-undermining process reaches a critical level, at which point a "punctuated equilibrium" will likely be observed, where change appears abrupt but is, in fact, the end result of an evolutionary process. Alternatively, parametric change may affect "the magnitude and nature of the exogenous shocks that will be necessary to cause the beliefs and behavior associated with that institution to change" (Greif and Laitin 2004, 639); the effects of endogenous processes will thus be indirect. Whether due to endogenous processes, exogenous shocks, or a combination of both, parametric change may lead to the creation of a new institution to replace the old. A more likely outcome, however, is "institutional refinement," because the "cognitive, coordinative, and informational content of institutionalized rules" (Greif and Laitin 2004, 649) make a complete departure from the past less likely.

This framework is useful for our purposes because it allows us to conceptualize both stability and change in the EU's language regime, in particular institutional stability and change that are endogenous. Specifically, it allows us to examine the extent to which the EU's language regime—the primary, secondary, and informal rules that govern multilingualism—are able to withstand or are induced to change as a result of sudden exogenous shocks, gradual exogenous parametric change, or endogenous quasi-parametric change.

Changing the EU's Language Rules

Key questions when considering institutional change as a result of either exogenous shocks or shifts in (quasi-)parameters are (a) what is required to change the formal institution, and (b) what it takes for practices and norms associated with multilingualism to change. Particularly important, in this regard, is identifying the actors capable of enacting formal institutional change. The first actor that could change the EU's primary language rules is the Court of Justice. The Court might rule, for example, that the language rules somehow conflict with the EU's founding treaties, or that Article 6—in theory or practice—is incompatible with the provisions for language equality in Regulation No. 1. Such scenarios might have been conceivable at some point in the past, but it is difficult to imagine it happening today. After all, the language rules have been in place for a long time without provoking ire in Luxembourg, and, when forced to adjudicate, the Court has confirmed the principles enshrined in Regulation No. 1, both by confirming the principle of language equality and the right of the institutions to maintain limited language regimes.

In the landmark case of *Kik vs. OHIM* (Case T-120/99, *Kik v Office for Harmonization in the Internal Market (Trade Marks and Designs) (OHIM)* [2001] ECR II-2235), the Court ruled that there is no "general principle of Community law that confers a right on every citizen to have a version of anything that might affect his interest drawn up in his language in all circumstances," because Regulation No. 1 must be considered secondary law and because such a principle would contradict the article in the EC Treaty that grants the Council power to change the EU's language rules. The Court thus confirmed that restricted language regimes in the EU institutions are legal, because "the language regime of a Community institution or body will often be the result of a difficult process which seeks to achieve the necessary balance between conflicting interests but also an appropriate linguistic solution to practical difficulties" (Athanassiou 2006, 12). More recently, Advocate General Maduro confirmed the view that an absolute principle of equality of EU languages does not exist and that there will be situations when languages will not be treated equally. The opinion states that

> it is necessary to accept restrictions in practice, in order to reconcile observance of that principle [of linguistic diversity] with the imperatives of institutional and administrative life. But those restrictions must be limited and justified. In any event, they cannot undermine the substance of the principle whereby Institutions must respect and use all the official languages of the Union.[14]

The opinion explains that certain restrictions based on administrative requirements are tolerable in the internal procedures of EU institutions and bodies when administrative efficiency demands the use of a limited number of languages. It also affirms a general commitment to language diversity, however, by emphasizing that such restrictions cannot result in a language regime that undermines the essence of linguistic diversity or the rules governing the external communications of the institutions. Indeed, it assigns the highest level of protection to the principle of linguistic diversity in communications between EU institutions and EU citizens (Athanassiou 2006, 12–13). The Court has thus recognized and "appears likely to do so again in the future" (Athanassiou 2006, 13) that the EU institutions' various restrictions on linguistic diversity are acceptable,[15] but that they must be limited, proportionate, and explicitly justified (Van der Jeught 2015).

The Court has also ruled to protect language diversity in other instances, for example in a series of cases in which the Commission tried to establish a limited trilingual regime of English, French, and German in competitions for the recruitment of administrators and assistants and in calls for proposals,[16] each of which the Commission lost (Gazzola 2016b, 547). In 2005, Italy brought a case against the Commission for publishing vacancy notices in English, French, and German only. The Court of First Instance ruled that there was significant risk that potential candidates whose native languages were not among those three would not learn of the vacancies and would thus be discriminated against even if they, in fact, spoke English, French, or German. Accordingly, the Commission would have to, at the least, publish short-form notices in all official languages, referring to the vacancy notices in English, French, and German. In 2010, however, the General Court ruled that candidates whose native language was not English, French, or German were at a disadvantage in terms of correctly understanding vacancy notices in those three languages and also with regard to the time it would take them to prepare and submit a job application. This, according to the Court, amounts to discrimination, meaning that recruitment notices must now be issued in all official languages.

In sum, previous rulings make it highly unlikely that the Court of Justice would overturn the EU's multilingual regime. Moreover, by ruling that Regulation No. 1 must be considered secondary law, it confirmed that it is the member states' prerogative to change the EU's primary language rules. This requires unanimous agreement by the member states, a principle that dates back to Article 217 of the EEC Treaty ("The Rules governing the languages of the institutions of the Community shall . . . be determined by the Council, acting unanimously.") and is enshrined today in Article 342 of the Lisbon Treaty. And despite the member states' apparent disinclination to substantively change the EU's primary language rules, there are scenarios under which the member states may be inclined to at least consider the possibility. There are three factors in particular the member states would likely be responsive to: public opinion, costs, and systemic dysfunction. In other words, if a critical mass of citizens became aware of, started caring, and negatively viewed EU multilingualism, the member state governments might find themselves reconsidering the rules. Similarly, if expending money on multilingualism were deemed unnecessary relative to the benefits of the language regime, the member states may be open to rule change. The same would be true, finally, if the EU language regime failed to fulfill all or some of its core functions: ensuring the symbolic equality of the official languages, safeguarding citizens' access to information, guaranteeing legal certainty in the application of EU law, and allowing actors inside the EU institutions to communicate effectively with each other. Put differently, in order to prompt changes to the EU's primary language rules, exogenous shocks or shifts in (quasi-)parameters would have to affect public opinion on EU multilingualism, make the language rules superfluous or redundant, or undermine the functioning of the language regime.

The EU's secondary language rules, which largely shape the use of languages in practice, are laid out in a variety of different intra- and interinstitutional documents. EU institutions are empowered by Article 6 of Regulation No. 1 to change or amend these secondary rules; the rules can be changed either by one institution (e.g., in the case of each institution's Rules of Procedure) or through interinstitutional agreement (e.g., in the case of the Joint Practical Guide for drafting legislation). Such changes are aimed entirely at the functioning of EU multilingualism inside the institutions, in that rules are maintained or altered to best accommodate the language needs of participants in EU politics. Formal secondary institutional change, in other words, is enacted to address (actual or anticipated) dysfunction in the operation of EU multilingualism. It tends to affect, in particular, the extent to which procedural languages are relied on more heavily relative to other languages, at the expense of language equality. In this regard, institutions are not only constrained by Regulation No. 1, however, but also by member states raising concerns about there being too great an imbalance in the use of languages (which they have done at various points in time) and by the Court of Justice's judgments regarding the EU's language regime. Within those constraints, however, it is the institutions that determine the parameters for actual language practices in EU politics, and thus the de facto balance between language equality (the symbolic, representational, and legal dimension of language) and favored status of some languages (the functional dimension of language). But it is important to emphasize in this context that the functional dimension of EU multilingualism is not simply about minimizing the number of languages. Indeed, it is not the case that using one or only a few languages necessarily results in better communication and a more efficient functioning of the language regime on the ground, as long as a critical mass of participants in EU politics is not sufficiently proficient in the relevant language(s). A key practical challenge for the EU's language regime is, therefore, to establish the right balance between the communication benefits that derive from shared language use and the communication benefits associated with continued multilingualism inside the institutions, which involves the continued reliance on language services. It is up to the EU institutions themselves to identify and (try to) establish that right balance in practice, again within the parameters of Regulation No. 1 and the budget allocations for language services.

An apparently obvious reason for the stability of the EU's primary language rules, as enshrined in Regulation No. 1, is that the unanimous agreement required among the member states sets an exceedingly high threshold for institutional change.[17] Even a cursory look at the history of the EU and the evolution of the European integration process reveals, however, that the unanimity rule does not guarantee permanence. Instead, we have seen the member states unanimously agree to wide-ranging and contested changes in EU policy (e.g. establishing the single market on the basis of the "four freedoms" of goods, services, capital, and people; wide-ranging reforms to the Common Agricultural Policy), the Union's institutional design (e.g., the empowerment of the European Parliament), and its decision-making rules (e.g., the introduction of the codecision procedure, changes to qualified majority voting rules). The possibility of a sole national veto surely discourages change, but it is not a sufficient condition for policy or institutional stability.

It is, moreover, not the case that the EU's primary language rules were seriously contested at any point in time and that it was only a possible veto that deterred a challenge to the status quo. Instead, as de Swaan put it,

> the subject of languages has been the great *non-dit* of European integration. There was much talk of milk pools and butter mountains, of a unitary currency, of liberalizing movements for EC citizens and restricting access for outsiders, but the language in which these issues were dealt with remained itself a non-issue. (De Swaan 2001, 144, 217)

Given the political sensitivity of the language question in the EU, it is not surprising that there is a distinct tendency of both EU and national politicians to avoid raising the issue (Mamadouh 1999; Phillipson 2003; Šarčević 2013; Strubell 2007; Wright 2000). National politicians across the member states are loath to accept the possibility of another language becoming formally more important than their own, even if they are willing to accept the reality that some languages are *informally* more equal than others. The potential loss of symbolic power is very much at play here (Loos 2000), as are concerns about possible electoral punishments (Wright 2009) and national countermobilization (Mamadouh 1999).

This is not to say that there was no contestation at all; when it occurred, however, it was in response to efforts to limit the number of working or procedural languages, not the number of official languages. In other words, contestation occurred regarding the EU's secondary, not primary, language rules: at stake were not the basic principles of language equality and the prerogative of the EU institutions to rely on a subset of languages in their day-to-day operations, but the relative use of different languages within those parameters. For example, the 1995 French Presidency of the Council made the proposal to restrict the number of working languages in the Commission to five, a suggestion that was met with immediate opposition by other member states and was dropped from the agenda (Wright 2000; Phillipson 2003). In 1999, Finland assumed the Council presidency and made no provisions for German interpretation at informal Council meetings. When Finland ignored German and Austrian protests, the two countries boycotted the first three meetings, and Finland gave in (Ammon 2010, 229; Phillipson 2003, 21–22). In 2001, Commission President Romano Prodi and Vice-President Neil Kinnock circulated the idea of making English the principal working language in the Commission, which the French and German governments, in particular, protested vehemently (Ammon 2010, 229). Prodi's response, offered in both French and German, reasserted the Commission's commitment to multilingualism (Phillipson 2003, 30). In 2005, it was the Italian government, in particular, that protested the decision of the Commission to limit the languages for its press conferences to English, French, German, and the language of the reporting Commissioner. The Commission left the limitation in place but conceded that other languages would be used when necessary (Ammon 2010, 229). Around the same time, the Commission triggered further dispute by changing its recruitment rules so that positions would only be advertised in English, French, and German, a practice that was ultimately scrapped following a ruling by the General Court (Gazzola 2016b, 547).

I am aware of only a single episode when actually limiting the number of official languages was briefly discussed. At the time of the EU's first enlargement in 1973, it was not even clear that English would become an official language and English texts be accorded equal authenticity (Šarčević 2007, 37). Upon its accession, Denmark was prepared to give up official language status for Danish and made the proposal that English and French become formal working languages, but only if native French speakers were forced to speak English and native English speakers French (Phillipson 2003, 223); in other words, nobody would use their native language inside the institutions.[18] This was "immediately rejected by the British and French," however (Wright 2000, 175), which led the Danes to insist on official language status for Danish. This set an important precedent, since Danish was the language of a minute portion of EU citizens. It would be difficult, thereafter, to deny official status to the language of any new member state upon accession (Clark and Priestley 2012, 162), even though concerns continued to be raised about the impact of enlargement on the functioning of EU multilingualism. Between 1979 and 1982, for example, members and committees in the European Parliament "studied the language question and expressed concern at the implications of the increase in the number of pairs of languages for translation and interpretation from 30 to 72" (Nic Craith 2006, 45; Wright 2000, 165–67). The EP ultimately passed a resolution rejecting calls for limiting the number of languages or introducing asymmetrical regimes, however. Concerns resurfaced especially in the run-up to the 2004 enlargement, when "serious doubts were raised, at least unofficially" not only about an increase in costs, inconvenience, and inefficiency, but also about most of the incoming languages being "small" and relatively unknown; "all proposals to reduce the number of official languages were flatly rejected by politicians," however (Šarčević 2007, 37). No serious consideration was given to ideas such as limiting the number of new official languages or granting the new languages a lower status.[19]

Simply put, there is little to suggest that the unanimity requirement is the main impediment to efforts at changing the rules. What we observe, instead, is the member states and EU institutions adjusting secondary language rules to ensure the continued practical operation of the language regime while preserving the basic principles enshrined in Regulation No. 1, including the safeguarding of the symbolic, representational, legal, and functional dimensions of EU multilingualism. They did so, at various points in time, in response to three factors: the EU's growing competences over time, the empowerment of the EP and the Court of Justice, and the various rounds of EU enlargement.

Institutional Stability and Change over Time

Starting with the Single European Act in 1987, the EU's authority to take policy action and enact legally binding acts has increased gradually with each treaty revision, and altogether dramatically. This resulted in a proliferation in the amount of EU legislation across a vastly increasing number of policy areas, as well as an expansion in the jurisdiction of the Court of Justice and, as a result, in the Court's case load. The same treaty revisions also successively expanded the European Parliament's role in EU lawmaking, while the Court of Justice was empowered not only through treaty change, but also through the evolution of its own case law. Most important, in this regard, are the Court's assertions of the doctrines of supremacy (prescribes that EU law takes precedence over the national law of the EU member states) and direct effect (gives individuals the right to invoke provisions from EU law before national and European courts). These developments, as well as the expansion of EU membership from 6 to 28 members and the resulting increase in the number of official languages, individually and jointly created a need for changes in the quantity and quality of EU language services: there was greater necessity for interpretation and translation covering increasingly consequential oral proceedings and written documents across a wider range of substantive policy areas and variation in national legal systems.

One way to think of these developments is as exogenous shocks, since they are external to the language regime itself and every moment of change (each round of enlargement, each treaty revision) could have served as a trigger for institutional change. Alternatively, the competences of the EU, the balance of power between its institutions, and the number of member states and official languages can be conceived as quasi-parameters that are stable in the short run but might have changed gradually over time so that they undermined the institutional stability of the EU's language regime. An exogenous shock might have resulted in change of the EU's primary language rules based on the recognition that the language regime was no longer viable. Since the member states are evidently reluctant to significantly increase their contributions to the EU budget, the likely outcome would have been a weakening of the language equality requirements to lower the demands placed on the language services. Quasi-parametric change, in contrast, might have had two consequences. First, it had the potential to successively undermine the proper functioning of the institutions by increasing the incidence of mistakes, miscommunications, and inefficiencies in the interpretation and translation processes. Second, it might have sufficiently

98 The Language(s) of Politics

widened the gap between symbolic language equality (in theory) and limited multilingualism (in practice) to "hollow out" a system built on the overarching premise that all official languages are formally equal. Eventually, either development could have brought about a tipping point where the primary language rules became susceptible to change.

Neither happened, however, and the primary language rules were instead affirmed as a result of these developments. For example, the supremacy and direct effect doctrines elevated not only the overall standing of EU law and of the Court of Justice, they also strengthened the importance of the legal dimension of the language regime, because legal certainty is particularly important when EU law trumps national law and can be directly invoked in national and European courts. As a result of this, the drafting of EU legislation and its equal authenticity in all official languages—as enshrined in Articles 4 and 5 of Regulation No. 1—took on additional prominence. Similarly, the empowerment of the EP significantly strengthened the representational dimension of the EU's language rules, as captured in Articles 2 and 3 of Regulation No. 1. The direct election of the EP, starting in 1979, and especially the subsequent increase in the institution's authority, meant that the right to information of the citizens who elect their representatives became more pivotal than they were before. Moreover, the representational dimension of language implies that it must be possible for a representative of the European people to hold elected office independent of foreign language proficiency; after all, how can citizens exert their influence through and receive information from their elected representatives about actual and possible EU actions and policies if said representatives are de facto excluded from policymaking? And how would it be justified to force citizens to select less preferred representatives because of their superior language skills, or to prevent them from running for office themselves because of limited foreign language skills? As long as the EU operated as an international organization, with power vested in the hands of national governments, such issues were of less concern than after the first direct EP election in 1979 and the subsequent empowerment of the only directly elected EU institution. Hence, the empowerment of the EP reinforced the symbolic and representational dimensions of EU language policy and thus the EU's primary language rules.

Finally, consider the impact of enlargement. Each round of enlargement had the potential to undermine the language regime, but at these moments of potential institutional weakness the member states recommitted themselves to the language rules by accepting the national languages of the incoming member states as official EU languages. The principle of formal language equality, and thus the symbolic dimension of language in the EU enshrined in Regulation No. 1, was reinforced with each expansion. That it was not even questioned when the prospect of the 2004 "big bang" enlargement promised to almost double the number of official languages is particularly notable: not even what might be considered the most likely moment of institutional change resulted in reconsideration of the primary language rules.

Instead, the member states repeatedly voted unanimously to change Regulation No. 1 so that its basic underlying principles would be preserved. That is what has happened each time Article 1 was amended to expand the list of official languages (in 1973, 1981, 1986, 1995, 2004, 2007, and 2013). After all, by adding official languages with each enlargement, the member states left the basic substance of Regulation No. 1 untouched, since *not* adding the national language of a new member state would mean that all languages would no longer be equal. In other words, it is through the addition of new official languages that the rules remain unchanged in their essence, when all it would have taken to undermine the EU's primary language rules is the veto of a single member state. *Multiple unanimous* votes—over the course of four decades—to preserve one of the core principles enshrined in the primary rules of EU multilingualism are a strong indicator of a stable consensus in their favor. The member states have continuously recommitted themselves to pairing a formal commitment to language equality with de facto restricted multilingualism inside the institutions, and they have purposefully and unanimously adjusted the primary language rules to preserve the EU's language regime.

Instead of the EU's primary language rules changing, it was the secondary language rules that were altered to address the consequences of the expansion of EU competences (more policy areas), the empowerment of the EU's supranational institutions (more policymakers), and enlargement (more languages). Those formal rule changes also coincided with and, to an extent, provided an impetus for informal changes of prevailing norms, conventions, and practices relating to language use in the institutions.[20] Such changes occurred, however, within the parameters imposed by the EU's primary language rules.

In response to various enlargements and the resulting increase in the number of official languages over time, but also in response to an increase in the competences of the EU following various revisions of the EU Treaties (European Commission 2010a), the institutions had to continuously work to balance the commitment to full language equality with the practical and budgetary constraints that came with the addition of new languages and EU competences. Already in the early 1980s, when the European Community was confronted with the imminent challenge of integrating Greek, Spanish, and Portuguese, there were concerns that "the Community institutions, as they struggle to maintain the linguistic regime, will begin to resemble the legendary Tower of Babel" (Brown 1981, 341). In 1984, the Commission advocated weighing the symbolic importance of language equality against "pragmatic formulas" based on "actual needs." In particular, a distinction was to be made between meetings of politicians with popular mandates and those involving officials, staff, and technical experts. For the latter, the goal was to allow all participants to express themselves sufficiently, in their native languages if necessary, but to restrict the language services provided to the minimum possible. In practice, this meant a strengthening of the already dominant French and the ascending English (Kraus 2008, 121–22).

Such considerations became ever more pressing and, in response to the "big bang" enlargement of 2004 in particular, the institutions had to make adjustments to their language services to ensure that needs were sufficiently met, quality maintained, and costs kept at bay (Duflou 2016, 95). This meant finding ways to make them more efficient, because the influx of languages was not matched with budget increases that would cover the increase in costs if no changes were made.[21] What is more, the doubling of the number of official languages brought about by the accession of the new member states in 2004 and 2007 was not only a budgetary problem, but also one of space and recruitment, since bringing in the new languages exacerbated the scarcity of meeting rooms with a sufficient number of interpretation booths and raised the difficult challenge of recruiting sufficiently qualified interpreters and translators from some small language communities (Duflou 2016, 106). While the institutions were quickly able to accommodate at least a few meetings per day with a full interpretation regime, the training and recruitment of qualified personnel would remain a challenge for several years to come (Duflou 2016, 107–8).

In the EP, preparations for the 2004 enlargement were led by a new working group under the leadership of Guido Podesta, an Italian Vice-President of the institution. The report the group presented in July 2001 was "unambiguous in supporting the multilingual principle," as the EP's former Secretary-General Julian Priestley later wrote, "but it also recognized the heavy extra cost to the Parliament's budget, even if some supplementary spending could be offset by rationalization measures and cutting out non-essential tasks" (Clark and Priestley 2012, 167). The report provided a blueprint, described by Clark and Priestley (2012) in some detail,

The EU's Language Regime — 101

for how the language services were to continue functioning after 2004. It estimated extra costs of 200 million euros and the need for 1,200 extra staff members, which were to start being recruited as early as 2002, easily accomplished for some languages and "painfully" slowly for others (Clark and Priestley 2012, 169). In the end, the influx of nine new languages in 2004 did not involve the type of horror scenarios some observers expected. While not a perfectly fluid transition, the language services proved resilient due to "a mixture of intense forward planning and basic pragmatism," and there were "few complaints," Priestley recalls (Clark and Priestley 2012, 169).

The system endorsed by the EP in its 2004 "Code of Conduct on Multilingualism" was one of "controlled full multilingualism," to keep the budgetary costs of language services to acceptable levels while ensuring "equality among Members and Citizens" (European Parliament 2004). According to this model, MEPs continued to have the right to rely on the languages they preferred, but adjustments were made to the language services to more efficiently meet their needs, using either existing but not widely used measures or introducing new ones (Gazzola 2006, 402). Today, the term "resource-efficient full multilingualism" captures a similar principle, whereby MEPs have a right to use the official language of their choice, while "the resources to be devoted to multilingualism shall be controlled by means of management on the basis of users' real needs" (European Parliament 2014). The Commission similarly reaffirmed in its preparations for the 2004 enlargement its policy of multilingualism based on the "real needs" of users, which had already been in place since 1984.[22]

After the 2004 enlargement, some of the same adjustments were adopted in the EP as in the other institutions (although with some nuanced differences based on the specific needs of each), such as relay, retour, and asymmetric interpretation. While relay interpretation (or indirect interpretation via the EP's three relay languages: English, French, and German) had already been used prior to 2004 and only became more frequently relied upon after 2004, the possibility of retour interpretation—or interpretation from an interpreter's native language into a nonnative one, most often English or French—marked a notable departure from the principle that interpreters interpret only into their mother tongues (Duflou 2016, 109). It was a "profound change in the post-2004 interpreting arrangements," but one that was then "unavoidable" and is now permanent (Duflou 2016, 109). As one of my respondent explained, it was once considered an evil but, out of necessity, no longer is (#1). Finally, asymmetric interpretation became a more commonplace practice, where participants speak their native language, but interpretation is only provided into some languages. One option is the so-called "SALT" (Speak All, Listen Three) system, which provides interpretation into English, French, and German only. The assumption behind this approach is that participants' passive knowledge of these languages suffices for them to understand the proceedings, even if they are unable to speak them with sufficient comfort (Wagner, Bech, and Martínez 2014, 102).[23] In both the Council and the EP, systems of interpretation "by request" are now in place for preparatory meetings (Gazzola 2006), and the latter has established "linguistic profiles" for parliamentary committees and other bodies to better anticipate and plan for language service needs. In the Commission, full interpretation is only provided for political bodies and limited or asymmetric regimes for technical representatives and staff.[24]

The institutions also introduced changes to their translation systems, among them the use of pivot languages that serve as bridges between lesser-used languages. As in relay interpretation, documents are translated into a pivot language and then retranslated from that language into others. In the EP, the pivot languages for translation are English, French, and German;[25] in the Court of Justice, they are English, French, German, Spanish, Italian, and Polish;[26] in the Commission, they are English and French;[27] and in the Council just English.[28] Also commonplace became so-called "aller-retour" or "two-way" translation, into and out of translators' mother tongues instead of into their native languages only (Wagner, Bech, and Martínez 2014, 103), often with a native speaker double-checking the text afterwards. The relay and pivot systems mean that translation and interpretation do not involve the theoretically possible but practically unworkable 552 language combinations that come with 24 official languages, which hugely cuts down on translation and interpretation costs by limiting the total number of language "pairs" and by making it unnecessary to train and recruit language service providers able to interpret or translate from Maltese into Estonian, for example. Other changes include the introduction of "linguistic profiling" in the translation of amendments, which are only translated into the languages of the relevant committee members and not necessarily into all official languages; the translation of verbatim reports of plenary proceedings on demand only; and greater reliance on new technologies.[29]

In addition, the EP and the Commission introduced length restrictions for different types of documents to cut down on translation costs and efforts (Gazzola 2006; Ginsburgh and Weber 2011; Tosi 2005). The Commission also started to carefully identify the documents that need translation into all languages and those that do not, with the highest priority given to legal acts and documents with major legal and financial implications (Ginsburgh and Weber 2011). As a result, the workload for the eleven "old" languages fell by 30 percent (European Commission 2010b, 46). The translation services in both the Commission and the EP also rely to a greater extent on freelance linguistic staff outside the institutions. In the Commission, for example, a distinction is made between core documents that have to be translated in-house and those that can be outsourced.[30] Moreover, efforts were made to ensure that draft texts were more concise, to aid with the translation of those texts (European Commission 2010b, 46). Finally, the institutions improved their use of specialized software and databases to facilitate the work of language service providers (Gravier and Lundquist 2016, 81). As a result of these changes, a reduced number of languages is used in most preparatory meetings across the institution today, based on the practical requirements of the participants, and preparatory documents are not usually available in all official languages. In general, the more formal, high-level, and public a meeting, the more likely it is to have interpretation into a greater number of languages.

As a result of the reforms that were implemented in response to the growing number of official languages, the EU was able to avoid the disproportionate impact that adding a large number of new official languages would have (such as the increase of possible language combinations from 110 when there were 11 official languages before 2004 to 380 after nine languages were added in 2004). Gazzola (2006, 400) calculates that the cost of translation increased from 523 to 807 million euros between 1999 and 2006–2007 (+65 percent), the cost of interpretation from 163 to 238 million euros (+69 percent), and thus the total costs for both from 686 to 1,045 million euros (+66 percent). In other words, the increase in the costs of language services was large, but not nearly as large as it would have been without reform.[31] Because of this reality and because the system continued to work reasonably well even after enlargement, the primary language rules were left untouched even in the run-up to 2004 and in its aftermath.[32]

One key consequence of the reforms, however, was that the institutions tilted the balance between complete language equality and efficient communication in favor of the latter without, however, sacrificing the formal commitment to language equality (Bugarski 2009, 110–11). The full language equality that exists on paper thus differs from the more limited multilingualism we observe in practice, as many others before me have observed (e.g., Mamadouh 1999; Longman 2007; van Els 2001, 2005; Wodak 2013; Van der Jeught 2015). This reality is at times criticized as hypocritical (e.g., House 2001; De Swaan 2007; Kraus 2008), and some commentators decry the disconnect between de jure language equality and de facto limited multilingualism in the EU. This discounts Article 6 of Regulation No. 1 relative to Article 1, however, when both provisions are part of the same regulation and thus equally de jure. From their earliest conception, the EU language rules have explicitly permitted a selective form of multilingualism under some circumstances, and even after twenty new official languages were added language services have been used pragmatically to ensure the participation of EU actors in policymaking processes without requiring secondary language skills. Interpretation is made available to those who need it in formal meetings across the institutions, and translation into all official languages is ensured for legal acts and particularly consequential documents, especially those that are aimed at or have consequences for the general publics across the member states.

Moreover, the EU and its institutions have continuously reaffirmed their commitment to multilingualism. The Lisbon Treaty charges the Union with supporting member state action to teach and disseminate the languages of the member states (Article 165.2), while respecting the responsibility of the member states for education policy, as well as cultural and linguistic diversity (Article 165.1). Similarly, the Charter of Fundamental Rights obliges the EU to respect linguistic diversity (Article 22) and prohibits discrimination on grounds of language (Article 22), making respect for linguistic diversity "a fundamental value of the EU" (Climent-Ferrando 2016, 5). The institutions have also reaffirmed their commitment to multilingualism, in particular when their obligations in terms of language services were set to increase disproportionately and they sought to dispel concerns about the implications thereof, as was the case in the run-up to the Union's 2004 eastward enlargement. The Commission, for example, reaffirmed its "commitment to multilingualism in the European Union" in its communication regarding the "A New Framework Strategy for Multilingualism" (COM/2005/0596 final), emphasizing that citizens must be given access to EU "legislation, procedures and information in their own languages" and that multilingualism was "essential for the proper functioning of the European Union." During the same time period, the European Parliament, in its "Code of Conduct on Multilingualism" (adopted by the Bureau on April 19, 2004), affirmed that "the right of Members to use in Parliament the official language of their choice . . . shall be fully respected" (Article 1.2) even under the new system of "controlled full multilingualism" that was to be implemented in preparation for the EU's imminent eastward enlargement (European Parliament 2004). The general principle of language equality thus remains firmly in place (Gazzola 2006, 394).

Potential Sources of Future Institutional Change

Brexit

The endurance of the underlying principles of the EU's language regime does not, of course, rule out future institutional change. Assuming that the decision to retain English as an official language after Brexit is not challenged in coming years, we in fact already witnessed one: English has been grandfathered in as an official language even though it was not registered as an official language by any of the current member states. English was registered by the British when they joined in 1973, allowing the other two countries in which English is an official language, Ireland and Malta, to register Irish and Maltese, respectively. Hence, English is not "associated" with any one member state, which sets it apart from the other official languages. To leave the basic underlying principles of the EU's language regime intact, English would have had to be dropped from the list of official languages, but that did not happen because it has become indispensable for the practical operation of EU multilingualism, as discussed in detail in chapters 4 and 5 (indeed, the general consensus among my respondents, prior to the UK formally leaving the EU, was that English would remain an official language and retain its status as the most important language inside the EU institutions). And so, in effect, Brexit was an exogenous shock that changed the EU's language regime, but in such a way that it continues operating largely as before (see chapter 5 for an additional discussion of Brexit).

While predicting other, future exogenous shocks would be an exercise in futility, there are a number of factors that are *quasi-parameters* and thus potential sources of endogenous institutional change.[33] I will briefly discuss several such factors that may, over time, result in institutional change by affecting citizens' attitudes toward EU multilingualism, by making the language rules superfluous or redundant, or by undermining the functioning of the language regime, since—to reiterate—the member states would be most responsive to public opinion, costs, and systemic dysfunction.

Politicization

EU multilingualism could come under stress if the issue, which at this point is flying largely under the radar, became politicized. This could happen, for example, because linguistic minorities in one (or more) member state(s) came into positions of sufficient political power to credibly push for an expansion of the number of official languages. The same might happen in reaction to EU-sceptics accusing the EU of being antidemocratic because of an alleged disregard for small and minority languages, although the more likely scenario is that EU-sceptic parties would make the opposite charge: that the EU was being wasteful in its spending on language services. In this context, EU-sceptic "rebel rousers" would politicize the language issue as part of a broader agenda of delegitimizing the EU in an effort to score electoral points with their national audiences. This might result in national governments that include EU-sceptic parties pushing for limits on EU multilingualism, in mainstream governments parties seeking new language rules to avoid a possible disruption of EU politics or the integration process more generally, or in fewer resources being committed toward multilingualism. The outcome of the latter would be a decrease in the effectiveness of those services or a widening of the gap between the ideal of language equality and the practice of limited multilingualism, or both. The EU language regime would be more prone to institutional change as a result.

Foreign Language Proficiency

Concerns about the cost of multilingualism may also drive institutional change if language services were to become increasingly perceived as superfluous or redundant. This may result, first, from changes in the foreign language capacities of EU actors or of the EU citizens who select them. At no point in time between the 1950s and today have EU actors or EU citizens at large possessed sufficient foreign language skills to make the EU's multilingual regime superfluous. Collectively, participants in EU policymaking have always required translation and interpretation from and into their native languages to operate inside the institutions, while citizens have been reliant on their native languages to interact with and receive information from the EU, its institutions, and EU actors. Hence, this parameter has not only supported the observed equilibrium, it has been a major part of its raison-d'être. It is conceivable, however, that people's command of foreign languages—especially of English, the primary shared language inside the institutions as well as in the international public sphere—will improve over time such that EU multilingualism will become superfluous or redundant.[34] Multilingualism would no longer be a necessity from a representational, legal, and functional point of view, because citizens would not need to receive information in their native languages, because the equal application of EU legislation would no longer depend on equally authentic versions in all official languages, and because EU actors would no longer be reliant on language services to participate in policy-making.[35] This would leave the symbolic value of language equality as the only reason for the existence of the EU's multilingual regime, but such "identity concerns" may ultimately fall victim to the efficiency gains provided by a single language (Laitin 1994, 622). What is today seen by many, if not most, EU actors as a matter of principle—the symbolic significance of language equality and the importance of multilingualism for the quality of democratic representation and legitimacy in the EU involves a commitment to multilingualism based on a "logic of appropriateness" (March and Olsen 2006)[36]—might well give way to more pragmatic considerations. This may happen more or less suddenly. For example, it is possible that we would observe a "punctuated equilibrium" (Baumgartner and Jones 2009) or "critical juncture" (Capoccia 2016) when the institution that has become slowly obsolete is abruptly transformed or eliminated. Alternatively, change may be creeping, in that the improving foreign language proficiency of EU actors leads to reduced reliance on language services, which in turn are provided on a less consistent basis, which results in the allocation of fewer resources toward language services, which creates an incentive for national actors (governments, political parties, voters) to "send" delegates with sufficient foreign language skills to the EU, which makes them less reliant on language services, and so on.[37] In other words, a negative feedback loop would transform the EU language regime over the course of time.

Machine Translation and Interpretation

Another factor that may result in EU multilingualism becoming redundant is an advance in computer translation and interpretation. Computer translation is making rapid strides and is already integrated as a default tool in the work environments of EU translators (#15), although at this time mostly as a processing tool that precedes and aids human translation or revision of texts. For this purpose, the Commission has its own machine translation web service called eTranslation, which processed almost four million pages for use in DG Translation in 2018. Translators in the EP also rely on machine-translated segments from eTranslation, as well as a computer-assisted translation tool that automatically matches new texts with translation memories containing previously translated text segments.[38]

Optimists foresee technology that is as good as or even better than human translators in the near future,[39] and it may not be too far off until smartphone apps provide for accurate and reliable on-the-spot interpretation. Such developments would not only reduce the need for language services, they would also make foreign language skills less necessary and useful for participants in EU policymaking. The consequences for EU multilingualism in terms of costs, personnel needs, and practice are potentially far-reaching. But important challenges remain at this time (and into the foreseeable future).[40] First among the problems with machine translation today, even as it is starting to approach or meet human-like levels of accuracy,[41] is that the mistakes it does produce tend to be more serious or dramatic than is the case for human translators. Among the reasons for this reality is that computers lack the common sense to recognize and correct a blunder that would obviously stand out to a human, as well as their difficulties with anything new or unusual (such as new words or concepts that were not included in their "training" data, typos, ambiguities, words with multiple meaning, idioms, and the like). Machine learning mitigates such problems, but whatever is nonstandard or calls for a "judgment call" will nonetheless continue to require human involvement for some time to come. There are also potentially significant questions about the legal ramifications of mistakes made by computers, as opposed to humans, or more generally about the extent to which such mistakes are tolerated, especially in a context in which *human* fallibility is broadly accepted as inevitable and inherent to a multilingual environment, as is discussed in detail in chapter 4.

Meanwhile, technology for translating spoken language is less advanced and more error-prone nowadays than is the case for written text. It is nonetheless likely that relevant software or smartphone apps will at least facilitate conversations in the foreseeable future. This may matter greatly in the EU context, for example with regard to the types of informal and spontaneous exchanges in the hallway or elevator in which a foreign language handicap can now be a genuine disadvantage. And while the technology would not allow for fluent conversation, because high-quality simultaneous or near-simultaneous machine interpretation poses special challenges in terms of speed and accuracy, its use will likely offer substantial benefits for some EU actors relative to the current status quo. Hence, the introduction of new technology might not undermine the current language regime, but reinforce it by helping to mitigate some of its shortcomings. It could also prove to be disruptive, however, especially looking further into the future, when some of the current weaknesses of machine translation of both spoken and written text may well be eliminated. While technology is unlikely to crowd out human translators and interpreters entirely anytime soon, it has the potential to have a dramatic effect down the road on how language service providers fulfill their tasks, for example by increasingly turning translators into revisers of machine-translated texts.

Institutional Dysfunction

The EU member states not only care about the costs of multilingualism when it comes to the basic necessity for EU multilingualism but also about the quality and effectiveness of the regime. In other words, they care about the proper functioning of the institution because they have an interest in the EU policymaking process operating reasonably efficiently and effectively. If the system became sufficiently dysfunctional, it may trigger institutional change.

Dysfunctional, in this regard, could mean that there is an undue amount of mistakes, miscommunications, inefficiencies, or other problems in the practical operation of the language regime, such that EU multilingualism becomes unsustainable in practice. Alternatively, dysfunction might mean that the system operates in such a way that it negates the basic premise of EU multilingualism. EU multilingualism combines a formal commitment to language equality with a practical reliance on limited multilingualism. If, over time, the system tilted so far toward reliance on English only, or English plus a small number of additional "big" languages (especially French and German), the commitment to language equality may be seen as a mere façade. This "hollowing out" of the system could reach a tipping point where the institution becomes susceptible to change.

Changes in Legal Multilingualism

Finally, changes in legal multilingualism may lead to changes in institutional multilingualism. One possibility is that divergences in different language versions of EU legislation are so frequent or substantial that EU law can no longer be interpreted and applied uniformly and reliably. In that scenario, multilingualism would no longer ensure the equality of EU citizens before the law but would, in fact, undermine legal certainty. At that point, limiting the number of authentic languages might be seen as preferable even at the cost of partial "linguistic disenfranchisement," which would open the door to formally limiting the number of languages used inside the institutions. We might observe the same outcome if the Court of Justice confirmed, over time, that there is an "original" language version of EU legislation that reflects "the intent of the legislator," against which others are judged when in conflict. Member state courts today generally rely only on their own language versions when adjudicating EU law, unless it is deemed ambiguous (Capoccia 2016). This reflects the Court's judgment in the Van der Vecht case of 1967, which states that national courts need to consult the other language versions "in cases of doubt"; it also stands to reason given that it is unrealistic to expect member state courts and tribunals to compare all the different official language versions before interpreting each judgment by an EU court (Šarčević 2013; McAuliffe 2013b). But the ruling is problematic from the point of view of legal certainty for individuals, as Šarčević (2013) argues, because it signals to EU citizens that their language version may not be reliable because of potential divergences between language versions. She foresees the possibility that "victims of multilingualism" may take their cases to the Court of Human Rights in the future (Šarčević 2013, 16). To date, the system has withstood these problems due to the Court striking "a proper balance when ascertaining the uniform meaning of the equally authentic language versions of EU legislation" (Šarčević 2013, 10),[42] but an increase in the number of "victims of multilingualism" would have the potential to shake the foundations of EU legal multilingualism and, by extension, of institutional multilingualism.

Conclusion

The evolution of the EU's language regime is marked by both continuity and change, an apparent disconnect this chapter sought to resolve and make sense of. By applying an institutionalist lens, it showed that the EU's primary language rules are remarkably stable, but that this stability is not coincidental: it is the result of adjustments in the practical operation of the language regime, through both formal modifications of secondary language rules and informal changes in the practices of language use inside the EU institutions. The evolution of the EU language regime is thus an example of institutional reproduction and change being two sides of the same coin (Thelen 1994; 2004). It is institutional adjustments that have allowed the EU language regime to successfully balance the symbolic, representational, legal, and functional dimensions of language over time, despite dramatic change in the EU's political system.

The EU's language regime is one of *uneven multilingualism* that operates under a *veil of formal language equality*. It is uneven in that certain languages have always been favored over others in the EU's everyday operations, which facilitates efficient communication inside the institutions, limits the cost of multilingualism, and allows EU multilingualism to evolve endogenously to best match the functional needs of different actors across the EU's core institutions. As long as these benefits are realized under a veil of formal language equality—as otherwise enshrined in Regulation No. 1—the member states are willing to accept de facto language inequality in EU politics. The member states are also quite aware of the symbolic power associated with language use in the EU and the potential volatility of the language question; hence, they profit from the language regime's success in *de*politicizing language choice, whether they recognize it or not.

Despite these benefits, the combination of formal language equality and uneven multilingualism is not usually seen in a positive light by observers of EU multilingualism. In fact, the ability of the EU institutions to mold their language rules and practices according to their particular needs is more often than not considered a problem, an "unresolved clash between top-down policy and bottom-up practice" (Wright 2009, 97) that reveals a pressing need for a new, more uniform language policy (see also Wodak 2013, 94; Van der Jeught 2015, 267; van Els 2001, 349). Skeptics thus see an inherent contradiction in the EU's language regime. Yet this apparent contradiction has been a feature, not a bug, of EU multilingualism since its inception, and critics tend to assume that an explicit, uniform policy would be preferable to the status quo. This is likely not the case, however, because the very incongruity in the language rules they decry allows EU actors to rely on "a range of pragmatic solutions that function as long as nobody explicitly discusses them," as a former German delegate to Coreper put it (referenced in Kraus 2008, 131–32). Moreover, each EU institution is able to rely on the language rules and practices that best match the needs of those working inside it, and those needs vary significantly. For example, politicians in the Council and the EP often use their native languages, either because their foreign language skills are lacking or because they seek to address domestic audiences; this is much less often the case among multilingual EU officials in the Commission. The EU's language regime offers sufficient flexibility to accommodate such differences. Last, but certainly not least, "resolving" the supposed disconnect between policy and practice in EU multilingualism would not be politically costless.[43] In fact, a debate about language rules would likely result in identity-based contestation and conflict, thus undermining a language regime that is broadly accepted by the member states, serves and protects political and linguistic equality within the EU (Nordland 2002, 48), and—for the most part—works in practice. As one of my respondents, a legal counselor in the

Permanent Representation of a member state, put it, "through a common working language, we get closer, but it will divide us if we do not have our own languages. It looks like a bit of a paradox, but it's how it works" (#68).

That EU multilingualism generally works and fulfills its core functions does not, however, mean that it is without consequence. In subsequent chapters, I focus on one particularly important consequence of the EU's language regime: it not only depoliticizes language as a potential issue of contention among EU member states, as discussed in the present chapter, it also depoliticizes EU policymaking in practice. I make this case, first, with regard to nonnative language use inside the EU institutions, and in particular concerning "EU English." I then discuss how reliance on language services has a depoliticizing effect.

FOUR

Foreign Language Use and Depoliticization

While European Union (EU) multilingualism tends to be associated primarily with the EU's translation and interpretation services, a similarly prevalent aspect of it is the reality that most interactions between individuals inside the EU institutions take place in a shared foreign language. This chapter takes a close look at nonnative language use among EU actors, with a particular focus on English as their main vehicular language. It argues that the use of a shared nonnative language for communication tends to depoliticize decision making inside and between the EU institutions by simplifying, standardizing, and neutralizing both spoken and written language. Notably—and in contrast to what we learned about the EU's language regime in the previous chapter—the depoliticization discussed in this and the remaining empirical chapters is *unintentional*. Depoliticization occurs inadvertently through foreign language use and reliance on language services, not by design.

The language used by nonnative speakers in the EU tends to be simple, pragmatic, and utilitarian. This is not inherently or necessarily depoliticizing, but in the EU it is, in that language largely serves as a mere instrument of communication rather than a political tool used to serve or advance a particular agenda. The main reason for this reality is that most people are unable to express themselves in a foreign language with the same competence, ease, and spontaneity as would be the case in their mother tongue. Their vocabulary, grammar, and syntax are simpler, and their ability to use idiomatic, rhetorically rich language is circumscribed. Expressing oneself takes substantially greater effort, which forces nonnative speakers to focus on getting their message or ideas across, rather than using elaborate, complex speech or writing in the process. Given their linguistic limitations, nonnative English speakers are also less likely to be original in their language use. While necessarily flexible and "loose" in their language given their own linguistic limitations and those of others, EU actors also tend to adopt commonly used words, phrases, and other linguistic constructs. This results in a standardization of language, meaning that EU actors are less distinguishable on the basis of their oral interventions or written texts alone. Simplification and standardization thus contribute to language being neutralized, because it is used similarly across nationalities, ideologies, and cultures. In other words, how an EU actor speaks or writes in a foreign language is less indicative of her national or cultural background, or of her political preferences.

Language not only tends to be simplified, standardized, and neutralized because of the limited ability of EU actors to express themselves, but also because of the limited ability of many to *understand* complex nonnative language. Hence, native or advanced nonnative English speakers may use comparatively more sophisticated language, yet avoid overly complicated linguistic constructs, idiomatic speech, or elaborate rhetoric, for the simple reason that others would have difficulty understanding them. For the sake of mutual understanding, language is thus kept simple even by linguistically gifted EU actors (although by some more than others).

The chapter reveals two additional depoliticizing consequences of foreign language use inside the EU institutions. First, participants in the EU's multilingual environment adjust their expectations of others' communication skills and are quite tolerant of foreign language handicaps. Indeed, foreign language use may even have deeper empathetic effects, for example through enhanced perspective taking and greater efforts at understanding others' communicative intent. "Hopping from language to language is a constant reminder of how others might see things differently," a Dutch official in the Commission recently observed (The Economist 2016). Second, reliance on foreign languages in political communication, deliberation, and negotiation entails that participants in EU policymaking tend to disregard politically charged language. The use of politically contested words is more likely ascribed to limited foreign language proficiency than to informed intent. Politicized, ideological, or partisan language thus becomes neutralized inside the EU institutions.

After reviewing a growing body of research in the cognitive sciences that shows foreign language use to systematically affect decision making, the chapter proceeds by considering EU actors' motivations for using a nonnative language as a medium of communication—most often English—rather than relying on their mother tongues paired with translation and interpretation. It then draws out how reliance on English simplifies and standardizes the language used inside the EU institutions, may enhance tolerance and empathy among participants in EU policymaking, and neutralizes politically charged terminology.

Decision Making in Foreign Languages

A coherent and growing body of research in psychology shows that the language in which information is delivered affects people's choices independent of the content of the message, and that the use of a foreign language has notable implications for decision making by affecting how people deal with risks, make inferences, and confront moral judgments (Hayakawa et al. 2016). The overall takeaway from this work, with notable implications for considerations of political contexts that involve nonnative speakers of a given language, is that while foreign language use may negatively affect individual decision making by depleting cognitive resources (Volk, Köhler, and Pudelko 2014), it also improves decision making and self-regulation (Hadjichristidis, Geipel, and Surian 2017) by making decisions more "rational," through reduced reliance on heuristic biases and emotional or intuitive cues, as well as through increased deliberation and greater utilitarianism (Hayakawa et al. 2016). This research demonstrates that "people make systematically different decisions in a foreign language compared to their native tongue" (Costa, Duñabeitia, and Keysar 2019, 1).[1]

Several experimental studies find that using a foreign language affects people's perception of risk and the choices they make as a result. For example, when confronted with potential hazards in a foreign language, such as "nuclear power plant" or "traveling by airplane," people consider the potential costs associated with them to be lower and the benefits greater than they do in their native language (Hadjichristidis, Geipel, and Savadori 2015; see also Hayakawa et al. 2019). This research suggests that foreign language improves decision making by making risk assessment more consistent. Foreign language use also reduces common decision biases and makes people less susceptible to framing manipulation. Keysar, Hayakawa, and An (2012), for instance, show that foreign language use reduces loss aversion, or people's tendency to prefer avoiding losses (not losing $10) to making equivalent gains (finding $10). Costa et al. (2014a) replicate this finding and further demonstrate that the foreign language effect extends to a variety of other heuristic biases in decision making, such as accounting biases (framing effects in the categorization of economic outcomes), ambiguity aversion, and intuition bias. Sunstein (2019) confirms that foreign language use reduces people's reliance on intuition when making decisions, while Hadjichristidis, Geipel, and Surian (2019) show that foreign language use suppresses superstitious beliefs. Díaz-Lago and Matute (2019) demonstrate that foreign language use reduces causality bias, or the illusion that two events are causally related when they are not: participants in their study were more accurate in detecting true causal relationships in a foreign language. Gao et al. (2015) find that foreign language use eliminates the so-called "hot hand" effect in gambling, whereby participants overestimate the likelihood of a positive outcome after a series of previous successes. Finally, Oganian, Heekeren, and Korn (2019) demonstrate that foreign language use reduces people's inclination to evaluate their personal futures overly optimistically.

Several studies show that using a foreign language also affects moral judgment, again with important potential implications in political deliberation and negotiation situations involving nonnative speakers. Bereby-Meyer et al. (2018), for example, show that people are less inclined to lie when they use a foreign language, likely because self-serving dishonesty is an automatic tendency that is suppressed by foreign language use prompting greater deliberation. Geipel, Hadjichristidis, and Surian (2015a) find that foreign language use leads to more lenient judgments of moral or social taboo violations, such as consensual incest or telling a lie, and to people having less confidence in these judgments. Costa et al. (2014b) show that this effect can also be observed with regard to more serious moral dilemmas, as people using a foreign language are more than twice as willing to sacrifice one life to save five than those using their native language. This effect has been replicated with a variety of languages (Geipel, Hadjichristidis, and Surian 2015b; Cipolletti, McFarlane, and Weissglass 2016) and found to be robust across several contexts and multiple confounding factors (Corey et al. 2017; Hayakawa et al. 2017). Moreover, when using a foreign language, people are more sensitive to outcomes and less sensitive to intention in experiments that pit positive outcomes against dubious intentions, and vice versa (Geipel, Hadjichristidis, and Surian 2016). Speaking a foreign language thus appears to lead to less activation of social and moral norms (Geipel, Hadjichristidis, and Surian 2015a) and more utilitarian decisions, as Hayakawa et al. write (2016, 792): when moral rules like "cause no harm" conflict with the utilitarian value of promoting the greater good, using a foreign language increases the weight of the latter over the former.

This body of research offers growing and converging evidence that foreign language use affects decision making, yet the underlying reasons for this phenomenon remain unclear (Hayakawa et al. 2016). One explanation for the impact of foreign language use on decision making is that it increases psychological distance, which leads to more abstract consideration and examination of a given social context (Corey et al. 2017). Another emphasizes the cognitive effort involved in using a foreign language, which disrupts the fluency of processing information. Foreign language use thus entails "a switch from emotional to analytic processing" (Hadjichristidis, Geipel, and Savadori 2015, 118) by raising attention levels, decreasing reliance on emotional or intuitive cues, and triggering more deliberate and rational responses. Put differently, foreign language use elevates processing that is "slow, systematic, and in some sense more voluntary" over processing that is "fast, automatic, non-voluntary, non-conscious, and sometimes associated with affect" (Cipolletti, McFarlane, and Weissglass 2016, 24).

The most prominent explanation for the various foreign language effects detected in experimental studies, however, is that foreign languages engage emotions less than native languages do (Corey et al. 2017; Hayakawa et al. 2017; Geipel, Hadjichristidis, and Surian 2015a, 2016), which results in greater utilitarianism and more rational consideration of risks and choices. There may be, in other words, a *foreign language detachment effect*, whereby the use of a foreign language provides a greater emotional and cognitive distance than the use of a speaker's native tongue would. As the author Emine Sevgi Özdamar, who was born in Turkey but has lived in Germany most of her life, put it, "my German words have no childhood" (Özdamar 2001, 131).[2]

Pavlenko (2012) offers a detailed review of an extensive body of research across several fields and empirical approaches (clinical, introspective, cognitive, psychophysiological, and neuroimaging), which finds that bilingual speakers process verbal stimuli differently in their respective languages. Emotional verbal stimuli are those that elicit heightened arousal, both physical (e.g., increased heart rate) and cognitive (e.g., heightened recall). Pavlenko (2005) suggests that differences in affective language processing between native and nonnative speakers stem from the coincidence of emotional socialization in early childhood with the process of language acquisition, when words and phrases become associated with particular emotions. In contrast, the context and process of acquiring a foreign language, most commonly in a classroom setting, does not provide the same opportunities for a similar integration of language and emotion. As a result, the literal meaning (denotation), associated meaning (connotation), or form (e.g., accent, double negation) of a verbal stimulus does not trigger the same emotional responses it would in native speakers (Pavlenko 2012). Words in a nonnative language thus become "disembodied" and are heard and used freely by speakers who do not experience the full affect (Pavlenko 2005). Moreover, these tendencies are more pronounced in late bilinguals and foreign language learners, meaning they are less likely to process language affectively and perceive words as emotional (Pavlenko 2012). While we of course do not have data on the timing and context of foreign language acquisition of EU politicians and officials, it is safe to assume that most do not acquire their foreign languages in early childhood, which would suggest that the foreign language detachment effect is quite common and pronounced in EU politics and other multilingual political arenas.[3]

The findings in this extensive body of experimental research, therefore, have important potential consequences in political contexts where decision makers engage with one another in foreign languages. Notably, these implications may go beyond decision making in a foreign language being more rational, deliberate, and utilitarian, in that foreign language use also entails a "positivity bias," as Hadjichristidis, Geipel, and Savadori (2015) suggest: foreign language use seems to mitigate people's tendency to weigh negative events more than positive ones. Such a positivity bias, they argue, may result from two (not mutually exclusive) processes. The first is that foreign language use tends to involve less negative affect. For example, negative emotional words and phrases have less emotional force in a foreign language (Wu and Thierry 2012), which may result in greater activation of positive than negative associations. Second, negative words have fewer opportunities for emotional grounding in a foreign language, because the adult social interactions experienced when acquiring a foreign language tend to be more positive than negative (Hadjichristidis, Geipel, and Savadori 2015, 118). Hence, the "consensus culture" some have observed in the EU institutions (see Lewis 1998; Heisenberg 2005; Pütter 2012; Novak 2013) may relate, in part, to a positivity bias induced by foreign language use.

Speaking and Writing in a Foreign Language

In very general terms, participants in EU politics have a choice of either using their mother tongues while relying on interpretation and translation when communicating with others, or of using a shared nonnative language, which for most actors is English. Both options have advantages and disadvantages that are a function of people's foreign language skills, the availability of language services in a given meeting, and the language skills and choices of those they are interacting with (even a person with limited foreign language skills might avoid interpretation, for example, if everybody else opts for direct communication using a vehicular language). Another basic factor is people's willingness to rely on a nonnative language in the first place; they have to be "pragmatic" linguists (Wright 2007).

The average foreign language proficiency of EU actors seems to have improved in the recent past. My own experience during frequent visits to Brussels and the EU institutions over the course of the past two decades confirms Wright's conclusion that "many non-native English users would score low on deficit model language testing but are communicatively competent, interact successfully and transmit their messages effectively" (Wright 2013, 264). My respondents also attested to improving foreign language skills. One European Parliament (EP) official, for example, highlighted that he has been seeing that "the ability of MEPs [Members of the EP] is improving, for so many of them. . . . Many of them do speak English now" (#11, also 14). His impression was shared by an MEP who has served several terms in office and hails from southern Europe, and thus the part of the EU that has tended to produce a greater number of MEPs with foreign language handicaps; she emphasized that "probably most of us are now as proficient in English as some native English speakers, and we'll become even better" (#44). While that may be an exaggeration, it is true that a growing number of people are "extremely fit" in their foreign language use and that their English, in particular, is "incredibly good," in the words of another MEP (#43). Part of the reason for this shift is that older EU actors make an effort to improve their language skills, for example by spending their vacation in another country in an effort to improve their language proficiency, as one former Commission official observed (#51) and as was confirmed by an MEP staffer, who highlighted that even some French MEPs "will talk about the English language courses they have been taking in Malta during their holidays" (#41). But the overall improvement of foreign language skills, in particular with regard to English, mostly reflects a generational change that progressively undermines what used to be a pronounced North-South split in foreign language proficiency (Wright 2000), since younger southern Europeans increasingly speak English as their second language and do so competently.

In oral communications, the obvious main advantage of using a shared language is that it allows for direct interactions between participants in EU policymaking (#9, 14, 43, 44, 58).[4] One MEP from a southern member state explained that

120 The Language(s) of Politics

> I know even with the mistakes I can do, it's much more effective when in a meeting I speak English, and everybody is listening at the real time what I'm saying, even with a mistake, than if I'm speaking [my native language] and they are waiting for the translation. And I've no doubt, for instance, the English translator speaks better English than mine, it's quite obvious, but the efficiency of the communication . . . [I get better results] with mistakes speaking English. (#47)

A respondent in the Council agreed with this assessment. He recounted that "in the beginning . . . I would speak [my mother tongue] because we don't want to lose our language . . . and I want people to know that it exists. Then, as the time evolved, I just realized that it would be far too difficult and I would lose out" (#67). He also recalls French delegates speaking French in the Council, "and then they repeat the same thing in English because no one understood anything." It is apparently not unusual that "people will sometimes say, 'I'm going to say this in English because I want to make sure that people understand exactly what I'm saying and the words that I'm using'" (#72, also 61). Another respondent confirmed that "you know when [the French] speak English then there is a problem. It means that they are not getting their message across and they will exceptionally say it in English to make the point as clear as possible" (#13, also 70). One high-ranking member state official tells a similar story about the German Permanent Representative: "I have witnessed at two occasions that the German ambassador decided to speak English. But this was just to be clear what he wanted to convey, first he said that in German, and then he repeated the same thing in English just to be sure that everybody understood very well" (#73).[5]

A more institutional solution to this problem is that

> when something gets extremely sensitive, or is considered extremely sensitive, Coreper will meet for breakfast or lunch, which is not a part of its formal meeting, but allows ambassadors to discuss with zero interpretation. Everybody speaks English directly, things where they are sure that they are only between themselves, and they are quite sure to get their message across. (#58)

The "trick" of moving from formal into informal session was also discussed by the Mertens counselor of another member state, who described that when his country held the Council Presidency

I was chairing several committees where you had a five-language regime, and what I did regularly when we had to negotiate actual texts is that I turned the meeting into an informal meeting. Then you are down to English. . . . Because otherwise people can complain, . . . "I want to speak French, I want to speak Spanish, I want to speak Italian, German." But if it becomes an informal meeting, they are fine, . . . People are kind of, "oh well, it was an informal meeting and the topic as such, it was better to have the informal format." So you resort to that sort of mechanism. . . . It's going to be much easier for the French delegation to say "it was an informal meeting, so, you know, don't call the Académie Française." (#71)

Aside from allowing for direct communication between participants in the EU policymaking process, using English can facilitate the business of legislating in that the documents negotiations are based on are usually (or at least more quickly and easily) available in English (#8) and because switching back and forth between languages may actually be more difficult than maintaining a discussion in a single shared language (#21, 60, 62). And while some EU actors consciously choose to stick to their mother tongues when negotiating technical matters because they lack the relevant vocabulary in English to make nuanced remarks (#45, 54, 55, 58), the technical jargon in some policy areas is already mostly in English (#71). For example, one Council official explained that in the areas of financial services or telecommunications,

everything is in English. So you would end up having pronouns in your mother tongue, and everything else is in English anyway. So people tend to just speak in English . . . It can actually be quite confusing for anybody who speaks decent French to hear something about technology on the internet being said in French. We wouldn't understand what it is. (#58, also 74)

Beyond these practical considerations, using English may also provide reputational benefits. Competent foreign language skills can impress others (#55) and "open doors" (#70, also #64, 67, 71, 76, 78, 79), although a Swede will likely receive less credit for speaking English than for speaking French, and a Frenchman will almost certainly receive more praise for speaking English than a Dutch person would (#55). Communicating with others in a foreign language also allows speakers to send the message that

"I am European" (#45, 55, 58), and it may be perceived as "charming," for example in the case for Commission President Jean-Claude Juncker (#33).

English is not only the primary language of oral communication; it also serves as the main written language in the EU. The overwhelming portion of source documents written in the EU nowadays are in English, and the percentage has increased steadily over time: in 2000, 55.1 percent of documents were originally drafted in English, a number that rose to 62 percent in 2004, 77.6 percent in 2012, and 81.3 percent in 2014 (Balič 2016a, 132). French, at this point, is lagging far behind as an original drafting language (5 percent in 2014 compared to 26 percent in 2004) (Ammon and Kruse 2013, 17; Balič 2016a, 132; Fidrmuc and Ginsburgh 2007, 1352).[6] But most creators of written texts in the EU are not native English speakers; in the Commission, for example, 95 percent of drafters reported writing primarily in English in 2009, when only 13 percent of them were native speakers (Robinson 2012, 9).[7] The drafting of legislative texts in English by nonnative speakers means that the process is simultaneously both monolingual and multilingual. It is monolingual in the sense that the various language versions of EU legislation are not drafted simultaneously. Instead, drafting takes place in one language, usually English, and the other language versions are de facto translations of this source text. This is not only because deliberation and negotiation of the substance of a text is generally more efficient in a single language, but because multilingual drafting is only feasible when the number of languages is much more restricted than is the case in the EU. After all, what sets the EU apart from other multilingual legislative settings like in Switzerland, Canada, or Hong Kong, is that legislation is equally authentic in 24 official languages, and it is not possible to "co-draft" simultaneously in that many language (Guggeis and Robinson 2012; Piris 2005).

Yet there are a number of ways in which a draft text invariably reflects the multilingual context in which it was created, starting with the reality that nonnative drafters may "introduce concepts and syntax structures from their own language" (Robertson 2012b, 7) and produce texts that include "grammatical mistakes or errors of idiom or register" (Robinson 2012, 9).[8] Moreover, nonnative drafters of a text tend to contemplate its substance in their native languages, or they at least mix their native and drafting languages. McAuliffe's respondents in the Court of Justice thus explained that they mix languages when conceptualizing texts, either by drafting "half [in their own mother tongue] and half in French" (McAuliffe 2013a, 488), or by straight-out translating "what I want to say into French instead of really working in French" (McAuliffe 2011, 104). Robinson similarly quotes a Court référendaire who explained that "all of my own reasoning and thinking about the case is done in my own language and then put into French when I come to the writing stage" (Robinson 2014b, 197). Much the same happens to nonnative English speakers in the other institutions, where groups of policymakers may also bring together "drafts in French, English, Spanish, Italian and German" and, on that multilingual basis, end up producing "compromise motions for resolutions," as Loos (2004, 16) describes in reference to meetings of political group advisors in the EP. In all those situations, the formal drafting language may be English, but the English text is influenced by multiple languages as it moves through the legislative process. Bengoetxea (2016) takes this argument even further when maintaining that a text is already the product of multilingual reasoning at the very early stages of that process:

> A draft regulation, directive and a decision of general application initiated in a German or French language draft might receive feedback from Polish or Portuguese delegations and is translated back with new languages additions. The proposal itself might be based on English language drafts elaborated by lobbies operating outside the Commission. Which, would we then ask, has been the language of the legislative initiative? In such cases, the draft is already a multilingual product of translation. (Bengoetxea 2016, 101)

The result are texts that differ from what they would look like if drafted by a native speaker; draft texts in the EU are reflections of a multilingual deliberation and negotiation process. They are "hybrids" or "depositories" of the multiple languages that have been relied on as the text was conceived, considered, contested, and drafted (see Schäffner and Adab 1997; Trosborg 1997; Dollerup 2001; Doczekalska 2009). The "core language versions" may "technically serve as the source texts" but they in fact reflect the "tortuous multilingual processes in which translators, interpreters, experts, national committees and politicians all over Europe have contributed to the product in their different tongues" (Dollerup 2001, 290). Some even argue that when a text is the result of multilingual negotiation, and thus the product of consideration in more than one language, no one language can legitimately be called a source language even if the text is produced in that language and then translated into others (Schäffner 1998, 87–88). The truth most likely lies somewhere in between, as Gibová suggests: it is appropriate to consider some source texts as "original," but there is not as sharp a contrast between "original" and "translation" given "an intricate

124　　　The Language(s) of Politics

tangle of mutually intertwined language versions of the given text" (Gibová 2009, 147). In sum, while the EU engages in multilingual drafting in relation to the final product (multiple equally authentic language versions), as opposed to traditional unilingual drafting paired with legal translation, this is not quite so clear-cut from the perspective of the drafting process (Stefaniak 2013). According to the former Director-General of the Legal Service of the Council, Jean-Claude Piris, in practice the EU uses a method that lies somewhere between codrafting (drafting in multiple languages at once) and drafting in one original language—usually English—with translation into other languages (Piris 2005, 23).

Simplification and Standardization through Foreign Language Use

Multilingualism introduces a degree of "messiness" into legislative drafting, since nonnative English speakers "focus primarily on achieving certain policy goals and regard the quality of drafting as merely of secondary importance" (Robinson 2014b, 197). But reliance on nonnative languages in drafting texts also contributes to a simplification and standardization of written language in the EU. One of McAuliffe's respondents in the Court of Justice, for example, explained that

> When you write in your mother tongue it flows more naturally, it is an unconscious exercise (language-wise), words and phrases flow from associations made by your brain by drawing on a lifetime's use of the language. . . . When you are writing in a language that is not your mother tongue you have to boil down the semantics of what you want to say into one thread, into the essential of what you want to say. (McAuliffe 2013a, 489)

As a result of their lack of mastery of the drafting language, nonnative speakers focus on making themselves understood by using simple, straightforward language; language is utilitarian and pragmatic. For the same reason, they are also more likely to revert back to shared common phrases or formulaic linguistic constructs. This can transform the source text by making it more succinct, but also by formalizing it (McAuliffe 2012, 209). The result tends to be a standardized text with a certain "alien" character, where the "original also reads like a translation" (Tosi 2013, 8). Some consider this to be a good thing. For example, one of my respondents in the EP recalled "an Irish friend of mine who used to work around the institutions" saying that

Foreign Language Use and Depoliticization 125

I get so fed up when I have to read native English speakers' texts on European affairs. I much prefer when a nonnative speaker has written it, because the limitations of his vocabulary also limit him diverting from the real substance of what he is trying to say. So the limitations in his vocabulary might help channeling a more clear message, more to the point. There is less hedging, there is less trying to encapsulate your argument in metaphors. It's more to the point. (#49)

Simplification and standardization are also driven by conscious efforts on the part of the EU institutions to improve the quality of source texts but offering explicit drafting guidelines. Even though these guidelines are not legally binding and are not always adhered to, they contribute to the common, formulaic style of EU legislation, as they impose a standardized and simplified lexical, syntactic, semantic, and grammatical linguistic framework. These drafting guidelines are provided in a variety of documents,[9] most importantly:

- Council Resolution of June 8, 1993, on the quality of drafting of Community legislation
- Declaration No. 39 on the quality of the drafting of Community legislation, adopted by the Amsterdam Conference in 1997
- Interinstitutional Agreement of December 22, 1998, on common guidelines for the quality of drafting of Community legislation
- Joint Practical Guide of the European Parliament, the Council and the Commission for persons involved in the drafting of legislation within the Community institutions; 2nd Edition 2013
- Interinstitutional Agreement of December 31, 2003, on better lawmaking
- Commission Manual on Legislative Drafting
- Manual of precedents, drawn up by the legal/linguistic experts of the Council
- Interinstitutional Style Guide
- "How to Write Clearly"; European Commission 2016
- English Style Guide; European Commission 2016

A particular emphasis is placed on draft acts being written in simple, straightforward language. The Joint Practical Guide, for example, calls for language that is "clear, easy to understand, and unambiguous"; "simple and concise, avoiding unnecessary elements"; and "precise, leaving no uncertainty in the mind of the reader" (Rule 1.1). It further specifies that "overly

126 The Language(s) of Politics

complicated sentences, comprising several phrases, subordinate clauses or parentheses" are to be avoided (5.2.2) and that "where necessary, clarity of expression should take precedence over considerations of style" (Rule 1.4.1).

These rules result in source texts that are standardized in their terminology, lexis, and structure (Trosborg 1997; Pym 2000; Biel 2007); they simplify, neutralize, and "de-culture" the text and, by extension, the other language versions that result from its translation. This tendency is reinforced by reliance on the wording of existing EU law and other sources written in EU legal language (Robinson 2012, 9), because drafters often "prefer the security of reproducing as closely as possible an existing text to the uncertainty of a new text" (Robinson 2014a, 266). Additionally, the Commission's Legal Service checks if the draft legislation complies with primary and secondary EU law already at the proposal stage (Robinson 2012, 8), which means that existing legal language flows into new draft texts. All this further drives a trend toward the standardization of written language in the EU.

We can observe a similar trend in oral English-language communications, which also take on a simpler, standardized, and more pragmatic quality due to nonnative speakers not having the same command over a foreign language that they have over their native tongues. One translator explained that

> when you use your mother tongue you have access to the whole range of instruments that a language has to offer. You can play with it. That's also possible when you speak a foreign language very well, but when you don't, you are not able to express yourself in the same way. (#35, also 81, 83)

Others concur that arguments made in a native language will likely be more sophisticated (#56), because "[you are] more at home in your language" (#78). When using a nonnative tongue, in contrast, people simply "are not able to speak a very elaborate, sophisticated language" (#20). There is, moreover, a strong incentive to be straightforward and literal, considering that symbolism and allusion imply a shared cultural and psychological context that is not given in a multilingual environment (Lakoff 1992, 103). The same is true of "value markers," which lack a shared meaning and are therefore consciously avoided by some; instead, EU actors' focus is squarely on making themselves understood and getting their main message across (#9, 12, 14, 21, 25, 37, 42, 71, 72, 74). "I communicate in a way that I think is understandable for [others]. . . . Consciously or unconsciously, I'm making that effort," explained one respondent (#21). The result is potentially profound for decision-making dynamics in EU politics, as a former EP official suggests:

> So much of the discussions that I sat through, in codecision sort of files, deliberately denatured or depoliticized the debate. . . . The language tends to move out of the sort of politically charged into the more bureaucratic sort of language, even though we know that language conceals political choice and political ways of doing things. But it means that it's difficult, people don't get excited about that, because it's harder to get excited about. Sort of tweaking Article 2 is not kind of the same as talking about, you know, "the struggling masses under the yoke of capitalism."[10] (#78)

As in the case of written language, some laud this simple and utilitarian spoken language. One Council official, for example, maintained that those who use their native language may end up rambling on, and that using English "makes communication more precise and clear, because it is focused on the essential" (#66). It also makes speakers sound "wooden and stiff" (#79), however, or lacking "the emotional part" (#47) or the "emotional ballast" (#42) of expressing themselves (also #14, 37, 74).[11] Language that is rhetorically rich, idiomatic, and nuanced gives way to language that is simplified and utilitarian—a mere means of communication—as nonnative speakers' primary concern is simply being understood and understanding others, as opposed to making "big speeches" (#68). Moreover, as Ban points out, "striking just the right tone in another language is difficult, and one can never be sure that the tone will be understood as it was meant"; hence, EU actors use language that is safely neutral and decultured, even at the expense of linguistic "richness, of nuance, and also of irony and sarcasm" (Ban 2013, 220).

The reality that irony and sarcasm are difficult to convey in a foreign language is one reason why participants in EU policymaking are advised to avoid making jokes (Fidrmuc and Ginsburgh 2007, 1353). Humor also often involves word plays or puns or reflects a particular cultural background (Ban 2009, 2013), and so "the thing which most people who worked a long time in the institutions tell you is 'jokes don't translate,' and anyone trying to use humor is very often ineffective in another language" (#79, also 36, 39). This applies to both nonnative speakers who unsuccessfully try to make jokes in a foreign language—which "takes a long time" to be able to do (#56)—but also to native or near-native speakers making jokes that are lost on their nonnative audience. For example, "if the British ambassador wants to make a joke, half of the audience will not understand," a former Commission official explained (#51). Many participants in EU politics thus avoid making jokes entirely because they do not feel sufficiently comfortable in the foreign language environment, even if they would be inclined to use humor in their mother tongues, for example in order to lighten the mood or to break up a tedious technical discussion.

In sum, reliance on a foreign language as a mode of communication makes policymakers focus on "getting their message across" when speaking and writing; it induces actors to be more succinct, precise, and focused (#27, 53, 66, 68, 69, 72). It also leads to use of language that is not only simplified, but also formalized and standardized. Finally, language tends to be neutral and lacking in emotion and spontaneity, not only because idioms and rhetorical devices as eschewed, but also because sarcasm and humor are avoided or fall flat with an audience of nonnative speakers.

Native English Speakers in a Multilingual Context

The language used inside the EU institutions thus lacks sophistication because of nonnative speakers' limited command, but also because participants in EU policymaking are always acutely aware of the possibility of information being lost. This means that even native or near-native speakers of a shared language tend to adopt the simple, pragmatic communication style of their nonnative counterparts, since embellishments are not only unnecessary and unexpected, but may actively prevent their counterparts from understanding what is being said. These realities weaken the natural dominance of native English speakers in verbal and written interactions, at least to an extent, despite the reality that, all else equal, using a native language gives speakers a leg up (van Els 2005, 273–74).

Native English speakers are advantaged for a number of reasons. To start, they do not have to put in the extra effort to operate in a nonnative language and thus expend less mental "bandwidth" on the same tasks, all else equal (#66, 68, 70, 72). Indeed, Costa et al. (2014a, 238) discuss research in the cognitive sciences that demonstrates how processing information in a foreign language is usually more costly and can "cause a disruption of cognitive fluency." In addition, Wright emphasizes that native speakers do not have to expend time and money on language learning and are thus "lib-

Foreign Language Use and Depoliticization 129

erated to study other things" (Wright 2009, 111). Native English speakers also do not have to deal with the discomfort that engaging with others in a foreign language might entail (#60).[12]

To what extent these advantages translate into greater policy influence is unclear; in fact, a number of both native and non-native English speakers among my respondents found the proposition questionable (#66, 70, 72, 78, 80, 81). One long-serving official in the EP said that:

> I don't really believe that the Brits really have politically, at the end, an advantage. You know, yeah, it's easier for them in their life but, politically speaking, I don't believe that it really gives them an edge. It's just easier for them. . . . There are a number of things that make the British members excellent [MEPs], I think on average better than others. But I don't think it's because they speak English. (#81)

One major challenge native speakers face is that the more sophisticated language they rely on—"I tend to use colloquialisms and idioms and sometimes make long meandering sentences," one native speaker acknowledged (#72)—is not as easily understood by nonnative speakers.[13] Several respondents discussed this challenge; one of them, for example, recalled a Council meeting in which

> We had the UK ambassador who was always using some word . . . and I think nobody understood what this word means. But he put all his story on some particular expression, and I was like "what?" . . . They told him please don't use this sophisticated word, because it's just in vain, nobody understands it. . . . We don't understand them, their English. (#63, also #15, 62, 76)

This reality is also captured in the commonly told joke that people in Brussels put on their headphones to listen to interpretation when the native English speakers start talking (#76).[14]

Hence, it can be "easier when English is a second language to all of the people" (#15), because nonnative English speakers better understand one another (#46, 47, 74, 76, 83).[15] One MEP thus explained:

> It is funny, because the native English speakers, sometimes we understand them, but they speak quickly or so formally that it is easier for a Spanish to talk with an Italian or with a Polish than

130 The Language(s) of Politics

with a British person. . . . We understand each other, because we all are learning languages. We understand the mistakes which a British person does not understand. (#47)

Similarly, a former EP official described being in a meeting

with all Director-Generals, some Directors, and the Secretary-General. And the language of the meeting was English. Two of the Director-Generals present were English. All the others we were of other nationalities. At a certain point an Italian Director-General said something; we all understood—except the two English. (#83)

Native English speakers, therefore, have to "acquire the language awareness that successful communication with a heterogeneous audience demands," as Wright (2013, 264) notes, meaning that native English skills do not automatically translate into an advantage. Only when native speakers are pragmatic and flexible in their language use can they wield influence (Wright 2007, 154).[16] They must actively and consciously adjust their language in order to get their message across (#72, 73, 74, 75), which in practice means that they have to "simplify their language" (#15, 21).[17] One native English speaker explained that "when I'm making a planned intervention, I will think about what I'm going to say and I will try to distill that into a couple of very clear sentences, just to ensure that people have understood me" (#72).[18] Another native speaker agreed:

"[It] of course leads to native speakers speaking slightly differently than they would do if they were speaking to another native speaker in these kinds of contexts. People may speak slightly more simply, and in phrases which are not trying to make life difficult, because obviously there's not much point in using a language if you can't communicate your meaning to the other person." (#78)

What Gets Lost—or Not—in a Foreign Language

Even if they are compelled to use simple language, some native English speakers are still able to express their ideas and arguments so that they are perceived as more convincing, professional, or charismatic (#38, 41, 43, 60, 62, 74).[19] To get at the question of how much nonnative speakers lose out in this regard, I asked my respondents to consider the example of Martin

Schulz, the former President of the European Parliament, who is known to be a charismatic speaker and competent politician in his native German. Does Schulz—or others like him—come across as similarly charismatic and competent when he uses a foreign language?

When Schulz (or other high-ranking EU politicians my respondents would think of) use a foreign language, it is usually English or French, and most of my respondents did not think that his use of a nonnative language has a substantial impact in how he comes across. It was not uncommon for respondents to perceive that "something gets lost" relative to Schulz using his native German, but there was a general agreement that this does not matter as much as one might think.[20] This assessment was particularly widespread among the policymakers I spoke to, while language service providers were—not surprisingly—more likely to suggest that Schulz would be better off sticking to his mother tongue and using interpretation.

Although some policymakers suggested that something gets lost when Schulz ventures out of his native German (#42, 43, 62, 64), it was striking that more did not think that Schulz is perceived and received differently when speaking a foreign language (#38, 39, 44, 66, 70, 75, 77, 78, 79, 81, 82). They emphasized that even to nonnative German speakers, Schulz comes across as "pretty charismatic" (#38) and "a skilled politician" (#77). Personality translates "very well and very easily" (#39), according to several respondents, because it is about more than "linguistic perfection" (#66, also #75, 78). One respondent explained:

> For example, in the parliament, Verhofstadt, he's a really good speaker but his English isn't that great. Sometimes he gets stuck, but he's so passionate that people still stay tuned to what he's saying. I think it's the same with Schulz. . . . You still get the sort of punch of what he's trying to deliver, and he's really good at it. (#70, also #82)

Two respondents offered examples of Schulz speaking to national audiences in Ireland and Italy, respectively, both highlighting the ability of Schulz to connect with audiences despite language differences.

> Schulz came on his official visit to Ireland . . . And one of the Irish MEPs said "oh my God, Schulz is a very terribly Germanic kind of figure, he won't go down well in Ireland." In fact, Schulz [was] tremendous. . . . Irish politicians saying "God, he's an impressive communicator" and so on, and he was speaking to them in English. And he really went down well. And then he . . . took part in a debate

with Irish politicians to a student audience, a student debate. And students really liked him. (#79)

Schulz makes quite a few mistakes in English, which is actually his third language, because his French is better than his English. But nonetheless, you get the guy, you get the man when he speaks English. . . . The extraordinary thing with Schulz is that he's up for it even in Italian and in Spanish as well. . . . I happened to be in Turin [when] Schulz was the star at this rally for the party leader who was hoping to become prime minister of Italy. And Schulz spoke in Italian, but from a text which he sort of prepared phonetically. . . . And I was staggered by the extent to which he was creating a real connection with his audience. (#81)

A first takeaway from the interviews is, therefore, that policymakers tended to believe that somebody's charisma does translate into other languages, which is notable in itself because such perceptions matter even if policymakers lack the skills to objectively evaluate differences between "Schulz in German" and "Schulz in a foreign language." But many also thought that this does not actually matter all that much in EU politics because the standards for what is expected of political actors in terms of their linguistic and rhetorical capacity are lower in the EU precisely because it is a multilingual environment (#25, 42, 49, 52, 53, 66, 67, 68, 76, 83). Most peoples' foreign language skills may be limited, in other words, but they are good enough for operating in the EU. EU actors are valued not because they are "good speakers, . . . It's because of their work. . . . It's because you are involved, it's because you are present when we need you" (#48). As one national counselor explained, "there's a kind of a tolerance. People know here that they do not aspire to be a Camus. . . . Giving great speeches, that's for national politics" (#68). Others agreed:

When I make a speech like Marc Anthony in Shakespeare's Julius Caesar, that's pure rhetoric. But in practice, when you are dealing with some legal text about tax policy, it is not about rhetoric. . . . It's about defining positions that reflect your interests but leave enough wiggle room for others. That's what's decisive. . . . In the EU, we talk to those who don't speak our language and try to explain our positions, we want them to understand our reasoning and what our objectives are. When I speak to my own population, especially in a political sense, via the media, then of course I have a different level

Foreign Language Use and Depoliticization 133

of linguistic possibilities, and of course there are different expectations. But . . . that's two different things. . . . We don't have those
expectations. You want to convey your ideas to others, you want to
hear their arguments. . . . So, I think rhetoric, and persuasion based
on the ability to express your ideas in a rhetorically refined way, that
may be important to an extent when you address your own people
in your own mother tongue, but when you are dealing with people
in other languages it just falls away. (#66)

In sum, the policymakers among my respondents emphasized that linguistic and rhetorical capabilities do not matter as much in EU politics as
one might think, because nobody expects rhetorical greatness in a multilingual political environment that is focused on the nitty-gritty of the
policymaking process rather than representational politics aimed at popular audiences. Hence, what is most important in Brussels, my respondents
emphasized, is being able to get your message across, however imperfectly
it may be delivered in a nonnative language (#42, 49, 53, 54, 57, 59, 66, 67,
71). What matters is being able to establish "a basic understanding on all
sides" (#42), and people like Schulz are able get their message across (#54,
71). That is what counts.

Foreign Language Use and Empathy

The example of Martin Schulz indicates that participants in the EU's multilingual political environment adjust the expectations they have of others'
communication skills. They do not expect rhetorical greatness, are quite
tolerant of foreign language handicaps, and take it as a given that others
will make mistakes or may cause confusion at times (#11, 17, 20, 21, 42, 52,
53, 60, 63 68, 82). A Commission official said, for example:

I would say the fact that when you enter into such a multicultural
environment, you kind of are maybe more tolerant. Because you
know that some people take more time to express themselves, and
you just, you know, it takes more time. If I've got meetings here
with my people, and I know I need to speak French, because there's
somebody from the administration, or somebody who doesn't speak
that well English, we could do it in French. And then some people
take more time to express themselves in French, so we just take a bit
more time. So, the increased tolerance. (#53)

EU actors also anticipate and are proactive about potential problems (#70). They are, as one counselor in a member state Permanent Representation, explained, "very careful" about avoiding misunderstandings (#75, also #25). According to one Council official, "everybody is very polite about that. . . . We are all trained here to understand nonnative speakers in their language. . . . We are really used to it here in Brussels, which is perhaps a reason why it works so well" (#60).

Part of being tolerant of others' language handicaps means accepting that it is difficult for nonnative speakers to be "diplomatic" in their choice of words (#38, 33) and that they may come across as blunt or hard-nosed (#16, 72). This effect may be exacerbated when somebody's speech in a nonnative language accentuates particular cultural differences (#69), for example when Germans use French with a directness that would be uncharacteristic of native French speakers (#37), or when they sound "very hectoring" speaking English (#29). But "in the end, you live with the fact that somebody is maybe not as good in his second language as in his native language" (#53) and you "put it in its context, if it's a German who says something, or a French or a Spaniard" (#82). Moreover,

> When somebody who is not perfectly fluent in English, or fluent but doesn't master the English language like an anglophone would, . . . then we are used to that anyway in the EU system. We are used to not paying attention to that anymore. We are used to paying attention to "what does it mean?" That's really what we, we always make an effort, when it's not an anglophone, to say "what does it mean? What did they want to say?" . . . I think that's how it works. . . . It works because we make an effort. You know it's not a national environment, it's an international environment, and, you know, 90 percent make this effort, so we are all aware that we are not speaking our language, so we are all patient, and we are all like okay, "what does he want or she want to say?" (#82)

Such observations confirm Wright's conclusion that, above a particular threshold level of language competence, "a certain degree of 'error' seemed to be disregarded by interlocutors as long as the speaker mastered the skills of accommodation and negotiation of meaning" (Wright 2013, 264; see also Hülmbauer and Seidlhofer 2013, 392–94).[21] This tolerance of others' limitations reflects a "very pragmatic" (#71) approach to language and communication. People are flexible in their use of language and tolerant of others being similarly flexible (#42), which makes sense insofar as worrying about delays or trying to correct little errors would get in the way getting their work done (Ban 2009). Most of the time, "you need to understand what the other is saying and not lose time," as an EP official put it quite simply (#82). This breeds a "spirit of cooperation," according to another respondent, where even political adversaries turn to each other for clarification (#64).

The realities and necessities of operating in a multilingual environment not only induce tolerance of limited foreign language abilities, they may also have a deeper empathetic effect. One respondent, for example, suggested that taking advantage of somebody else's linguistic handicaps would be unacceptable in EU politics; "that would be one of the few things where people would really wince," he said (#41). More generally, multilingualism demands a high degree of good will, and the very willingness to display linguistic flexibility ensures a basic effort at "inclusion of the other" (Habermas 1998) and of listening to the other side (Kraus 2008, 124).[22] Some of my own respondents similarly suggested that foreign language use signals openness to other cultures and perspectives (#17, 55, 56, 78), increases a common understanding and empathy (#76, 80), and breeds trust (#59, also 71). A long-serving party official in the EP explained:

> In a national monolingual environment people are much more interested in being opposition in government and attacking the other. Here you don't really start out to attack necessarily. . . . Because you're dealing with somebody across the table who doesn't understand your language, who's probably never been to your country, you've probably never been to his. (#39)

These impressions—that multilingualism induces tolerance and empathy toward others—have been recognized previously by analysts of EU multilingualism (Kraus 2008, 124; van Els 2001, 346–47). More recently, such propositions have also found grounding in cognitive research that shows foreign language use to preferentially activate positive associations (Wu and Thierry 2012) and to induce people to be better listeners.[23] Lev-Ari and Keysar (2012), for example, find that listeners expect the language of nonnative speakers to be less reliable in conveying their intentions and, as a result, adjust the manner in which they process what they hear. Moreover, multilingual exposure promotes effective communication by enhancing perspective taking and helping people effectively interpret others' communicative intent, as Fan et al. (2015) suggest. Their experiments with monolingual and bilingual children reveal that monolinguals misinterpret a speaker's meaning "dramatically more often" than either bilingual children or monolingual children who had been exposed to a multilingual environment (Fan et al. 2015, 1).

Another line of research suggests that native speakers have a tendency to discriminate against speakers of socially marginalized varieties of their language, relative to speakers of a standard or prestigious variety (Pavlenko 2012; Bresnahan et al. 2002; for a review see Lippi-Green 2012). Differentiating between standard, prestigious, and socially marginalized varieties of a language, however, is very difficult for nonnative speakers; it therefore stands to reason—even seems likely—that nonnative speakers would not be in a position to similarly discriminate. I am unaware of experimental research that tests this proposition, but Doerr (2012) finds that in the context of preparatory meetings of the European Social Forum, linguistically heterogeneous European meetings reflect a higher inclusivity within deliberation compared to the national level. National discourse arenas that are monolingual, her analyses reveal, "worked according to a kind of unspoken, implicit, and familiar logic of codes through which participants interpret each other," reproducing, for example, class inequalities, accents, and rhetorical abilities (Doerr 2012).

Discounting Politically Charged Language

My conversations with EU actors revealed another depoliticizing effect of multilingualism: it leads people to disregard politically charged language. In my interviews, I asked respondents to consider situations in which the term "austerity" is used and how it affects communication and interaction. Austerity is a term that has gained in prominence over the past decade and a half. It is politically charged but does not always have a clear and obvious translation into other languages. In German, for example, the most direct translation of austerity is *"Austerität,"* yet this term was not commonly used until recently, when it gained visibility in the context of the euro crisis. Heine (2015), for example, emphasizes that the term was only known to "readers of specialized macroeconomic literature" until "not too long ago." He also shows that the term was used only 24 times in the German weekly newspaper *Die Zeit* in the 36 years between 1970 and 2006; in the nine years that followed, it appeared 67 times.

Austerity can be translated into German as *"Austerität,"* but the term would likely still be perceived by many as technical and obscure. It also has a largely negative connotation; for example, Heine's 2015 article in the

German conservative daily newspaper *Die Welt* was titled "This word lets the global left shake with fury" ("Dieses Wort lässt die globale Linke vor Wut beben") (Heine 2015). Alternatively, austerity may be translated as *"Sparkurs"* (savings plan), *"Sanierungsprogramm"* (restructuring program), or *"Spardiktat"* (savings decree), three possible translations with very different connotations and political flavors. A similar difference in emotional resonance exists in possible translations of austerity into French as either *"austérité"* or *"rigueur."*[24] *"Austérité"* in Old French means "sternness," "harshness," or "cruelty" and thus connotes an element of punishment for past excesses.[25] In contrast, *"rigueur"* implies strictness in calculation or following rules, which suggests a need for intellectual honesty and clarity in accounting or economic assumptions. The term "austerity" is thus politically ambiguous as well as controversial.

I asked my respondents to consider a situation in which an EU actor uses the term austerity (or *Austerität*, or *austerité*, or an equivalent in another language). How would this be perceived? What kinds of reactions would it elicit? The response, especially among the policymakers I interviewed, was that EU actors tend to converse freely without too much consideration of the potential ambiguity and controversial nature of particular terms (#1, 6, 43, 44, 52, 58, 60, 62, 63, 66, 67, 68, 70, 73, 74, 78, 80). As one national counselor put it, "you know it's not always the best option, but you just sort of go with it so that you don't get stuck in language issues when you really need to deal with the substance issues" (#70). After all, one MEP explained,

> when people use foreign languages, they can't use terms with the specificity and nuance that they would in their native tongue. You would have to be incredibly precise even in English . . . and that's not usually the case. (#43, also 63, 68)

Hence, one interpreter in the Commission emphasized, "codes in languages matters, but can't here" (#17). Instead, "we are all loose with our language," according to a party group advisor in the EP (#39). Indeed, nonnative speakers will not only lack precision, but regularly use English terms incorrectly (#11, 44); in a multilingual context, however, it is generally considered imperative that "you give [a nonnative speaker] the benefit of the doubt" (#68). Participants in EU politics are "aware of the fact that they have to work differently and act differently and speak differently in a multilingual context" (#21) and that it is "impossible to take into account every possible connotation in every possible language" (#15). And so people often do not know why somebody might be using a particular term (#9) and therefore disregard it. This finding is notable in terms of levels of contestation, intensity of debate, and the polarization of opinion in EU politics. It is also instructive in that it helps illuminate the question if simplified language is necessarily depoliticized. One might reasonably presume, for example, that the simple language used by nonnative speakers is more blunt and, for that reason, more likely to be inadvertently politicizing. That, however, is exactly why it would be discounted by others.

The term "austerity" thus appears to be an example of a "disembodied" word that is "used freely by speakers who do not experience their full impact" (Pavlenko 2012, 421). In these regards, communications in the EU institutions share characteristics emphasized in research on "English as a Lingua Franca" (ELF), which involves "normalizing" potential trouble sources and adopting "a principle of 'let it pass'" (House 2003, 558). Similarly, EU actors do not get hung up on the use of particular terms (#11, 46, 58, 60, 62, 66, 67, 73), as the following short quotes demonstrate:

I have never seen [that] somebody got upset about the use of a term like austerity. (#60)

Nobody is going to be worried about whether we say bailout or whether we say assistance program. (#58)

It does not trigger much [controversy] when you use such a term, where you know that's a sore spot. . . . You know that and say it anyway. (#66)

[People] are familiar with that kind of speaking and kind of discount it, I think. (#78)

It was quite rare for respondents to suggest that the use of politically charged terms may trigger a negative reaction. Only one member state counselor said that "a particular country might feel offended by the choice of term" (#64), and a single respondent in the EP maintained that "every time I speak [about] austerity, my German colleagues go berserk. They are very offended indeed." This last respondent, however, hails from one of the member states in southern Europe that were hardest hit by the euro crisis, and she represents a leftist party.[26] Hence, the reaction she experiences might be the result of others not giving her the aforementioned benefit of the doubt when she uses the term austerity. In what appears to be an exception from the norm, from her mouth austerity is perceived as a "fighting term."

Foreign Language Use and Depoliticization 139

One important implication of these realities is that political and ideological differences become less overt, as subtleties in language choice are erased and "partisan language" rendered moot. For example, in a monolingual context like the United States, the use of the term "undocumented worker" is largely limited to Democrats, while Republicans would speak of "illegal aliens" (Thompson 2016).[27] In the EU context, similar terminological markers of ideology might be "refugee" (left) vs. "economic migrant" (right), or "irregular" (left) vs. "illegal migration" (right). When nonnative English speakers on either side of the political spectrum refer to "irregular" or "illegal" migration, however, it might simply be a result of their inability to grasp and express the relevant nuances in a foreign tongue. As in the case of "austerity," their particular choice of words would likely be discounted rather than taken as indicative of ideology or partisanship. As a result, participants in EU policymaking may incorrectly assume that a mutual understanding or common ground for agreement exist when they, in fact, do not (Grynaviski 2014).

Conclusion

Foreign language use, this chapter argued, depoliticizes politics. It simplifies the language used in policymaking, standardizes it, and has a neutralizing effect. It also heightens empathy among policymakers by making them more conscious listeners and encouraging perspective taking. Finally, politicized language is discounted by participants in multilingual politics, because politically charged terms are often not used with intent by nonnative speakers.

The main shared language relied on by nonnative speakers inside the EU institutions is English, and much of the discussion in this chapter has focused on its use in the EU policy process. Not considered thus far, however, has been the proposition that a particular kind of English prevails in Brussels, an "EU English" that is distinguishable from standard English and fulfills its communicative function by providing a common basis for interactions, collaborations, and transactions between EU actors. The next chapter thus turns to a more focused investigation of the kind of English used in the EU institutions.

FIVE

"EU English" and Depoliticization

In the words of a Council official,

> [EU English] works great, a lot better than proper English. . . . It is a much more *simplified* version of the language. . . . In reality, it's *not real English*, it's an international convention of words that are *used in a certain context* and *with a certain meaning*. A very *simplified vocabulary*, allowing for very *rapid communication*. . . . I think it's a *very short and crisp form of communication* that we've developed. . . . We *don't really bother with the things that are unnecessary*. . . . It's a very barbaric use of English, no doubt, but a very *predictable* one . . . There's a lot of *standardized* forms of communication. (#58; my emphases)

The idea that there is a particular kind of English used inside the European Union's (EU) institutions is not new. Indeed, most people who have spent some time in Brussels' "EU bubble" would intuit that there is something different about the way people speak English. Similarly, to readers outside the EU institutions, EU texts often have an unfamiliar and sometimes strange quality. The most obvious aspect of EU English—but not the only one, as this chapter will show—is its vocabulary, a major component of which are terms that are specific to and closely associated with the EU. Examples include the *subsidiarity* principle (which prescribes that the EU shall only take action when a given objective cannot be achieved by the member states), the *Acquis Communautaire* (the complete body of EU law), or *comitology* (the area of EU secondary legislation, which is enacted under the executive duties of the Commission). A second category of EU vocabulary are words that have a particular meaning in the EU context that differs from their regular usage. Examples are the *transposition* of EU legislation (the process by which it is implemented in and by the member states) or the *cabinet* of a Commissioner (their private office or group of personal advisors), which is pronounced the French way (kabinɛ) in the EU institutions. The third category of EU vocabulary are words or phrases that are irregular but still intelligible to outsiders, for example the use of "aid" in the plural ("we seek to provide aids to victims of floods and other natural disasters"). Finally, there are terms that are used sufficiently out of order that their meaning is incomprehensible or misleading outside the EU context. Examples include the use of "delay" instead of "deadline" ("In order to meet the delay for translation, additional lawyer-linguists are added to the team"), the use of "eventual" instead of "possible" ("to avoid the eventual imposition of fines, members states shall receive sufficient advance notice"), or the use of "elaborate" instead of "to draft" or "to write something up" ("Additional background information shall be elaborated in due course"). EU English also involves unusual or irregular constructions, such as "with the aim to" ("Provisions are included in the regulation with the aim to reduce emissions from small vehicles") or when the possessive form is replaced with "of" constructions ("there are major problems with the argument of Mr. Leclerc").[1]

EU English has variably been referred to as Eurospeak (Bellier 1997; McCluskey 2002; McArthur 2003; Phillipson 2003; Magistro 2013), EU language (Robinson 2014b), Eurorhetoric (Koskinen 2008), EU officialese (Creech 2005), an "EU sociolect" (Dollerup 2001), or Bruxellish (Chaudenson 2001). It is also sometimes called "Euro-English" (e.g., Balič 2016a; Crystal 1999; McArthur 2003), which can cause confusion because that term more commonly denotes the English of nonnative speakers across Europe, as opposed to specifically in the EU and its institutions (Berns 1995; Jenkins, Modiano, and Seidlhofer 2001; Mollin 2006; Seidlhofer 2011). To avoid this confusion, I will use the term "EU English."

For a similar reason, I refrain from using the term "lingua franca," which is frequently used loosely to describe EU English, but its precise meaning does not actually apply in the case of the EU.[2] The term "lingua franca" refers to a communicative medium among speakers of different languages (Hülmbauer and Seidlhofer 2013, 388), and "English as a lingua franca" (ELF) thus to a communicative medium based on an "'open source' code of English" (Hülmbauer and Seidlhofer 2013, 391). However, a lingua franca is more spontaneous, flexible, and unstructured than EU English.

As House (2003, 557) describes, "each combination of interactants seems to negotiate and govern their own variety of lingua franca use." Similarly, Hülmbauer and Seidlhofer (2013, 390) explain that English as a lingua franca "cannot be pinned down to certain features but has to be flexibly mobilized in ever-changing contexts of linguistic diversity." When people enter the EU's institutions, however, they are becoming part of a linguistic environment in which much of this "negotiating of meaning" has already taken place. This makes English language interactions inside the EU institutions quite different from a spontaneous meeting of "a group of tourists in a seaside taverna" (Seidlhofer 2011, 18). Rather than having to establish a common basis for communication in each interaction from scratch, new arrivals in Brussels learn to adhere to the EU English that is already prevalent inside the institutions, as discussed in more detail below. This does not mean that there is no need to adjust to particular counterparts' language capacities, which of course can vary widely. Indeed, some of the spontaneity and flexibility that is associated with lingua franca use does come into play inside the institutions; if there were no such flexibility and adaptation, EU English would not be particularly useful as a communicative medium, after all. For the most part, however, EU English is not "ad hoc"; instead, there is a "locally relevant" linguistic framework in place, including the "customary conventions" that a lingua franca lacks (see Hülmbauer 2011; Seidlhofer and Widdowson 2006).

A final point of conceptual and terminological clarification is warranted up front: I am entirely agnostic as to whether EU English constitutes a new variety, form, register, or genre of English, which is a point of contention among some analysts of language use in the EU. Vuorikoski (2005, 231), for example, concludes that speeches in the European Parliament (EP) plenary "share features that characterise the EP discourse as a specific genre"; Bugarski (2009) and Pozzo (2012) consider EU English a "new variety"; Tosi (2013) describes a "form of international English unmarked by cultural specificity"; and Robinson (2014b, 185) maintains that EU English is "its own particular language." Others question these propositions (e.g., McCluskey 2002; Grzega 2005). Balič, for example, concludes that "a particular variety of English . . . has not been developed within the EU institutions to date" (Balič 2016b, 103) and that EU English "must be regarded as EU jargon due to its technical, administrative or legal nature and not as a separate non-standard form of English for EU institutional settings" (Balič 2016a, 131). These conclusions follow neither obviously nor inescapably from her empirical results, however, which highlights one important challenge with the comparison of text corpora to identify a new language variety: there are no agreed upon parameters or criteria of what constitutes a

"EU English" and Depoliticization   143

new "type" of English. As Mollin (2006, 100) puts it, "how different does it have to be to be different?" As a political scientist, I do not have the expertise to confidently take a position in this debate, and I defer to my colleagues in other fields. But whether or not EU English constitutes a new "type" does not have a particular bearing on my argument or conclusions, because my ambitions are more modest. I merely seek to help establish that participants in EU politics use English in a particular way that enables and facilitates communication within the context of the EU's core institutions, and what the consequences are of using EU English. Whether or not EU English constitutes a "new variety" or the like is secondary, in this regard, as long as it serves the pragmatic function of providing a common basis for interactions, collaborations, and transactions between EU actors.

This chapter looks closely at the use and characteristics of EU English, which my respondents describe as a standardized language shared by EU actors that is simple, neutral, and utilitarian in the sense that it involves a specialized, technical vocabulary and jargon that reflects the particular needs of its users. It also shows that EU actors, including native speakers, have to adjust to EU English upon arriving in Brussels and highlights the role of language service providers in disseminating EU English. It contributes to the limited number of empirical studies focused on identifying features of EU English by analyzing English-language oral interactions between policymakers in the European Parliament concerning one particular legislative proposal. This analysis of spontaneous, natural speech in one of the EU institutions is, to my knowledge, the first of its kind and reveals that EU actors tend to use shorter words and sentences than their counterparts in two native-English legislative chambers. Their speech is, moreover, lexically less rich and lacks complexity: EU actors use English at a seventh-grade reading level on average, compared to the eleventh-grade reading level used by native English lawmakers elsewhere. The analyses also show that EU actors tend to use ideologically neutral language. These findings are notable and instructive, but far from definitive due to important data limitations; much additional research is warranted to confirm their robustness. Finally, the chapter considers the potential consequences of Brexit for the use of English inside the EU institutions.

Characteristics of EU English

EU English is a key component of the EU's multilingual regime that develops endogenously in response to the particular needs of participants in EU policymaking, rather than being imposed "from above." After all,

English (whether the standard or EU kind) is not *formally* the main working language inside the institutions. Its dominance is, instead, driven by linguistic pragmatism, and this pragmatism is also evident in the endogenous development of EU English. In a multilingual context, Longman writes, "the temptation will always be to work in the most convenient manner" (Longman 2007, 198), and a simple, utilitarian form of English offers both convenience and efficiency. The endogenous evolution of EU English reflects, first, the reality that for most speakers of EU English the language is foreign. As discussed in chapter 4, the uneven competence of nonnative speakers imposes a simplicity on the language, since a higher-level version of English may exclude some actors and thus stand in the way of effective communication. Second, the competence of the EU in many technical policy areas encourages the formation of a professional EU jargon, much of which is in English (Bellier 2002, 104). Third, nonnative speakers introduce particular words, concepts, and syntax structures that reflect their own languages; the influence of French is particularly notable in this regard. Some such foreign influences are spontaneous and fleeting, while others become more widely adopted over time and even travel across languages inside the institutions. In the short term, foreign influence may simply be experienced as deviations from EU English, which are commonplace in the halls of the EU institutions and thus considered acceptable. Over time, however, such deviations can become integrated into EU English (Jenkins, Modiano, and Seidlhofer 2001, 14). Finally, EU English arises out of the need for all language versions of EU legislation to be equally authentic, because certain concepts or expressions may become dominant in EU English not because they are the best "fit" in linguistic terms, but because they translate well into other languages. They may, for example, be less ambiguous than a linguistically more appropriate alternative. Along these lines, Robertson maintains that one reason why "EU texts look and feel odd and unfamiliar to native speakers" is "the way in which legislative texts are constructed" (Robertson 2011, 56), including the harmonization of terms across languages. This harmonization may happen when other languages are "put into the 'mould' of the source language text," but also when the (usually EU English) source text is "bent" to "suit other languages" (Robertson 2012b, 11–12).

The nature of "EU English" was one of the most common points of discussion in my interviews with a large number of respondents, often without my prompting.[3] Some of my respondents' general descriptions are worth quoting at some length:

"EU English" and Depoliticization 145

I would say that much of the communication in this Parliament is done through a, if you consider the English language as a bandwidth, it would be a very narrow portion of it that's being used. So everybody speaks kind of the same English, which avoids up to a certain extent problems and miscommunication, as long as you stay on professional topics, and on familiar topics. But once you go beyond that, the potential for miscommunication becomes much more. . . . It's neutral, it's simpler, and yet it's made up of all this jargon. (#49)

I think most of the people in the Commission use this Euro speak, which is a sort of written English that is technical. And because you tend to avoid misunderstanding, we all stick to the same expressions, the same words, and in the end it might be a very small number of words and verbs that we use. That would be a poor language, but at least we know we understand each other when we speak this. Outside, this language does not exist . . . In the real world it doesn't work. (#55)

The English that is spoken . . . tends to be a slightly, kind of bastardized version. . . . A rather particular form of English emerges, which is not quite, you know, it isn't actually the English of the native speaker, but it's perfectly adequate for the purposes for which it's required. (#78)

One of the most common ways to describe EU English was by emphasizing that it is not "real," "normal," or "British" English, or by highlighting the lower quality of the kind of English that is used inside the EU institutions (#41, 43, 51, 55, 56, 62, 66, 68, 70, 72, 73, 78, 79, 82, 83).[4] Respondents thus emphasized, for example, that EU English does not have "the same structure, the same vocabulary, the same meaning" as British English (#83), and that they "are conscious of the fact that it is not true English . . . but it is English that everybody understands" (#66). Indeed, one of the key features of EU English is that it includes systematic deviations from standard English that are taken for granted by its users. As one of my respondents put it, "you don't notice [certain mistakes] as a mistake anymore. . . . You just kind of integrate that as normal speak" (#58). Balič (2016a, 2016b) investigates this proposition in more detail. Her survey of Commission officials asked respondents to indicate if several deviations from standard English identified in corpus-based analyses of EU texts were

146   The Language(s) of Politics

acceptable or unacceptable use of English. The goal of the exercise was to establish if there is "a community of speakers who are not only developing and regularly using distinctly non-standard patterns of English but who are, moreover, genuinely and openly accepting them as 'appropriate' in their minds" (Balič 2016a, 138–39). This is an important consideration, because the existence of a community that thinks of itself as speaking a particular variety is viewed by some as more meaningful than the existence of "objectively identifiable linguistic features" (Seidlhofer 2011, 83). Balič finds that almost all the deviations from standard English are rated as acceptable by both nonnative and native speakers among her respondents, although this finding has to be interpreted with some caution for the latter group because of the small number of native English speakers in her sample (Balič 2016b, 131).

My respondents also emphasized the simplicity of EU English compared to regular English (#42, 49, 58, 62, 64, 66, 73, 81, 82), which is of course one of the key features that allows it to serve as a medium of communication among nonnative speakers (see also Ban 2009, 2013; Crystal 1999). Is is "simpler . . . more common sense" in the eyes of a national counselor (#62).

> [EU English] is basic. . . . It's not refined. . . . We usually do concentrate on the substance, so what really counts between us is to understand what the others mean. We're not going to listen so much, pay attention so much to the style, because we aren't here for the style, we're here for politics. (#82)

> Nobody would venture to using very kind of colorful expressions. If you want to be understood by everyone, you have to speak relatively clearly and slowly. . . . If they want to be influential with everybody, they have to adapt to the way they speak. . . . I suppose it's a kind of Esperanto type of English. (#64)

> If I try to write my reports in Brussels-English, they will be, let's say, two pages. If I try to write my reports in proper English, I might gain half a page. On the other hand, if I try to write them in any other language, I will gain at least another page. (#58)

Another characteristic of EU English highlighted in my interviews was the more limited vocabulary and specialized jargon it involves (#1, 27, 42,

46, 49, 56, 58, 62, 68, 69, 74, 76, 83). "Certain words mean something different than they would in another normal context," according to a national counselor (#76), in part because "sometimes there are even new words invented" (#62) and also because of the lingering influence of French (#56, 61, 75). One Mertens counselor explained that "you get this mix of English and French. . . . It's become more or less like a new language. It's so common that . . . it doesn't strike you as something strange" (#75). EU English is thus denationalized or acultural (see also Bugarski 2009; Tosi 2013).

Finally, EU English has been described as neutral or homogenized (Roberts 2006; Phillipson 2016), which is, in part, due to its being standardized and shared across nationalities and ideologies. But it also results from the technical nature of much EU legislation, which "imposes certain language," a former high-ranking Commission official explained (#51, also #42, 51, 55, 72). The personal staffer of a Member of the EP (MEP) further elaborated this point:

> What's spoken here, the kind of English that's spoken, . . . it's a technical language, one must say. It has particular terms that keep coming up, so that everybody pictures the same thing, even when they seem strange to an outsider. . . . This technical language that has developed is very helpful. It is a strange lingua franca that everybody knows how to handle. (#42)

Adjusting to EU English

New arrivals in Brussels do not immediately know how to handle EU English, however. They have to adjust and become familiar with reading, speaking, and writing it. "Brussels-speak takes time" as one interpreter put it (#6, also 39, 51, 55, 58, 62, 70, 81, 83).[5] When newcomers first get to Brussels, "they come with an imported language, which restrains their possibility to exchange with the audience"; but very soon, they "develop another language. . . . The first concern for newcomers is to get integrated and to adopt the language style to be accepted by the mainstream; that's almost a prerequisite," according to a respondent who spent decades in the Commission (#51).[6] What happens if they resist was conveyed by a current Commission official, who recalled others telling him that "we don't understand" a new colleague who proved reluctant to change how he spoke (#55). To avoid such problems, "we need to stick to those words because

148 The Language(s) of Politics

they've already been commonly accepted, so it's easier to go with those" (#70). This leads to "textual uniformity" (Tosi 2013, 9) and a standardization of language in the EU institutions.

For some respondents, adopting EU English happens organically and perhaps even unconsciously,[7] while others describe making a deliberate choice. One national counselor from one of member states in central and eastern Europe, for example, explained

> What I started to do when we negotiated the regulation of Erasmus+, for example, I started to speak English, European English, because it was easier for me. It was more understandable, and I could actually get some of the changes that I couldn't get otherwise. (#62)

Notably, it is not only nonnative English speakers who have to adjust to using EU English; native English speakers also end up adopting it (#55, 58, 62, 63, 72, 73, 79).[8] One native English speaker involved in policymaking in the Council, for example, acknowledged that she "absolutely" uses EU English, "that's a Brussels-only thing, you just get sucked into it" (#72). A Commission official similarly described that:

> Most of the UK officials I know here, they claim themselves that they don't speak English anymore. They speak the Euro speak, and they say that when they come back home for summer holidays or Christmas, it takes them a few days to just come back to. (#55)

A particularly interesting and instructive quote came from a retired EP official:

> The fact that I haven't lived in [a native English country], for example, since the '70s, maybe what I think is normal English is no longer. . . . A lot of people say to me, you know, especially now that I live in [a native English country again], "my God, you have an incredibly kind of neutral English." And I wonder if it was magnified by having most of my parliamentary career . . . having to speak English to nonnatives, and maybe that affected the way I spoke English. . . . I couldn't put my finger on it and say that's why I speak English the way I do, but probably I did have to. I'm not conscious of ever dumbing down the quality. (#79)

Language service providers play an important role in the spread of EU English (and EU language more broadly) in that they teach incoming policymakers EU-typical terminology, concepts, and phrases and more broadly how to talk and write the "Brussels way" (#2, 3, 15, 62, 46, 61). One MEP assistant thus described making an effort to read documents in English in order to learn the right terms to communicate with others (#38). A party group advisor in the EP acknowledged that policymakers learn policy-relevant vocabulary from the lawyer-linguists sitting next to them (#46), while a national counselor explained that "when we drafted the texts, we usually relied on advice from the Council's Legal Service, just because they could propose us the best solution for the problem from the linguistic per-spective" (#61). Such dynamics were confirmed by a lawyer-linguist, who explained that part of their job is to make sure newcomers understand what a word or concept "means in EU legalistic terms" (#19). Sometimes this even includes teaching native English speakers what a particular term in EU legal English means. For example, a national counselor recalled a situation in the Council in which the UK delegation asked to change a term in an English-language text,

> And the Council Legal Service—[who was of] British origin—answered "sorry, it is bad English, I agree with you, my father wouldn't understand that. But here in Brussels we use it in a very specific format and it has been mentioned in hundreds of legal text." . . . So that was interesting, the negotiation between two native speakers. (#61)

Learning EU language also happens passively, however, through repeated exposure to its use by language service providers and other partic-ipants in EU politics.[9] This is especially true when it comes to specialized EU jargon and legal language (McAuliffe 2008, 2010). Beaton (2007), for example, shows that simultaneous interpretation from German to English involves extensive structural and lexical repetition and the recurrent use of certain collocations and specific vocabulary. Over time, those are adopted by nonnative speakers who are not otherwise exposed to standard English, as well as by native English speakers who adjust their way of speaking and writing to the prevailing language norms inside the institutions (see also Abélès 1999, 115).

Written text, as opposed to spoken language, plays a particularly impor-tant role in the creation and spread of EU language. Robertson emphasizes the influence of written texts for the "separate oral dimension" of EU legal language, where the latter is linked and subordinated to the former (Rob-ertson 2010c, 2). One national counselor illustrated this point when she explained that "when you actually start talking about a file, you switch to

150   The Language(s) of Politics

English. Maybe because the language is limited and also because you deal with the file in English in here, so yeah, you have the terminology already in English" (#70). As discussed in detail elsewhere, written texts in the EU are highly standardized, using set wordings and patterns that are carefully constructed in all languages (Robertson 2012b). This standardized written language—including particular phrases, constructions, and simplified semantic and syntactic patterns (Biel 2007)—then informs how people speak. Stritar and Stabej, for example, report that their interview respondents in the EP and the Court of Justice acquire "the vocabulary necessary in debates" through work with English and French documents (Stritar and Stabej 2013, 186).

Notably, this dynamic implies that written language in the EU tends to innovate spoken language, rather than the other way around.[10] This makes language service providers not just teachers, but also creators of EU language; some even consider themselves "language innovators" who set modes and change trends (Tosi 2003, 56). As a result, "what you see is that sometimes there are even new [EU English] words invented, which make sense to everybody but the Brits" (#62).[11]

Analyzing EU English

Most references to EU English in existing research are made more or less in passing (e.g., Ban 2009; Ginsburgh and Weber 2011; Clark and Priestley 2012), and there are few empirical investigations of the phenomenon. Some are qualitative, such as Bugarski's (Bugarski 2009), which highlights differences between EU English and standard English in terms of lexis and terminology. A handful of studies rely on corpora of EU text, such as Trebits (2008), which aims to identify and describe those lexical elements that are indispensable for EU-related work. Comparing her "Corpus of EU English" (CEUE) to the British National Corpus (BNC), Trebits finds that many words in the former may be considered EU-specific and not part of a general English vocabulary, and thus concludes that "EU English has developed into a special language . . . [that mirrors] the different functions and multiple activities of the EU as a cultural, political and historical reality" (Trebits 2008, 40). The analyses in a follow-up article that compares the use of conjunctions in the BNC and the EUROPARL7 corpus (Koehn 2005), which is extracted from the proceedings of the EP, indicate that there is "considerable difference in the use of some causal, clarifying, and additive conjunctions in the two corpora" (Trebits 2009a, 206). Finally, her investigation of phrasal verbs (a phrase consisting of a verb and another element, such as an adverb or preposition) reveals that about half of the most frequent phrasal verbs in the EU corpus are also among the most frequent in the BNC (Trebits 2009b, 477). Jablonkai (2009) compares corpora of official EU texts to online EU news and finds them to be notably different in terms of EU-specific vocabulary, discourse patterns, and text organization. Balič (Balič 2016a, 2016b) also relies on the EUROPARL7 corpus.[12] She finds pronounced differences between the EU-specific corpus and the BNC when it comes to EU vocabulary in particular, which she describes as "generally very technical, complex, and not easily understood by the general public" (Balič 2016a, 136). But she also identifies particularities in EU English when it comes to countable nouns (e.g., aid and competence used in the plural), the use of "of" constructions instead of the possessive (e.g., "the aim of the Communication of the Commission is to . . ."), and lexical bundles (e.g., "I should like to . . ."). Finally, Rabinovich et al. (2016) investigate differences between the language used by native speakers in the EUROPARL7 corpus, the language of advanced nonnative speakers, and translations of native speech. They find that the nonnative English used inside the EU institutions and translations have in common that they "exhibit poorer lexical richness, a tendency to use more frequent words, a different distribution of idiomatic expressions and pronouns, and excessive use of cohesive devices" (Rabinovich et al. 2016, 1871). EU English, in other words, more closely resembles EU "translationese" than native English.

Aside from offering insights drawn from my interviews, I make a modest contribution to the body of research on EU English by analyzing a corpus of EU language that is different from the ones that are commonly used. The problem with existing text corpora is that they do not capture spontaneous, natural speech, but focus on written texts or reflect oral discussions that are "based on pre-drafted speeches or other written documents that may or may not be proofread by [native speakers] of English" and are then "read out in more formal settings" (Balič 2016b, 80). Hence, Balič emphasizes that informal EU meetings or discussions would be "a more promising source of English usage within the main EU institutions," but she maintains that due to confidential information that may be discussed, obtaining those is "absolutely impossible" (Balič 2016b, 80).

It is entirely true that getting hold of records of such informal meetings and discussions is extremely difficult, but it is not impossible. I was, in fact, able to gather, transcribe, and rely on video recordings of closed-door negotiations between rapporteurs and shadow rapporteurs in the EP concerning one particular legislative proposal. Due to the highly sensitive nature of the negotiations, I was only granted access to those records under the strictest conditions of confidentiality. I am thus unable to identify any of the participants in the meetings, the legislative proposal in question, or even the general policy area. The data themselves are also not without problems. There is only a relatively small number of speakers, which raises important questions about generalizability. Moreover, an even smaller number of speakers dominates the discussions, which makes the results reported below sensitive to the inclusion or exclusion of certain speakers from the corpus of text. Hence, the findings have to be interpreted with caution and considered preliminary and indicative at best. That being said, the data are so rare and unusually difficult to acquire that they are worth analyzing despite these significant caveats.

Meaningfully analyzing English-language speech in the EP's multilingual environment requires a monolingual, native English comparison case to establish if EU English is meaningfully different from "regular" legislative (or administrative/bureaucratic) English. For this purpose, I relied on publicly available video-recorded proceedings in the Irish Parliament and the UK House of Lords focused on a similar policy area as in the EP. Those videos were carefully transcribed by the same person as the EP data, to ensure consistency and comparability. The comparison cases were selected from a variety of different options, including video coverage of legislative proceedings in other native-English legislatures in the United States, Canada, Australia, New Zealand, and Scotland. The problem with those alternatives was that the only publicly available video footage is of formal meetings and debates in standing committees and the like, which for the most part involve legislators reading prepared statements rather than speaking freely. In the case of the Irish Parliament and the House of Lords, however, video recordings are available of proceedings that were more similar in style and substance to the EP data, namely deliberations in which lawmakers spoke freely when engaging in back-and-forth interactions with one another about particular legislative proposals. At one stage of the legislative process in Ireland, for example, groups of lawmakers engage in a general discussion of the scope of a piece of legislation. The format is not identical to the EP data, in that lawmakers scrutinize the proposed bill in general terms, rather than directly negotiating detailed compromises; the interactions are similar, however, in that participants engage directly with each other using spontaneous, natural speech. The House of Lords data were selected because their format is similar to the Irish case.

Altogether, the transcripts consist of more than 150,000 words of text.

Table 5.1 shows the total number of sentences, tokens (overall number of words),[13] and types (unique words). The corpora were processed for analysis by stemming words, converting all words to lower case, removing punctuation and numerals, and removing stopwords (i.e., "useless" words), including utterances like "ums" and "uhs" (the incidence of which was similar across the corpora).[14]

Based on the intuition that longer words and sentences indicate complexity of language—because they are harder to construct and comprehend and especially difficult to use extemporaneously in a spoken setting—EU texts ought to use shorter words and sentences. This is confirmed in the data (table 5.2): the average sentence in the non-EU corpus is 27.4 percent longer than in the EU corpus and the average word contains 5.7 percent more syllables, a small substantive difference but still potentially meaningful given that English is prone to shorter words to begin with.

Next, the type-token ratio (TTR) was calculated, which is a standard measure of lexical richness that divides the number of types (unique words) in a text by the number of tokens (overall word count). The smaller the TTR, the lower the lexical diversity of a document in that fewer unique words are being used. The average TTR for the EU texts is smaller than for the non-EU texts (see table 5.3), indicating that the EU texts include fewer unique words. While the difference in TTRs across the corpora of only 0.03 seems small, it is comparable in size to other significant differences across similar political texts (e.g., Rabinovich et al. 2016). Based on this measure, EU English is less complex than standard English. Consideration of Flesch-Kincaid scores (column 2 in table 5.3), which measure the grade reading level of a text (Kincaid et al. 1975), leads to the same conclusion.[15] Using weighted measures for words per sentence and syllables per word as indicators of complexity, F-K scores correspond to grade levels in

TABLE 5.1. Sentences, Tokens, and Types

	Sentences	Tokens	Types
Non-EU	4,008	110,460	13,281
EU	5,574	123,192	11,723

TABLE 5.2. Sentences and Syllables

	Average number of words per sentence	Average number of syllables per word
Non-EU	23.69	1.49
EU	18.59	1.41

TABLE 5.3. Lexical Richness

	Average type-token ratios	Average Flesch-Kincaid scores
Non-EU	.22	11.23
EU	.19	7.21

the U.S. system. For example, a score of 7.1 would indicate comprehensibility for the average U.S. seventh grader, and a sixth-grade reading level is considered conversational English. Based on F-K scores, the non-EU transcripts are much more complex than the EU documents: the former are on average at an eleventh-grade reading level, while the latter are on average at a seventh-grade level.[16]

Next we consider the incidence of adjectives and adverbs in the two texts, which are often unnecessary to convey basic meanings and may thus be less common in the EU texts. These analyses rely on natural language processing (NLP) algorithms to tag each word's part of speech.[17] Because the algorithm generates counts of parts of speech, table 5.4 reports the results as the percentages of each corpus that consist of adjectives and adverbs, which partially capture lexical density (Lu 2011). Contrary to expectations, however, EU texts include *more* adverbs and adjectives than the non-EU texts. There is some disagreement among linguists about the extent to which these sorts of modifiers heighten or hinder the readability of texts, suggesting that their usage may not be an indicator of linguistic complexity (Aziz, Fook, and Alsree 2010; De Clerq and Hoste 2016; Lu et al. 2019). There is also a substantive difference between adjectives such as "good" or "one" and more precise words, which means that parts of speech measures, taken alone, may be poor indicators of the complexity of a text. It is nonetheless surprising that the EU text includes a greater proportion of adjectives and adverbs.

It is similarly unexpected that the EU texts include *fewer* disfluencies than do the non-EU texts. Based on the list of misused English words and expressions in EU publications compiled by Gardner (2016), three customs "disfluency dictionaries" were created: one containing all items on Gard-

TABLE 5.4. Adjectives and Adverbs

	Adjectives	Adverbs
Non-EU	3.1%	3.2%
EU	3.3%	4.5%

ner's list;[18] one with "of" and "do" removed (as these are such common words that it is not possible to separate actual disfluent usage as part of phrases from "correct" use); and one including only words and expressions that seem, a priori, unlikely to appear in standard English. The numbers of disfluencies in the texts, based on these three dictionaries, are presented in table 5.5, which shows that there are *more* disfluencies in the non-EU documents than in the EU documents. This finding may be a particular feature of these data, but it may also result from some EU-typical disfluencies being regular words that happen to be used incorrectly in the EU. For example, it is possible that "to ensure," which in the case of the EU is often used instead of "to provide" (Gardner 2016, 30) happens to be used more often (and used correctly) in the non-EU texts but is counted as a disfluency. That the difference in the number of obvious disfluencies in the EU and non-EU texts is negligible (column 3) suggests that this is at least part of the explanation. It is also possible, however, that the lower incidence of disfluencies is suggestive of a general difference between written and spoken EU English that warrants further consideration and analysis.

The final analysis focuses on the ideological content of the EP corpus using the Wordfish scaling model (Slapin and Proksch 2008)[19] to consider the proposition that EU English has a notably "neutral" quality. We find some support for this proposition when breaking the EP texts down by speaker, as shown in figure 5.1: with few exceptions, MEPs cluster around zero, indicating that they use ideologically neutral language.

It is, again, important not to put too much purchase on these results. The data are too limited to reach definitive conclusions and the results sensitive to the exclusion of those speakers who dominate the discussion. The findings are, therefore, indicative at best, but they do suggest that there may be something to the proposition that spoken EU English is less complex than standard English used in comparable circumstances by native speakers, and that it tends to be ideologically neutral (which is particularly notable since the speakers analyzed here are politicians who are directly elected by EU citizens, not career EU officials). A lot more research is warranted to confirm these preliminary results and to further investigate the

TABLE 5.5. Disfluencies

	All Disfluencies	Without "Of" and "Do"	Obvious Disfluencies Only
Non-EU	3,918	787	339
EU	2,814	721	336

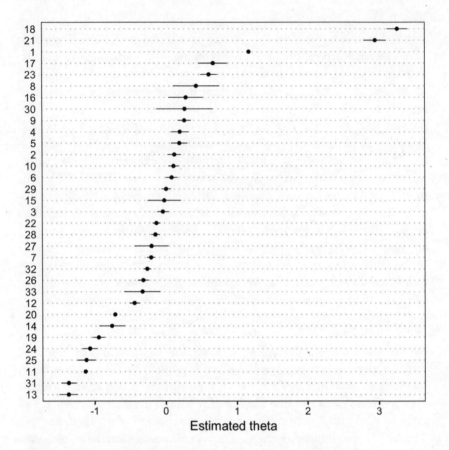

Fig. 5.1. Ideology in EU Speeches

unexpected findings regarding the use of adjectives, adverbs, and disfluencies in EU speech. Interpreted with due caution and in combination with previous research, however, the results suggest that the English used inside the EU's core institutions is different from standard English.

The Impact of Brexit

The UK's departure from the European Union raises obvious questions about the future of English, and in particular EU English, in the EU institutions.[20] The general consensus among my respondents was that Brexit would have little impact on the dominance of English in EU politics and that English would surely not disappear as an official and main working language of the EU (#37, 38, 43, 44, 47, 52, 53, 54, 55, 56, 57, 58, 59, 60, 61, 62, 63, 65, 66, 69, 70, 71, 72, 73, 74, 75, 76, 78, 79, 80, 82, 83).[21] One MEP put it succinctly: "I heard all these stupid stories about, because of Brexit, we're ditching English; absolutely ridiculous" (#44, also 54, 82). Respondents pointed to a variety of (not mutually exclusive) reasons for this, first that English is the main language people are able to speak in Brussels (#37, 52, 55, 56, 65, 71, 75, 78, 79) and therefore the main language that people share (#43, 47, 61, 66, 78). It is "the most common bridge" (#47), while not enough people speak or share even the other "big" languages like French or German (#52, 54, 56, 59, 70). And this is unlikely to change, given that 97 percent of lower secondary students are learning English across the EU (outside the UK), compared with 34 percent for French and 23 percent for German; in primary school, 79 percent are learning English and only 4 percent French (The Economist 2017). And so English will retain its status, "in spite of wishful thinking of some" (#71).[22]

Several respondents did indicate, however, that even if English were not to disappear, it may be losing importance (#49, 50, 56, 61, 62, 63, 67, 72, 77), as Commission President Jean-Claude Juncker suggested in May 2017 (BBC 2017). "What the status of English will be, we don't know yet," one respondent said (#49). He and others suspect that there might be an increase in the use of French (#49, 56, 61, 62, 63, 72, 77) or German (#50, 61, 62, 63), but perhaps also in some of the other languages, like Italian or Spanish (#63). One respondent also suggested that MEPs may be more inclined in the future to use their native languages instead of English (#43). And so, despite the consensus that English will not disappear, it may be that "more things would be done in more languages," as one counselor in a Permanent Representation speculated (#63).

It is also possible, however, that Brexit will reinforce the use of English inside the EU institutions because it will no longer be associated with one particular member state (#52, 65, 78, 79, 81), in particular one that also happens to be large and often recalcitrant.[23] "Funnily enough," one EP official suggested, "it might very well entrench its use, on the grounds that you'll no longer have the one dominant nationality going around using their English, and even the French might feel more relaxed about using English" (#78). In contrast to English, one Mertens counselor explained,

> any other EU language will have this national aspect, that you are giving more weight to some specific country. For example, if you say that we will use French more, Germans will not be happy about this,

158 The Language(s) of Politics

and if you say we use German and French, the Spaniards and Italians and Poles will not be happy about this. (#65)

English may thus come to be seen as a neutral medium of communication inside the EU institutions, or a "third party's language" that "creates a sense of relative equality" (Liu 2015, 16).[24]

While those outcomes are uncertain, it stands to reason that Brexit will affect the kind of English used inside the EU institutions. As highlighted above, my respondents already consider EU English to be different from standard British English, and with fewer native speakers around it is likely that nonnatives will continue to "take possession of the language, or at least they become co-creators of the specific variant of the working language required in that organisation" (van Els 2001, 340; see also Berns 2017; Modiano 2017).[25] Nowadays, there are often native English speakers in the room who can help select the right term or expression or who can correct mistakes as they happen in the deliberation or drafting process (#46, 54, 62, 64, 70, 75). A smaller number of native English speakers might, therefore, result in a strengthening of EU English, since the ratio of speakers of standard English to EU English will change dramatically (#59, 72, 79, 83). Hence, one Mertens counselor maintained, it is quite possible that "English becomes more and more Euro English" (#72).

Conclusion

EU English is a simple, utilitarian, specialized, and standardized language used inside the EU institutions. Those who speak or write in EU English express themselves using less colorful, complex, and lexically rich language, which also tends to be ideologically neutral. EU English is therefore meaningfully different from the "regular" English used in native language parliaments, as the linguistic analyses suggest. It is more than "just" bureaucratic jargon with a specialized vocabulary.

The focus of this chapter was on EU English as the primary vehicular language inside the EU institutions, but it is important to emphasize that some of the insights offered here may travel to other languages as well. The respondent in the EP who talked about people only using a narrow "bandwidth" of English, for example, emphasized that "it's the same thing for French," which "everybody masters up to a certain degree a professional fluency" (#49). One implication of this observation is that there may not just be a particular "EU English" or a particular "EU French," but more broadly a particular way of speaking and writing in the EU, across languages.[26]

English is dominant, however, and it levels the linguistic playing field in the EU institutions in that "everyone has the same way of speaking in this place" (#67). "We all communicate in the EU mother tongue, so to speak," explained one national counselor, so people "basically don't notice the fact that some people maybe do not express themselves as eloquently as they would have had they spoken their mother tongue" (#80). That is one important implication of the use of EU English inside the institutions. The particular characteristics my respondents associate with EU English are also consequential: they, once again, have a depoliticizing effect. EU English is simple and utilitarian, a tool that is used pragmatically to communicate information, as opposed to an instrument for signaling or advancing a particular political agenda. It also contributes to the standardization of both written and spoken language in the EU, making users less distinguishable and distinctive from one another. Finally, EU English is decultured and neutral, and thus less indicative of particular EU actors' national or ideological backgrounds or political agendas. All this has important potential implications for the quality of political deliberation and contestation inside the EU institutions, but also for the EU's relationship with the European people, because a bland, technocratic, depoliticized language likely contributes to a gap between the EU and its citizens (a theme that will be revisited in the concluding pages of this book).

These insights should be read in conjunction with those offered in chapter 4. Indeed, the deep dive into EU English presented here is an extension of the previous chapter, in that both dealt with foreign language use in the EU institutions. The next chapter shifts focus toward the second way in which EU actors commonly communicate with one another, namely in their native tongues while relying on the EU's extensive language services. This dimension of institutional multilingualism in the EU, as will be seen, has its own (and once again unintentionally) depoliticizing effects.

SIX

Translation, Interpretation, and Depoliticization

While many interactions in the European Union (EU) institutions occur between nonnative speakers of a shared foreign language, especially (EU) English, the other primary mode of communication is through interpretation and translation. As described in chapter 2, the EU's language services are extensive and generally seen as the best in the world. They are also recognized as such by my respondents, despite some complaints about occasional and for the most part inconsequential problems. In this chapter, I examine how reliance on interpreters for oral interactions and translators for written texts impacts policymaking. My focus is not, however, on how language services affect the "logistics" of political processes, for example by causing delays or by imposing deadlines, but on how translation and interpretation affect the language of politics in the EU. The chapter argues that reliance on language services, again, entails a depoliticization of policymaking through the simplification, standardization, and neutralization of (both source and target) language.

Translation, my respondents highlighted across institutions, is not an exact science: there are always multiple ways to transmit each word, phrase, or sentence uttered or written in one language into another. Translation and interpretation thus involve constantly making difficult choices. For translators, the main challenge is having to choose—often under significant time pressure—not *a* term, but *the right* term in the given context. Especially when translating legislative or legal texts, they have to overcome the inherent uncertainty of the translation process to produce texts that are equivalent across languages, so that their interpretation leads to the uniform application of EU legislation across member states (Strandvik 2014). Interlingual concordance ultimately trumps style, and the safest way to ensure equivalence is for translators to rely on "precedent" rather than to seek creative linguistic solutions. Hence, they use existing documents and shared terminology databases as well as common phrases and formulations, all of which results in a standardization and simplification of the target language. Another depoliticizing effect of the equal authenticity principle is that it allows little room for ambiguity in the source text. The need for consistency in the legal effect of EU legislation therefore constrains the ability of political actors to use purposely vague or ambiguous language when negotiating and drafting legislation, thus blunting a popular tool for forging political agreement.

Interpreters also face terminological challenges, but the equivalence of source and target language is necessarily less of a priority in simultaneous interpretation than in the translation of written texts, because oral interventions are fleeting, and translations made on the spot are held to a lower standard. What is particularly challenging for interpreters is transmitting not just what is said, but also what lies behind a given utterance, such as meaning, intention, culture, or personality. They have to (try to) do justice to the speaker, in this regard, and they have to do so immediately. The difficulty in this is heightened by rapid speech and the reading out loud of prepared statements, highly technical subject areas, and the use of idiomatic speech, humor, and occasionally inappropriate language, which many EU actors try to avoid using, as discussed in chapter 4, but which are of course not completely eliminated from EU actors' speech. Given these challenges, simultaneous interpretation necessarily edits and processes speech, generally by making it functional and simple rather than rich and expressive. It has a depersonalizing effect and replaces rhetorical devices, elegance, finesse, and nuance in the native source language with standardized phrases and formulations in the target language.

Finally, the EU's language services have an additional, indirect effect on the nature of language in the EU institutions: EU actors are aware of and adjust the way they speak and write in anticipation of translation and interpretation. To ensure that their messages are conveyed more easily into other languages, they "speak for interpretation" and "write for translation" by using simple language and commonly accepted phrases. In other words, it is not only that the process and practice of translation and interpretation simplifies, standardizes, and neutralizes the *target* language, the *expectation thereof* leads to a simplification, standardization, and neutralization of the

162 The Language(s) of Politics

source language—not always completely or by everyone, but enough that it was a recurrent theme in my interviews.

This chapter first discusses the challenges associated with interpretation and translation, to illustrate why it is that language services necessarily and inevitably transform what is conveyed in the source language. It then explains how EU actors adjust their speeches and writing in order to make them more "translatable," before closing with a discussion of how multilingualism limits both intentional and unintentional ambiguity in policymaking. As in previous chapters, I provide detailed information drawn from my interviews not only to support my argument, but also to offer a wealth of descriptive information on language services, their role, and their impact in EU politics.

Simultaneous Interpretation of Spoken Language

Interpreting is not word-for-word translation, which in most cases would produce just nonsense, but the faithful transmission of a message, captured in one language and then accurately rendered in another. [Translation and interpreting] are very similar in that they both involve the understanding of language and the underlying meaning [. . .] Unlike translators, interpreters have to deal with fleeting messages, and they have to do so in real time, with very little room for second guesses, let alone elegant style. Linguistic knowledge, in any case, is just the tip of the iceberg. (European Parliament 2003, as quoted in Vuorikoski 2004)

Interpretation in the EU institutions is always a challenging job, as the interpreters I spoke to expressed in detail and as my other respondents readily acknowledged.[1] Difficulties are, in part, a function of the structures of the source and target languages. It is, for example, more difficult to translate across language families, such as from a Romance into a Germanic language (#17, 26); it is more difficult when sentence structures differ between two languages (#17, 24, 61); and it is more difficult yet if one language, such as English, has a particularly extensive vocabulary (#17, 34).

Other challenges go beyond such structural features, however, and apply no matter what languages are involved. Particularly testing are the difficulty of translating idiomatic expressions (#15, 20, 61, 64) and the need to convey more than just what is said, since part of the message lies in the speaker's tone of voice, emphasis, and other expression. One respondent explained that:

> It's very important to provide and translate whether there is some irony, whether the speaker is excited, whether he or she is simply saying things in a very matter of fact way. You have to render that because all of that is part of the message. . . . This is why I think it's very important for an interpreter to be as much translator as a communicator and an actor. . . . You really step into the shoes of the person you are interpreting, and you get a completely different personality basically with each speaker that you are interpreting. You're changing personality a certain way every five, ten, fifteen minutes. (#8)

Another concurred:

> The interpreter's goal is to become that person. If the person is agitated, they become agitated. He's not a newsreader. . . . But you also have to do it credibly. Your communication is across cultural boarders. Italians speak a lot, fast, and get invested in their speech, sometimes they are quite emotional. You also have to interpret this culture. If you do exactly the same thing for a Dutch person, it would be odd. You have to convey the emotional context appropriately. It's not easy. (#13)

In the end, people should not "realize that they are listening to an interpreter" (#17). To gauge the difficulty of this endeavor, I again used the example of Martin Schulz in my interviews. How much of Schulz's personality or charisma, for which he is known when speaking his native German, get lost in interpretation? Most of the language service providers I spoke to were of the opinion that even though interpretation is rarely perfect, it is possible to both transmit a message and convey somebody's personality via interpretation (#5, 7, 8, 14, 18, 22, 24, 26, 29, 34, 35). Some policymakers agreed (#12, 16, 39, 60, 82), emphasizing, for example, that

> Even if [Schulz] speaks German, when he gives a general statement, you hear the way you speak even if it goes via interpretation. I don't think there is a lot of loss, from the body language and from the message being passed. . . . And actually the interpreters sort of pass it also. You can hear from the way they interpret. . . . Our interpret-

ers are really excellent. I'm so impressed. . . . So you get the message across even if it's done via interpretation. (#60)

Aside from praising the quality of interpretation, this last respondent—a Council official—made another notable point, which helps explain why charisma and competence can be transmitted even when somebody's remarks go through interpretation: that a speaker can still be heard and seen. Body language, tone of voice, sentiment, and passion are, therefore, not totally lost on the audience. This was emphasized by service providers and policymakers alike (#5, 7, 14, 34, 20, 60, 70, 74), despite the delay that inevitably disconnects what is being said from "their body language, from their gestures, from their attitude" (#58, also #34, 74). This, however, can be a double-edged sword. The reality that the speaker's body language, facial expressions, pitch, and volume are "separated" from their words can "feel weird," in the words of another Council official (#58), especially when a discussion is more political than technical (#61). This disconnect can also result in the loss of important information, as another frequent participant in Council meetings recalls:

Last week there was a meeting of the Coreper, where it's a very restricted language regime [of English, French, and German], and I was again listening to the English translation, and the German ambassador was speaking. And he said something that clearly was of utmost importance, but from the English translation I couldn't get it. (#64)

In general, policymakers were more likely than language service providers to emphasize the "depersonalizing" effect of interpretation (Longman 2007, 198) in that at least some of Schulz's charisma and expression may get lost in the interpretation process (#20, 46, 47, 56, 58, 63, 65, 71, 72, 74). One respondent likened the use of interpretation to the dubbed version of a film (#18, also 47, 79). "The feel will be different" (#20), I was told, because interpreters "have to deliver a message very quickly, to avoid delay as much as possible, fully and accurately, and it may be that they are sometimes too focused on not losing any part of the words communicated" (#58). A Mertens counselor elaborated on this point:

For example, the French ambassador speaks in French [in Coreper], and I mean he's an incredibly impressive person, and you can tell again just by listening to him that he is saying something in very

Translation, Interpretation, and Depoliticization   165

beautiful language. But I don't speak French particularly well, so I listen to it through interpretation. And while, again, the interpreters do a fantastic job, you do know that you're not getting things presented exactly in the way that he is. . . . For example, one of the things that is lost is people's tone. Sometimes, very, very rarely, but sometimes we do have, for example, an angry or an exasperated exchange. And that isn't interpreted. You can tell from the person who is saying it, from their body language and the tone of their voice, but . . . you tend to get a, not a monotone, but certainly it's an emotionless interpretation of that. So you do miss out on that a little bit. (#72)

This quote is instructive, in part, because it stresses the high quality of the interpreters and recognizes the difficulty of their jobs. Yet it also emphasizes what another respondent called "the distorting prism of interpretation" (#81), which is particularly pronounced in the case of relay interpretation (e.g., of Greek via German into Swedish) (#81). Indeed, even if a skilled interpreter is able to successfully convey words *and* expression when interpreting a speaker directly, this inevitably becomes more difficult when interpreting "on relay."

The challenge of accurately conveying the expression or charisma of a given speaker in part relates to their different cultural backgrounds.[2] Italians were singled out by several respondents as being "more emphatic" (#33), but "would never say something directly," so transmitting "the deeper meaning" is a problem (#79). This is further complicated by interpreters having to stay true to the speaker while at the same time being conscious of how what they are saying will be received by their audience. One interpreter acknowledged that "playing to the audience" can influence what is conveyed:

The way people talk in southern Europe includes more redundancies and more repetition. But when interpreting into German, I cannot include every embellishment and every diversion and every repetition, because the Germans will not take me seriously anymore, because it is too different. (#35)

Some interpreters feel that they have to be able to transmit expressive speech just as well as highly technical subject matters (e.g., #8), while others acknowledge that they tend to tone it down. One interpreter in the European Parliament (EP), for example, maintained that

166 The Language(s) of Politics

> Some [interpreters] are more extroverted than others. We don't do "over the top" here though, there's a certain amount of decorum you have to keep. Some people might not find it appropriate. Some stay calmer in order to keep up with the message, so it probably depends on the meeting context. . . . And then you probably think more about making the message, preparing the message for your colleagues, not doing the emotion because that wouldn't help them.[3] (#3)

Also challenging is that nonnative speakers will use English and put the interpreters in the position of having to comprehend and then convey what is being said (#8, 11, 16, 17, 14, 47), and that speakers sometimes switch between languages and force different interpretation teams to suddenly become involved (#14). One interpreter in the Commission, for example, explained that "you've got to try to divine [the speaker's] intention" and, at the same time, "make certain allowances for that person's limitations in the language. And you have to second-guess sometimes what is he trying to say, rather than just translating the words" (#18, also 16). For example, when a native French speaker uses the term "public service" in English, his likely reference point is the French concept of "service publique"; the interpreter has to convey that these apparently equivalent concepts actually have slightly different meanings and connotations (#37, also 43, 51, 61). One possibility would be to use the French term in the English translation, as a signal to the audience, but interpreters can only use this instrument sparingly; after all, their audience would generally not appreciate a translation peppered with foreign words.

Especially challenging for nonnative speakers are so-called "false friends," or instances where there is an apparent but actually misleading resemblance between words in different languages, as in the case of "public service" versus "service publique."[4] As a result, one respondent explained, "when translating from English into French, we have to pay attention to the nationality of the author" (#33). Similarly, the intent of a speaker may not be to send a political message when using a politically charged term; as highlighted in chapter 4, the term "austerity" might be used purely descriptively by a nonnative speaker. Interpreters have to make a choice on the spot, which can lead to complaints, as one interpreter explained, and "reactions to things that we tone down or cause more offense than we meant to. . . . Hopefully you picked the right one!" (#22). Because of the uncertainty involved, that same interpreter suggested that she would opt for the more neutral option when in doubt. Others agreed, because it is "important not to put intentions in the speaker's mouth" (#7, also 35). As a result, what is conveyed may have "its edge taken off," as one Member of the EP (MEP) put it (#43).[5]

In other situations, however, interpreters may actually correct or improve what is being said in subpar English (#5, 11) and make a mediocre speaker sound better (#18). Interpretation offers "a processed version" of what is said, with interpreters "editing the hesitations, the redundancies" (#18), perhaps turning an overly blunt comment "into something less direct" (#35), or livening up a boring speech (#79) and "making it better than it actually is" (#82). One Council official maintains that

> we often have interpreters who make sense out of political speeches that don't make sense. . . . That has happened to me with a certain prime minister who is no longer in office, whose manner of expressing himself was not very coherent, but the interpreter made it coherent. (#58)

Hence, the "distorting prism of interpretation" sometimes manifests itself in the interpreter's *improvement* of somebody's speech.

The difficulty of conveying meaning, expression, and intent across languages is exacerbated by its happening on the spot, an inherent challenge in simultaneous interpretation. "The interpreter doesn't have the time to find the best possible expression" (#8), which can lead to interpreters relying on standard phrases to transmit what may, in fact, be carefully chosen, nuanced wording by the speaker. Beaton's analysis of simultaneous interpretation of German into English in the EP plenary confirms this impression, highlighting a "trend toward institutionalization of the English rendering of individual phrases" (Beaton 2007, 283). This is perhaps even more likely to occur nowadays than in the past, because of a greater incidence of participants in EU meetings reading out prepared statements at rapid speed, rather than speaking freely (#1, 6, 14, 16, 17, 18, 44, 49, 64, 73). EU actors are often allocated short time slots to make their interventions; for example, MEPs are often limited to as little as one or two minutes of speaking time, in which they try to communicate as much information as possible. People may also read prepared statements to more comfortably offer remarks in a foreign language, or because they want to go on public record with a carefully drafted statement.[6] Reading prepared statements, especially at high speeds, aggravates the already difficult job of simultaneous interpretation because the syntax of written speeches systematically deviates from oral language and may result in nonconformance between originals and their interpretations (Vuorikoski 2004, 208, 229).[7]

168 The Language(s) of Politics

Interpretation, of rapid speech or otherwise, is particularly challenging when highly technical subject matters are discussed, which is frequently the case in the EU (#1, 7, 15, 17, 22, 35, 54, 59, 62, 71, 73, 79). Interpreters are assigned based on the languages they interpret from and into and the linguistic needs of the participants in a given meeting. This means they must use specialized vocabulary in a wide range of policy areas; "you start out with olives and you end up talking about mopeds" (#22, also 18). Policymakers were quick to emphasize that you could not expect the interpreter to know "all of the terminology" regarding "culture, education, youth, finances, foodstuff regulations" (#62), but it can prove to be an issue nevertheless, for example when an interpreter covering a meeting on "the financial framework is not a financial specialist. . . . You get the wrong term and you might totally lose the context of the speaker" (#64, also 62).

Interpreters can rely on their cooperation with translators and lawyer-linguists to find out the proper terminology in a given situation and to ensure that a term is used and translated consistently in oral proceedings and written documents (#8, 13). This is only possible, however, if they have sufficient time to plan and prepare for their assignments, which is often not the case for interpreters in the Commission, the Council, and the EP. Unlike in the Court of Justice, where interpreters are almost always given sufficient time to prepare for their assignments and also have access to translations of relevant legal documents (#22, 24, 25, 26, 35), interpreters in the other institutions are often assigned to meetings at short notice. Interpreters thus have to be highly flexible when covering technical language, jargon, or specialized terminology in a meeting to which they may have been assigned at the last minute (#7).

Another important challenge for interpreters is humor, which is difficult to translate for the reasons highlighted in chapter 4.[8] Whether nonnative speakers of a language hear a joke directly or via interpretation, it often does not have the desired effect. Precise interpretation is difficult, under these circumstances, above and beyond the "regular" difficulties of interpretation. Another such challenge is when a speaker insults somebody else, which is a rare and unusual occurrence but does happen. One respondent indicated that she was taught in interpreting school to deal with insults by translating them "one level under" the harshness of what was actually said, or "slightly milder, yes, to lessen the blow a bit" (#22, also #1). An example of this was offered by a former EP official, who recalled an episode when John Prescott, the then-leader of the British Labour delegation, exclaimed "That's a load of crap!" and the French interpreter conveyed it at "ça n'est pas juste [That's not fair]!" (#79) But in order to pull this off "you have to find the right kind of tone; you have to know how to insult people" (#22). Interpreters also have to take into account, in such instances, that nonnative speakers may not be fully aware of the connotations of their choice of words, and that an apparent insult might be accidental rather than intentional. One MEP offered the example of others casually saying "fucking this [or that]" in English, which he "wouldn't dare" use in his mother tongue (#44, also #76).

Not everybody agreed with the idea of softening harsh language or insults, however. Several interpreters told me that "the customer has the right to be insulted" (#7); that "we are not censors. If it is said, you say it" (#13); and that "we are not here to sugarcoat things, we enable communication by transmitting what has been said" (#35). Some indicated that they might add "says the speaker" when inappropriate language was used, to indicate that what they are conveying was, in fact, said and to simultaneously distance themselves from the insult (#7, 35, 82). Not translating the insult at all is not an option for these interpreters, however, in part because it would be a problem if somebody only found out after the fact that they had been insulted (#8).[9]

The list of challenges interpreters face in their daily tasks is, in sum, substantial. They have to convey not just the speakers' words, but also their personality and charisma; they have to recognize and transmit what nonnative speakers of a language might be *trying* to say; they have to interpret what speakers are saying (or reading) at rapid speed; they have to competently cover highly technical subject matter, often without sufficient opportunity to prepare in advance; and, at least at times, they have to deal with humor and insults. And they have to achieve all of this while interpreting on the spot and often via relay interpretation.

It is thus inevitable that interpreters mediate communication between political decision makers in the EU, rather than serving as passive transmitters of what is said (Beaton 2007, 271). In some instances, this may lead to a *politicization* of proceedings, not a depoliticization, since the original message might be distorted enough that it becomes unduly controversial. This, however, tends not to be the case, for a number of reasons. First, potential distortions are generally factored in by EU audiences and speakers are given the benefit of the doubt; second, interpreters "take the edge off" when in doubt so as to not inadvertently cause a stir; and third, reliance on go-to phrases and substituting the "correct" terminology standardizes the output of language services, which tends to have a depoliticizing effect.

It is, ultimately, not surprising that the linguistic characteristics of interpreted texts in the EU systematically differ from native language texts, as

Rabinovich et al. demonstrate. EU "translationese," even when produced by native speakers, "gravitates toward non-native language use" (Rabinovich et al. 2016, 1877), meaning nonnative language and interpretations are closer to each other than each is to native language. Both tend to exhibit less lexical diversity and richness than native language, and they both tend to use common words more frequently, use idiomatic expressions and pronouns more carefully, and disproportionately use cohesive devices like sentence transitions. In linguistic terms, therefore, interpretations in the EU differ from native language interventions and more closely resemble nonnative speech. Interpretations also have in common with nonnative speech that they struggle to convey "elegant style" (Vuorikoski 2004, 19), "wit" (Abélès 1999, 113), and the "rhetoric devices used by the speakers, such as figurative speech," which is "frequently not conveyed, or it is conveyed in such a manner that the effect of the device is lost" (Vuorikoski 2004, 183). The former Secretary-General of the EP thus describes the "simplifying and sanitizing" effect of interpretation on "parliamentary oratory," whereby the EP's plenary sessions in particular "lose the sparkle and excitement of some national, monolingual forums" (Clark and Priestley 2012, 178).

It is not just rhetoric and figurative speech that are affected by the interpretation process, however, but also argumentation and reasoning. Vuorikoski shows that the target texts in simultaneous translation "lose much of the specificity" in a speaker's line of reasoning (Vuorikoski 2004, 153) and fail to consistently convey a clearly planned argumentative structure, claims supported by specifying examples and references, particular terms and concepts, and logical connectors (Vuorikoski 2004, 182–83). Carefully formulated argumentation, nuances, and finesse thus get "diluted" (Vuorikoski 2004, 207). The result is, once again, that the language used in political discourse, deliberation, and negotiation tends to be functional and simple, rather than rich and expressive—in this case because of the interpretation process, rather than the use of a shared foreign language by nonnative speakers.

Translation of Written Texts

Translators and lawyer-linguists in the EU produce texts that are consumed by a great variety of readers, including lawmakers in the Council and the EP; civil servants both in the EU institutions and in the member states; technical experts in the public and private sectors; national lawyers, national courts, and the Court of Justice of the EU; and members of the general public. The main challenge they face is inherent in their professions and summarized succinctly by a translator in the Court of Justice: "translation is not an exact science. There are many correct ways of translating one source text" (#33). In what follows, I describe how this fundamental challenge manifests itself in the work of both translators and lawyer-linguists.[10]

There are a great many language combinations at play in the translation of EU texts, even with the extensive reliance on translation via pivot languages after the 2004 EU enlargement. A number of respondents discussed the relative difficulties of translating from or into different languages and shared their impressions that, for example, English is particularly difficult because of its vast vocabulary (#34), French because its "eloquence" conflicts with the prevailing desire for concision (#28), and German because of a terminology that tends to be "very specific" compared to other languages (#30). There was no clear consensus, however, on which languages are most difficult to translate; translators offered the convincing explanations that the relative difficulty of translation depends on how closely related two languages are, the extent to which they reflect shared legal traditions, whether EU terminology is more or less easily integrated, and other such contextual factors (#30, 32, 36). The use of pivot languages also comes into play, since translation can be more or less difficult if it goes through a particular pivot language. McAuliffe, for example, emphasizes that translators covering pivot languages in the Court of Justice tend to use "simple" and "watered down" language, the "audience" of which includes "non-native speakers" (McAuliffe 2008, 814). One English translator described having to sacrifice "the purity and the richness of the English language" because "we have to use easy words" that are not "difficult for other, non-native-English speakers to understand" (McAuliffe 2008, 814). In other words, a text is consciously simplified and standardized in the translation process. Nonetheless, one Bulgarian translator described how English can be a challenging pivot language for him when the substance of the text deals with company law and corporate taxes, because the structure of corporations in much of Europe is "more or less similar," yet differs in important ways from the UK. Translation of a text with this subject matter first into English and then from English into another language can make the final text "almost unintelligible" (#27, also 34).[11]

In the Commission, the Council, and the EP, the most important challenge for EU translators is ensuring the equivalence of terms and concepts across the official languages,[12] which of course matters a great deal more when the text is legislative or legal in nature than when it is a declaration or merely informational (#9, 34). When translating the word "worker," for example, translators have to take into account that the term, as a legal concept, does not have the same meaning in all languages (#28). Or when translating "misdemeanor" into French, a choice has to be made between "*contravention*" or "*délit*" (#21)—a distinction that depends on whether the infraction was committed with intent or not—and with the knowledge that any translation will be approximate at best because of the grounding of the terms in common and civil law traditions, respectively. This challenge is lessened in the Court of Justice, since "we are at the end of the line, and the terminology comes from the file, from the written document, so we have absolutely no influence on that," in the words of one translator in the Court (#24, also 35).

Terms that are challenging to translate are often of a technical or legal nature. It can also turn out to be an issue for translators if the meaning of a term changes over time or when a new term replaces one that used to be relied upon, which is not unusual in some policy areas, like economics and finance (#19).[13] To help translators become and remain familiar with specialized terminology, the Commission tries "to specialize and keep translators . . . systematically work[ing] with a specific DG, like agriculture for instance," but this system revolves around core teams of two or three translators whose competences match the relevant issue area, whereas most translators are "generalists" (Robinson 2014b, 200) who cover multiple topics (#15).

Translation in the EU frequently involves decisions to use a term that is "close enough" to the original; to rely on EU jargon or legal language because a particular term or concept does not exist in the target language; or to invent and introduce new terminology in the target language. One way of avoiding the problem is to use Latin or Greek words, or words rooted in Latin or Greek, across language versions (#32), but that is of course not always possible and also makes EU texts less intelligible, which is already seen as a problem in the EU's communication with its citizens.[14]

In general, there is a preference for not inventing new words (#21),[15] but there is quite often simply no equivalent for a term in one or more of the other official languages, especially (but not only) when a member state is fairly new and has yet to develop the relevant EU-related jargon (#2, 24). An example was offered by a translator from one of the member states that most recently joined the EU, who described the difficulty of translating the idea of something being sold "over the counter" into her mother tongue, since no equivalent term existed in the still young market economy of her native country. She thus opted for using the English term in the translation. Some language groups, however, are more open to accepting and adopting "foreign" terms than others are (#2), and it is possible that she would have felt more inclined to create a new term had she been translating into a different language.[16]

There are other reasons, in addition to situations when there simply is no equivalent in a national language, where it makes sense to invent a new term. One situation is when there is a seemingly equivalent term in a national language that actually has a different meaning in the European context, and another when the purpose of using a term that is new, foreign, or grounded in EU jargon is to send an explicit signal that the term has a specific meaning. "Oftentimes you have to choose a word that is not the best, just to make it stand out, that this is something that could have a different meaning," one translator explained (#27, also 9, 31). At the same time, however, translators try to ensure that national officials and "an average lawyer not familiar with EU law" are able to understand and correctly interpret the new term (#28, 34). Hence, the denomination of a new term is not done haphazardly, especially if it relates to legislative language that concerns more than one EU institution. In that case, denomination happens following consultation involving translators and lawyer-linguists across institutions, because "we all have to say the same thing"; terminological choices are, moreover, entered into the IATE database, which formalizes their use for present and future (#2) and entails a "generalization of language" (#19).

While readily acknowledging the challenges that come with translation in the EU—many of which they considered to be inherent to multilingual policymaking—the language service providers I interviewed were eager to emphasize that the translation process is highly institutionalized and professionalized and, as a result, works quite well. The difficulties are real, but it is "not really a problem" (#7) because "one learns" how to handle them (#25). Moreover, one lawyer-linguist made the crucially important point that small divergences across translations often do not have legal consequences, especially if equivalence is assured by considering the broader context within which a particular term is used. She explained:

> There are always terms that cannot be expressed 100 percent in another language, but in lawmaking that's not necessarily a problem. You always have to think about it in legal terms: does the content change? . . . In the end it is about the extent to which ideas are converted into concrete facts and that can be derived from the context. So when you don't find a word that's 100 percent equivalent it's not that big a deal because in the context the idea is clear and it won't have an impact on the legal provision. (#9)

Despite this reality, the translation of legal terms is particularly difficult because of the need to balance national legal terminology and European law terminology (#31), and also to appropriately capture differences in national legal language (#15, 36, 47). Comparison of legal terms is thus "triangular," according to one translator in the Court of Justice (#28): between the draft and target legal language, and between each of those and EU legal language. This comparison is complicated by differences in legal traditions, especially between civil law and common law systems (#29, 30, 32). Indeed, Šarčević (2012a) maintains that the difficulty in translating a legal text depends primarily on the extent to which the source and target legal systems are related and only secondarily on the similarity of the source and target languages. Hence, translation in the EU, which involves multiple diverse legal orders, differs from legal translation in a polity that is multilingual but has a common legal order, like Belgium (Biel 2007, 146–47). One Commission official made this very point and emphasized that as a result, conceptual mismatches are "inevitable" in the EU, and translators are often not to blame when they arise (#15).

Legal terminology may differ even if two countries share the same language. There are, for instance, differences in the meaning of certain legal terms between France, Belgium, and Luxembourg, between Belgium and the Netherlands, between Germany and Austria, and between Greece and Cyprus (#24, 19). To offer just one example, the German term "*Rechtsmittel*" (appeal, legal remedy) has a different meaning in Germany and Austria (#9). The challenge for translators and lawyer-linguists is not only that such terms need to be translated so that there is equivalence across different language versions, but also that EU policymakers interpret particular terms based on their national background and legal languages (#19). For example, a German may assume that the term "*juristische Person*" (legal person) has the same meaning in European law as it does in Germany, when this is not, in fact, the case (#9). Similarly, a French speaker might suppose that the concept of "parental responsibility," when used in an EU context, means the same as "*responsabilité parentale*," when in fact its content is broader than in French national law (#31). This complicates not only the translation of documents when translators have to figure out the intent of the drafter, but also poses a challenge for lawyer-linguists when they participate in legislative negotiations. After all, their responsibility is to ensure that lawmakers understand what the implications of their decisions will be. It is under these circumstances that the otherwise excellent terminology tools translators and lawyer-linguists have at their disposal reach the limits of their utility, since they do not (and indeed cannot) always provide unambiguous answers (#27, 31).

Translators thus face tremendous challenges in their work, especially when they must produce translated texts under significant time pressure (#9, 15, 17, 29, 31). But they have a number of strategies for dealing with these difficulties, starting with the identification of relevant terminology in existing EU documents, especially existing legislative texts, Court of Justice case files, or treaties (#5, 24, 25, 27, 28, 33, 36). This not only facilitates the translator's job, but it also helps ensures consistency with earlier texts (Wagner, Bech, and Martínez 2014, 117). There is also cooperation across language services within institutions, within "language communities" (i.e., language service providers from across the institutions who share the same language) (#2), as well as across institutions, to help with terminology choices and ensure the consistent use of terms and concepts. Lawyer-linguists in the Court of Justice, for example, offer training on particular national legal terminology (#24) and are contacted "by colleagues . . . [who] ask them what the best choice would be" (#23), including by translators in the other institutions (#2, 32). Meanwhile, when interpreters first come across a term that is unclear or ambiguous, they may give translators and lawyer-linguists a heads up (#8). Often, however, the problem is that a term is genuinely ambiguous; it cannot simply be solved by considering different terminology options, because the correct choice of words depends on the drafter's (or drafters') intent. When this happens, translators and lawyer-linguists will try to contact the drafter(s) of the document to establish this intent (#2, 5, 15, 36), which "happens relatively often" (#2) but can be difficult because texts are frequently "altered by many different hands" and so "no-one has absolute ownership" (Robinson 2014a, 266).

Despite these practices and efforts, translation remains a challenging process, and my respondents confirmed the list of difficulties put forward by Robinson (2014b): technical language and jargon, different meanings of legal terms, the identification of intent and meaning, and ambiguity. They also struggle with the difficulty of ensuring both clarity and style and the need for equivalence across languages. The tension between the certainty demanded by the equivalence of language versions and the inherent linguistic uncertainty of the translation process tends to produce legislative and judicial texts that are "created within and for the purposes of the EU legal order" (Radulescu 2012, 321) and thus are functional, rather than accessible, engaging, or elegant. As Šarčević puts it:

176 The Language(s) of Politics

Since translation errors are frequently due to the inability of translators to render the intended ideas while respecting the genius of each language, even highly skilled translators are cautious about being creative with language, sacrificing comprehension to give priority to strict interlingual concordance. (Šarčević 2012b, 93)[17]

The result of this balancing act is, inevitably, that nuance, expressiveness, and even meaning are affected by the translation process. The "voices" of EU actors tend to be modified, standardized, and neutralized, which takes the political tone out of policymaking and makes individuals and their policy agendas less distinguishable from each other. An illustrative anecdote, in this regard, was offered by Eleanor Sharpston, a former Advocate General at the Court of Justice. She described a rare occasion in which she had drafted an opinion in Spanish, which she was later able to compare to translations into French and English. The Spanish and French were "more or less aligned," Sharpston recalled in a public lecture in 2014. "[T]hen I started reading the English; and after a few pages I thought, 'This woman is being evasive. She's not quite telling it the way it is. She may have sounded like Sharpston-in-Spanish, but she doesn't sound like Sharpston-in-English'" (Sharpston 2014, 20–21).

Speaking for Interpretation and Writing for Translation

EU actors are generally aware of the effects of interpretation and translation on spoken and written language, since both are embedded into the process of deliberating, negotiating, and drafting legislation. It may take them a little while to learn to adjust, but reliance by EU actors on language services means that in the end, they tend to adapt the way they speak and write in anticipation of their words being interpreted or translated.[18] This applies for the most part when people use their native languages, but also to EU actors who use a foreign language at a high level of proficiency. Reminiscent of what we learned about foreign language use in chapter 4, this involves a simplification, standardization, and ultimately depoliticization of language in the EU, as one respondent explained in reference to the interpretation process:

Most people won't understand it when you make a great speech, a political speech with a lot of passion and emotion, because it is not going to come across [in interpretation]. So that already forces you

Translation, Interpretation, and Depoliticization   177

to focus on policy content. . . . A lot stays at the level of [policy] content, and many things don't get politicized in most cases. (#42)

Policymakers, in particular, discussed how anticipation of simultaneous interpretation affects how they speak.[19] One member state counselor, for example, explained that

We really need to think about how we write a speech so that the interpretation stays with it and can really deliver the message as it was intended. . . . It means that the speeches need to be really concise, and you really need to make your point clearly and you can't go into too much detail. . . . We get training [from the interpreters' unit] on how to deliver a speech if you do it in your own language. (#70)

Another counselor offered a similar statement:

If [the ministers are] aware of the fact that they should be translated, they speak really slower, and then everything gets translated and everything is perfect. You have some people who are unexperienced who come for the first time. . . . They try to speak like at home, they speak very fast, and then it gets lost a little bit in translation. (#73)

A third one explicitly highlighted how anticipation of interpretation constrains him linguistically when he explained that he cannot be as precise in his native language because the interpreters "will copy and paste the usual phrases in English. . . . I know that the phrase that will come will be the standard one" (#61). The result is, once again, is that there is little room for rhetorical richness, for nuance, or for wit, and also that language with particular partisan or ideological connotations is again rendered neutral. Political speech is not only "amputated" by the act of interpretation itself, but also in anticipation thereof (Abélès 1999, 113).

A similar dynamic applies to written language. The previously discussed guidelines for drafting legislation are based in large part on the idea that improving the quality of the source text will facilitate and help improve the quality of subsequent translations. The Joint Practical Guide, for instance, explicitly states that draft texts "must fit into a system that is complex, multicultural and multilingual" (Rule 1.2.1) and that "draft acts shall be framed in terms and sentence structures which respect the multilingual nature of Community legislation" (Rule 5). Further, it elaborates that

- "The person drafting an act of general application must always be aware that the text has to satisfy the requirements of Council Regulation No 1, which requires that such acts be adopted in all the official languages";
- Draft texts "shall be framed in terms and sentence structures which respect the multilingual nature of Union legislation"; "must be particularly simple, clear and direct"; and "avoid overly complicated sentences."
- Terms should be avoided that "are too closely linked to a particular national legal system" and be replaced with more neutral terms. Aesthetic aspects are of distinctly secondary importance, in this regard. (Biel 2007, 149)

Consideration of how other language versions of the draft text are expected to read thus influences the drafting of the source text, especially for languages that serve as pivots for translation into others (Visconti 2013, 45). The source text may thus be "bent" to suit other languages, while the other language versions are *simultaneously* put into the "mould" of the source language draft (Robertson 2012b, 11; my emphasis). In the words of one Commission lawyer-linguist, "the drafter has to take into account constraints of other languages and avoid any 'idiolinguistic' solutions" (Kaduczak 2005, 38). Broadly speaking, the result is "a certain degree of deculturalisation" (Gibová 2009, 149) and the construction of standardized texts that can be treated as "functionally and, it is hoped, semantically 'equivalent'" in all languages (Robertson 2012b, 11), so that EU legislation can be uniformly interpreted and applied in the member states (Baaij 2012a). The pressure on drafters, translators, and revisers to produce such texts is considerable (Šarčević and Robertson 2013, 182) and results in texts that "feel different" because they are "drafted with an eye to translation" (Robertson 2010c, 3). As the primary drafting language, "EU legal English is neutralized to the greatest extent possible, thus enhancing its translatability" (Šarčević 2015, 9).[20]

Participants in EU policymaking are not formally required to and, in fact, often do not consciously follow the drafting guidelines, but they recognize that "you have to be mindful how it is going to be translated" (#84), according to a high-ranking official in the Court of Justice. Anticipation of the need for translation can thus significantly impact how EU actors write. Lawyer-linguists play a critical role in all this, since they provide linguistic assistance in the drafting process and participate in a process of consultation between the original authors of a text, translators, legal experts, and policymakers (Pym 2000). Lawyer-linguists nowadays even have the opportunity to revise the language of the base text, as long as no substantive changes are made (Šarčević 2013). Indeed, Stefaniak (2013) explains that the stages of drafting, translation, and legal revision increasingly overlap today, when they used to be sequential in the past. The result is that, for example, in the Commission,

> it is not uncommon for the translators to be working on the translation, the lawyers on the legal substance, the editing service on the quality of the source text, and the DG requesting translation on the final version of the text. This leads to numerous versions of the same text: some passages are added, others are deleted, concepts are redefined and terminology is changed. (Stefaniak 2013, 62)

It even happens that a draft act is adjusted to the translation, since an "original" text drafted by a nonnative speaker may be of lower linguistic quality than the "translation"; original draft texts may thus be "corrected to align with the 'translations'" (Kaduczak 2005, 39). This was confirmed by one of my respondents, a budget counselor for one of the Nordic member states, who emphasized that "translation can help improve a text because problems are caught" (#64).

The Constraining Effect of Multilingualism on Politically Expedient Ambiguity

One important consequence of EU multilingualism and the reliance on language services is that it limits ambiguity in policymaking. It does so, in the first place, by providing multiple language versions of a text, which means that something that appears ambiguous in one language may be "clarified" by what other language versions say (#4). But this is not always the case, especially when policymaking is still under way, and one of the most common challenges for translators and lawyer-linguists is to identify and correct substantive or linguistic ambiguity. These efforts, in turn, leave less room for ambiguity in the creation of legislation than would be the case in a monolingual environment. As was explained in one interview, "compared to making legislation—which I used to do—in my own country, I think you have to accept . . . a literal preciseness working with EU legislation, [more] than you would accept if you only had one language" (#56).

Ambiguity in draft texts seems to be accidental more often than it is

180 The Language(s) of Politics

intentional, and there are a variety of reasons for unintentional ambiguity. The first is that the primary drafting language in the EU is English, and "drafting in English is very, very ambiguous at times" (#2) because the language has a vast vocabulary compared to many others and thus provides for a multitude of synonyms to choose from (Robertson 2011, 64). The selection of one term over another can have a substantial impact, however, especially once that term is translated into other languages. And it is further complicated by the reality that "the drafters, the politicians, are not native English speakers, and so they don't know themselves what is meant"; they use whatever term they happen to know, take their best guess, or leave the text purposely vague because they are unsure about the best choice of words (#9, also 33). One Commission official involved with quality control in language services explained that

> it is very often not a question of intentional ambiguity but rather of sloppy drafting, or drafting carried out under very tight time pressure by nonnative speakers. . . . It's a real problem because mostly it's nonnative speakers, and mostly there are several people intervening in the drafting process. And mostly everybody is working on a very tight time constraint. So this means that the default option is to suspect that this is just unintended ambiguity. (#15)

The need for legal certainty of legislation that is equally authentic in all official languages means that ambiguity in legislative drafting is particularly problematic in the EU context and is therefore subject to special scrutiny. First among those efforts are the aforementioned drafting guidelines that put a particular emphasis on drafting being "unambiguous," as well as "clear," "simple," "concise," and "precise, leaving no uncertainty in the mind of the reader" (Joint Practical Guide, Rule 1.1.). But most important is the role of lawyer-linguists in detecting and correcting ambiguities, which they increasingly do while participating in the policymaking process.[21] One policymaker, for example, highlighted that "it happened to me several times, [being told] 'please do not write this because it will not translate into Portuguese'" (#68). This is explicitly part of the lawyer-linguists' job, as one emphasized: "that's why we are there for the negotiations" (#9). Another lawyer-linguist highlighted that:

> One of the reasons that we started attending the trilogues in the beginning was because you'd end up with an agreement in front of you with ambiguities, and you would say to whoever was around,

Translation, Interpretation, and Depoliticization 181

"well, we want to change these ambiguities because they are causing issues in translation," and then all of the sudden you can't change it! (#4)

Most frequently, lawyer-linguists are confronted with accidental ambiguities that the politicians themselves are not aware of. Once lawmakers learn of more appropriate choices of wording, however, and better understand how the English draft text would translate into their native languages, they are often quite willing—even eager—to adjust their language (#9). But there are instances when politicians prefer sticking with ambiguous wording, most importantly when they are reluctant to revisit a text that has already been negotiated (#22, 56). Ambiguity, in such instances, is initially accidental and becomes intentional only after the fact, when it is left in the draft legislation because it turned out to be politically convenient. One example offered by a German staffer in the EP was that both "misuse" and "abuse" were translated into the German version of a legislative text as "*Missbrauch*," an ambiguity both he and his boss found opportune (#41). At the extreme, such ambiguity can help prevent an unraveling of an agreement that has already been struck.

Such post hoc intentional ambiguity is different from what we might call *calculated* intentional ambiguity, however, which is purposeful in the sense that relevant actors build it into the draft legislation *with the intent* of facilitating agreement. Hence, not all intentional or "constructive" ambiguity (Piris 2005, 24) is created equal, even if its appeal for policymakers is the same: it is "a lubricant of politics" that offers "the opportunity to skip over especially contentious issues" or "to paper over disagreements by blurring differences" (Sharkansky 1999, 9, 10, 19).[22] And indeed, several respondents discussed how ambiguity can be politically expedient (#2, 4, 27, 31, 44, 78):

Often agreements are based on ambiguity. To be able to get an agreement, you play with the fact that actually a word means one thing to one person and another thing to another person. (#78)

[You] see stuff come out which is not clear and not fixable, but people will adopt it because they know it was the compromise struck by the groups. (#4)

Sometimes they try to be very precise, sometimes they try to be vague because they can reach an agreement. (#27)

182 The Language(s) of Politics

When ambiguity is intentional, lawyer-linguists are expected to accommodate it, because "translation of legislation must . . . be just as precise and clear as the original—or just as imprecise and unclear" (Robinson 2014b, 185–86). And so one advantage of their participation in legislative negotiations is that lawyer-linguists have the opportunity to learn when ambiguity is accidental and when it is not; indeed, they are supposed to be made aware of ambiguity that is left on purpose (#2, 9). They may still try to correct the language by proposing alternatives that are more easily translated, but lawyer-linguists are ultimately bound by the intent of the lawmakers and may be forced to find a way to translate the ambiguous draft text so that it is similarly ambiguous in the target languages. After all, the equivalence of text has to be assured even in the face of ambiguity of the original (#9, 31, 36), as one respondent explained:

> Sometimes we must tell our colleagues in the translation unit that they must keep it ambiguous, because they are trained to improve also the text and sometimes we have to tell them that we don't want the text improved. It doesn't sound right, it doesn't sound good, it's not logical, and we have to tell them "that is the intention." (#15)

Post hoc intentional ambiguity is less likely than accidental ambiguity in EU negotiations, but it probably occurs far more often than calculated intentional ambiguity. Indeed, calculated intentional ambiguity does not appear to be a systematic feature of multilingual lawmaking in the EU, for a number of reasons. To start, when I explicitly asked about ambiguity in my interviews, respondents were, almost across the board, unable to offer examples of instances when ambiguity was somehow "snuck into" legislation. One exception was an EP official who recalled an episode from "almost 20 years ago" when

> there was a compromise text tabled by the German Council Presidency and Spanish rapporteur of the committee. And it was tabled not in German or Spanish, but in English and French, in two versions. So you had four languages involved. And the English and French versions of the compromise reached by the Spaniard and this German didn't correspond. They thought they were so clever! (#16)

The same respondent believed, however, that this "wouldn't happen today, because [the lawyer-linguists] would be on to them before they even

Translation, Interpretation, and Depoliticization 183

put pen to paper." He continued to explain that "Parliament's machinery wasn't so geared to sorting out these problems. . . . We've gotten a lot more professional in the last 15 years on that front. . . . In those days it only came at the last moment, just before plenary, and everything was sealed" (#16).[23] The answers I received from other respondents about incidents of calculated intentional ambiguity confirmed this suggestion. I heard, for example:

> I would say that is very rare, I've never seen it. [Question: Really?] Really. I really can say I haven't seen it. (#5)

> Theoretically that is possible [but] I don't think anybody could give you a concrete example. (#39)

> In theory it could happen, but in practice I don't remember. (#65)

It is, of course, possible that my respondents were unable to provide examples of calculated intentional ambiguity simply because such instances, when successful, go unnoticed. This cannot be ruled out, but there are good reasons—besides efforts by lawyer-linguists to spot and eliminate ambiguities in legislation—to believe that reliance on calculated intentional ambiguity is neither systematic nor widespread. The first is that EU legislation tends to be technical, which means that introducing ambiguous language is "not that easy" because concepts have particular meanings and cannot simply be altered (#61). There is, in the words of one high-ranking representative of a Permanent Representation, not actually much room to "play" with language beyond "marginal maneuvers" (#65). Moreover, legislative negotiations do not happen overnight, and there is typically not one moment in time when one particular term is set in stone and can no longer be challenged or adjusted. And since ambiguity can be identified and corrected at various points in time, it is difficult to "sneak" purposely ambiguous language through the prolonged legislative process, in particular because not everybody necessarily has an interest in the ambiguous legislative language. As one EP official put it, there are so many people,

> all reading it and they scope for [problems]. . . . There's so many stages in it, even if you're Clever Harry and you wrote something that you feel is ambiguous enough for everyone to interpret in their language, the likelihood of it getting through all of those hoops, and then the same thing over in the Council, is almost zero. (#39)

Finally, calculated intentional ambiguity presupposes that policymakers are able to identify which particular term or concept will produce the desired level of ambiguity, to figure out how the relevant wording would translate into the other official languages and how it would then be interpreted in different national legal systems, and to anticipate what the likely implications of ambiguities in the different languages would be upon the implementation of the legislation. All this would be a tall order for any legislator, never mind legislators who are nonnative speakers of the drafting language (#9). Moreover, politicians "don't have control over how [something] is translated" (#12); the final choice is up to lawyer-linguists and translators. They may consult with the drafter to determine intent, and perhaps even check with national authorities to identify terminology options, but they are not bound by the input they receive (#2). What guides translation is "absolute fidelity to the original text" (#28).

At times, there may be pressure by member states or MEPs to use a particular term or concept. One lawyer-linguist, for example, recalled "a whole big conversation with somebody from the member state who was outraged that we are not obliged to follow their realities" (#2). Another emphasized that sometimes MEPs have a particular term in mind that reflects the legal system of their member state, and that "some experienced MEPs who had huge experience in national politics are tougher to persuade" in those circumstances. But it is the role of the lawyer-linguists to "make sure they understand what the term means in EU legalistic terms" so that you do not end up with "a term that can only be understood in one specific legal order" (#19). And indeed, a counselor in a Permanent Representation emphasized that lawyer-linguists in the Council only accept a small portion of requested changes; "they are quite precise whether they accept it or not" (#61).

Policymakers may thus try to anticipate what the translated text may say, and they may even try to confer with lawyer-linguists about it, but lawyer-linguists would be loath to participate in efforts to purposefully introduce ambiguities because this would contradict their role in EU policymaking, just as they would see it as overstepping their authority to eliminate ambiguity that is intended by the legislator (Biel 2007, 158). One lawyer-linguist responded forcefully when I raised the possibility of lawyer-linguists helping lawmakers produce an ambiguous text, emphasizing that they would "reject this because we are not a political service. Our responsibility is to ensure that all texts say the same thing. . . . So it could not be reconciled with our mission" (#9).

None of this is to say that there is no ambiguity in EU legislation, but rather that when ambiguity arises it is most likely accidental and, when intentional, more likely to be post hoc than calculated.[24] This pattern is driven in important ways by both the reality that most EU policymakers are not native English speakers and by the involvement of language service providers. Nonnative speakers are more likely to be ambiguous by mistake, but they are also likely to adopt changes to their texts proposed by lawyer-linguists because of their limited language skills. Those limitations also generally prevent them from successfully inserting ambiguity on purpose, for the reasons outlined above; the EU's multilingual context thus makes calculated intentional ambiguity less likely. The involvement of lawyer-linguists, meanwhile, decreases the incidence of accidental ambiguity and also of post hoc intentional ambiguity because they offer alternative wording that is less ambiguous and more easily translated. More generally, their role as "guardians" of language equivalence and their presence in EU negotiations imposes a constraint on the ability of policymakers to be intentionally vague or ambiguous. The need for legal certainty across all language versions of EU legislation thus actively limits the ability of policymakers to be overly "creative" with their language and thus takes some of the politics out of policymaking in the EU.

Conclusion

Translation and interpretation lead to a depoliticization of EU policymaking by contributing to the prevalence of a "language of politics" that is simplified, standardized, and neutralized. It is important that this is not to be interpreted as a critique of the language services, which I have come to admire ever more throughout the process of researching this book. In fact, the dynamics I describe in this chapter are all but inevitable; it was, in part, to demonstrate this reality that I provided as much detail as I did about the difficulties associated with interpretation and translation in the EU.

Translators routinely face difficult terminological choices. They not only have to transmit the substance of one language version of an EU text in another, they must convey it so that the texts will produce equivalent legal outcomes in the member states. This need for interlingual concordance means that translators tend to rely on existing documents, terminology databases, and standard phrases and formulations in their work. When balancing linguistic and legal considerations, the latter prevail. One consequence of this reality is that there is less room for ambiguity in EU policymaking, because the need for language equivalence curtails the ability of politicians to use vague or ambiguous language to paper over disagreements. The challenges for interpreters are of a different nature. Conveying—on the spot—not only substance across numerous highly technical policy areas, but also meaning, intention, culture, and personality, is hugely demanding, especially when EU actors tend to speak or read prepared statements at a rapid pace.

This chapter has argued that as a result of these difficulties, reliance on language services simplifies, standardizes, and neutralizes the target language in the translation or interpretation process; what is more, the anticipation thereof leads EU actors to speak and write so that the source language is itself more likely to be simplified, standardized, and neutralized (and if they do not, depoliticization occurs through translation and interpretation). This reinforces the tendencies toward a simplification, standardization, and neutralization of language described in chapters 4 and 5, which are driven by the language handicaps of nonnative speakers. The "language of politics" in the EU is, in sum, a function of both foreign language use for communication *and* reliance on language services.

SEVEN

Conclusion

Kjær and Adamo (2016) highlight that multilingualism in the European Union (EU) can mean many things,

> A democratic value to be protected, a fundamental right of minority groups, an obstacle to deliberative democracy and a hindrance to legal certainty and the possibility of uniform law, a cultural asset of Europe to be promoted and protected, a competitive advantage of businesses on the market and a prerequisite for the free movement of EU citizens." (Kjær and Adamo 2016, 2)

This book adds another dimension: multilingualism is a key feature of EU politics that systematically affects political and policymaking processes. Multilingualism depoliticizes politics and policymaking in the EU, with important potential consequences for issue salience, perceptions of political similarities and differences, polarization of opinion, intensity of debate, and the resonance of arguments and evidence.

Argument and Evidence: A Brief Review

Multilingualism influences the very nature and flavor of politics and policymaking in the EU, but its depoliticizing effects are only purposeful when it comes to the language rules themselves. The institutional framework for multilingualism in the EU builds on the formal equality of all national languages, while allowing for the uneven multilingualism that helps ensure effective communication between EU actors and contain the already substantial costs associated with high-quality language services. This arrangement, as argued in chapter 3, provides for a strong equilibrium that the member states have little incentive to change. It thus successfully defuses the potentially highly volatile "language question" in EU politics, even though it is recognized that not all languages are, in fact, equal. Language equality is a fiction, in other words, but EU multilingualism works in part *because* of the "veil of formal language equality," not despite it.[1] Under the veil of language equality, the EU language regime has evolved into an effective system that combines a main shared working language with the best, most extensive (and most expensive) language services in the world, which political actors can fall back and rely on as needed.

The other depoliticizing effects of multilingualism, however, are unintended and exogenous to human agency, as they result from the linguistic limitations of those involved in EU policymaking and the transformative effects of translation and interpretation. This means neither that most EU actors do not possess excellent foreign language skills, nor that the EU's language services are deficient. Rather, it is necessarily the case that people are more constrained in a nonnative language than in their mother tongues, and the very nature and inherent challenges of translation and interpretation are necessarily distorting. The depoliticizing consequences of foreign language use and reliance on language services are, therefore, unintentional. Yet they affect EU policymaking all the way from the initial conception of EU legislation in the Commission to its adjudication by the Court of Justice.

As the empirical chapters demonstrate, multilingualism reduces the political nature of and the potential for contestation in EU policymaking in a number of important ways. Chapter 4 made the case that EU actors' reliance on shared nonnative languages for political communication restricts their linguistic repertoires. Either because of their own language handicaps or to accommodate those of others, EU actors use simpler linguistic constructions, eschew rhetorical embellishment and idiomatic language, and rely on commonly used and understood expressions and terminology. Moreover, foreign language use induces greater tolerance and empathy toward others, and it compels participants in EU policymaking to discount political language and apparent expressions of political differences because they might reflect only what their counterparts are able to say or write, rather than what they actually mean. Reliance on shared nonnative tongues thus leads EU actors to focus on "getting the message across" using simple

Conclusion   189

and utilitarian language, which depresses the political tone of their communications with others and decreases the intensity of political debate. It also makes them less distinguishable from one another based solely on what they say or write and masks their national and political backgrounds, preferences, and priorities. These effects are amplified by the use of "EU English" as the most common shared language in EU politics, as chapter 5 showed. As others before me have argued, and as my own interview data and corpus analysis suggest, EU English is distinguishable from standard English by being more neutral, utilitarian, standardized, pragmatic, "decultured," and de-ideologized.

Reliance on translation and interpretation has similar effects, as the conveyance of written texts and oral interventions in another language inevitably constricts, condenses, and transforms. The indirect nature of communication, moreover, reduces spontaneity and intensity of debate. As described in chapter 6, due to the manifold challenges of their highly demanding work, interpreters and translators tend to express complex messages in more straightforward terms; fall back on standard terminology, phrases, and expressions; and avoid politically charged or emotional language. Nuances in meaning are subdued as a result, differences muted, and a degree of uncertainty left about a speaker's or drafter's true intentions. Moreover, EU actors anticipate these effects and "write for translation" and "speak for interpretation" as a result, which again makes the source language more straightforward and less complex. Finally, the need for equivalence across languages constrains politicians' ability to use vague or ambiguous language to obscure disagreement; they may be "loose" with their language when deliberating and negotiating but are compelled to deliver an unambiguous final product. Altogether, reliance on language services once again depoliticizes political language: both input and output languages are more utilitarian and simple; decision makers are less distinguishable based on their spoken and written language; and what they say or write is less indicative of their national backgrounds and political agendas.

EU Multilingualism Is Imperfect, but It "Works"

EU multilingualism builds on extensive reliance on (EU) English as the main vehicular language inside the EU institutions, but it allows participants in EU policymaking to fall back on their native languages. This system does not work perfectly, but it works quite well according to most of my respondents. They also offered little evidence that the problems they

190 The Language(s) of Politics

experience occur systematically or have notable negative consequences, and they considered it possible (if more difficult) for those with limited language skills to participate and wield influence in EU politics (see chapter 2). One quote by a Council official summed it up nicely:

> It is pretty remarkable that we don't make more mistakes which can be attributed, at least indirectly, to language than we do. And that this place churns out legislation and speeches like any other government, frankly, but no worse than any other government or organization around the world. It's true that we take refuge in . . . sort of platitudes, common phrases, or extremely technical language. . . . But, I mean, when you consider the range of issues which the EU institutions deal with, from high politics to efficient agriculture and environment and all sorts of things, it works. It works. (#56)

We ought not dismiss such statements, because it is those inside the EU institutions who are most directly "affected" by multilingualism. Moreover, despite the frequent criticisms of the EU's language regime, they confirm what previous empirical research has tended to find (Abélès 1999; Bellier 1997; Horspool 2006; McAuliffe 2008; Stritar and Stabej 2013; Wodak 2009).

This is not to say or to imply that there are not areas where EU multilingualism falls short and improvement would not be possible and desirable. It is important, however, to take as a baseline for consideration of potential improvements that EU multilingualism generally "works," to ensure that relevant efforts focus pragmatically on improving performance, rather than on realizing unattainable ideals (Krzyżanowski 2014, 118). They also ought to avoid trying to fix what are inherent or inevitable consequences of multilingualism. For example, accommodating more than one language will necessarily slow down workflow, some misunderstandings and mistakes are unavoidable, it may at times not be possible to provide interpretation when meeting rooms with a sufficient number of interpretation booths are fully booked, and divergences in meaning between the various language versions must be accepted as an inevitable fact of EU multilingual lawmaking, as it is by "most lawyers" (Šarčević 2013, 10).

The severity of some of the negative consequences of multilingualism, however, depends in part on the choices made collectively by the member states when they contribute to and allocate resources through the EU budget. Indeed, despite the system working reasonably well, there are problems associated with EU multilingualism that could be improved or

Conclusion 191

fixed by "throwing money at it," or at least by not decreasing funding for language services. But that is exactly what has been happening relative to the number of official languages. The translation service in the Council, for example, employs about the same number of translators today, when there are 24 official languages, as it did in 2002, when there were 11. The most recent cuts followed the 2014 Staff Regulations, which prescribed a 5 percent decrease in personnel.[2] Staff numbers in the Commission's DG Translation have also dropped in recent times, from more than 2,500 in 2012 to just under 2,300 in 2018, a decrease of about 10 percent.[3] These changes are partially compensated through increases in resource efficiency, by adapting demand management, and by making use of innovations in new technologies.[4] Nonetheless, some of my respondents had the impression that the quality of language services has declined as a result of budget cuts (#71), because it has affected the number and availability of language service providers (#39, 61, 78), led to greater reliance on freelance translators and interpreters (#42, 83), and increased time pressures for translators, in particular (#34). As a result, in the opinion of one translator with experience in several of the EU institutions, "we are moving away from an ideal that we were already relatively close to" (#34).

Among the problems that greater investment in language services would help mitigate is, for example, an increasing number of English-only EU websites that include information of general concern to EU citizens (Barbier 2018, 337–38), which are problematic not only because of their exclusionary nature, but also because they may trigger or augment feelings of frustration among speakers of other languages (Laponce 2004, 592). Another is that the EU is not consistently providing documents to the national institutions of the member states in their native languages. As Ammon and Kruse (2013) demonstrate, the frequent unavailability of translations into German makes it difficult for an institution like the German Bundestag to effectively scrutinize and monitor EU policymaking on the basis of foreign-language documents. Hence, it is not surprising that the Commission receives "regular complaints" from the German Bundestag, which "wants more translations into German," as one Commission official acknowledged; but he also pointed out that "on the other hand, all member states want to cut our budget!" (#15).

Another issue identified by my respondents is that policy-relevant documents are not always made available in the same timely fashion for all official languages. In the European Parliament (EP), for example, translations into the "big" languages are generally accessible quite a bit earlier than for the "small" languages. As a result, Members of the EP (MEPs)

192 The Language(s) of Politics

are sometimes forced to make decisions on the basis of a foreign language version of an amendment or legislative text, or they have to make decisions quickly when their own language version only becomes available at the last minute (#4, 47, 54). This problem is particularly pronounced for so-called "compromise amendments," which consolidate and replace all proposed amendments in an effort to facilitate agreement. MEPs can block a vote if a translation is not available (#16, 39, 47),[5] but they of course would only want to use this option sparingly for the sake of expediency. Further budget cuts could exacerbate such problems and may ultimately affect the quality of language services provided. Interpreters are already complaining that they do not have sufficient time to prepare for their assignments, and there is a danger that lower quality translation would result in a greater incidence of discrepancies between the equally authentic language versions of EU legislation and of a proliferation of retrospective "meaning-changing" corrigenda of what are supposed to final legislative texts (Bobek 2009). This, in turn, would undermine confidence in the uniformity of EU law (Šarčević 2013). Ensuring proper funding for language services is thus distinctly in the interest of the EU member states. They would also be well advised to ensure that resources continue to be available for foreign language courses, especially for incoming MEPs. While the institutionalization of the EP over time has resulted in a professionalization of its members and a greater number of "career MEPs" (Daniel 2015), turnover continues to be quite high (Daniel and Metzger 2018). Since "learning the ropes" in the EP involves adjusting to a multilingual environment and learning the language of politics in the EU, ensuring access to language lessons is particularly important.

Implications, Contributions, and Extensions

Implications

One way to think about the impact of multilingualism on EU politics concerns institutional, political, and social hierarchies. Foreign language skills may not be a prerequisite for influence, but they are an important asset and give skilled linguists a comparative advantage (chapter 2). Wright emphasizes one way in which this matters: language proficiency increases political actors' ability to build, maintain, and use social networks (Wright 2000, 173), which not only affects the flow of information (see Ringe and Victor 2013; Ringe, Victor, and Gross 2013), but also social and political hierarchies inside the EU institutions. Language skills may also be a determinant of who gets selected into positions that grant policy influence; those who capably speak English (and to a lesser extent French) may be more likely to be selected as rapporteur or shadow rapporteur in the EP, for example. Moreover, if it is actors in institutional leadership positions who tend to have strong foreign language skills, multilingualism would be reinforcing formal hierarchies. Allowing EU actors to rely or "fall back" on their native languages mitigates these potential effects, but they do not fully level the playing field.

Multilingualism may also flatten hierarchies, however, for example if actors who are otherwise disadvantaged in the formal institutional structure are empowered by their language skills. Foreign language proficiency may provide a shortcut to becoming influential, and those who are younger or have less seniority may well benefit from this possibility. More generally, "the possibility of subversion which comes from the uncertainty created by the multiculturalism and multilingualism lighten the formal hierarchy and give spaces for the individual to find his space," as Abélès put it (1999, 114). Hierarchies are also flattened in that the standardization and simplification of language serve as "equalizers" between those who are skilled communicators and those who are not. Expectations about rhetorical sophistication and fluency of speech are lowered in a multilingual environment, and poor communicators are given the benefit of the doubt. Social hierarchies that stem from somebody having a nonstandard accent in a given language may similarly be weakened in a multilingual context, since nonnative audiences are unlikely to share the (often negative) associations and perceptions of native speakers. A final way in which hierarchies are flattened by multilingualism was described by some of my respondents in the Council, where national ministers are more likely to suffer from language handicaps than national officials based in Brussels. This reinforces the tendency in the Council to make decisions at the working party or Coreper level, if possible, rather than leave detailed substantive negotiations to national ministers when they come to Brussels for formal meetings of the Council of Ministers. The ministers may "fine-tune" those decisions, but most of the politically relevant groundwork has already been laid by lower-level officials, in part because of the language factor (#18, 59).

Hence, multilingualism has potential tangible consequences for political and social hierarchies inside the institutions, but its impact on EU politics is also at once more fundamental and more subtle: the existence of a shared "language of politics" means that political actors in the EU communicate and interact with one another in ways that are distinct and particular.

The EU's shared language of politics contributes to the socialization and acceptance of individuals into a common political community and provides a basis for the EU's political culture, whether defined as the "root beliefs about political arrangements" (Laitin 1977, 4), "the particular pattern of orientations to political actions" (Almond 1956, 396), or "all publicly common ways of relating within the collectivity" (Chilton 1988, 431).[6] Language is so central to political culture that a change in language means a change in culture (Laitin 1977, 4). The standardization associated with EU multilingualism contributes to the EU's political culture, for example, by standardizing terminology, which not only limits substantive ambiguity but also dampens the cultural particularities associated with words in the different EU languages. Most consequential for the EU's political culture, however, is the depoliticization multilingualism entails. The EU's language regime thus relates to the proposition that there is a "consensus culture" or "consensus norm" inside the EU institutions (Lewis 1998; Heisenberg 2005; Hayes-Renshaw, van Aken, and Wallace 2006; Pütter 2012; Novak 2013). Part of what this idea involves is that EU politics tends to be less antagonistic and confrontational than national politics and that "consensus" is a feature of EU political identity. The depoliticization that comes with multilingualism may well be a contributing factor to this.[7] Language helps "conceal a bit the political choices that are taking place," as one long-serving EP official confirmed (#78), which does not mean that a problem is no longer political, only that it is dealt with in a less confrontational manner. For the reasons highlighted throughout the preceding chapters, multilingualism diminishes the expression of political differences and leads to political choices being considered, deliberated, and negotiated using less political and politicized language, all of which has the potential to influence perceptions of political differences and the intensity of contestation and debate. In fact, the reality that EU actors perceive multilingualism to have these effects may actually matter in and of itself, whether or not they are real. In the end, testing the proposition that multilingualism contributes to a culture of consensus is challenging due to possible endogeneity and is not something that can be done with the data at hand. It is, however, suggested by those data and warrants further consideration. The same is true of the consequences this implies for policy outcomes, in that a shared language of politics may facilitate policy agreement, not only because it mutes differences, but also because it standardizes what makes people persuasive. Most importantly, multilingualism entails that the substance of political actors' contributions is prioritized over style, rhetoric, and fluency (chapter 4), which means both that linguistic shortcomings are tolerated and actively discounted and that "great speeches" are rare. Most EU actors are unable to show off rhetorical prowess in a nonnative language. But even if they could, great speeches would not "translate" when transmitted by interpreters, and audiences in the EU institutions generally do not possess sufficient language skills to appreciate them. Hence, "the biggest tool of the politician is blunted here," in the words of one respondent in the EP (#49). The focus is squarely on "getting the message across."

Language in the EU institutions is thus "rationalized" in part through its focus on policy substance. This is potentially profound, especially when considered alongside the previously discussed research in the cognitive sciences about foreign language use and decision making (see chapter 4). That research suggests that foreign language use makes decision making more rational, deliberate, and utilitarian by increasing deliberation and self-regulation, making risk assessment more consistent, and reducing reliance on intuition, framing, and a variety of heuristic biases (including loss aversion, accounting biases, ambiguity aversion, intuition bias, and causality bias). Foreign language use also makes people more sensitive to outcomes than intentions and affects their moral judgment, generally leading to more utilitarian decisions, which again has the potential to influence political deliberation and negotiation.

Making decision making more deliberate and rational is potentially quite positive in a policymaking process. But there are downsides, including at a most basic level the suppression of meaningful political differences: political problems are depoliticized, at least to an extent, not because they are not genuinely divisive, but because they are debated in a multilingual environment. One former Commission official's evaluation was particularly blunt in this regard and is worth quoting in detail:

> Pick ten speeches of Commissioners today and just compare the language. . . . You wonder if those people have a personality of their own. It's very frightening how people have inhibited their own thinking. . . . Most of them would be normal politicians with strong ideas and so on, but it would not permeate in their speeches. Their speeches were standard; it could have been delivered by a machine. . . . [MEPs] are sort of deprived of their way of thinking and expressing themselves, they are losing part of their soul. And I think a main characteristic of the European Parliament in that respect, it is really a soulless institution. . . . It's a place where you

196 The Language(s) of Politics

cannot have real debates. . . . People seem to agree, but in fact they keep their nuances for themselves. . . . It's completely unconscious, no cynicism. And it's sad, it's very sad. (#51)

Despite impressions that debates in the EP have become more vigorous over time (#79), these concerns are far from negligible. They raise the crucial question if political language in the EU is not in fact crippled rather than merely rationalized, which "shrinks our capacity to understand the world," as a current Commission official put it (#55).

Multilingualism thus reinforces some problematic tendencies in EU politics, especially when it comes to jargon and technical language. But legal and legislative texts generally cannot be made more straightforward and comprehensible without misrepresenting their content and consequences (Wagner, Bech, and Martínez 2014). After all, these texts are created within and for the purpose of the EU legal order, which "comprises a systematic body of law that is internally self-coherent, self-consistent and internally self-referent" (Radulescu 2012, 321). This is a greatly constraining factor in the production and translation of texts, which in turn affects spoken language (see chapter 5), and it will almost certainly leave some people feeling put off and disconnected from the EU. But not all texts are of a legislative, legal, or technical nature, and the EU would be well advised to ensure that communications aimed directly at the European people are devoid of "EU-isms" to the extent possible. This is particularly important because there is already a widespread perception that the EU is too distant from its citizens and that its representatives are part of an unaccountable elite disconnected from the concerns of regular people.

Multilingualism thus has an important "external dimension" that deserves further consideration, especially as it relates to the EU's quest for political and democratic legitimacy. For much of the European integration process, the EU's predecessor organizations flew below the general public's radar. Deals were cut by insulated political elites, the impact of which was not obvious to most people, and public opinion was accordingly quiescent. Those were the days of the so-called "permissive consensus," during which the EU was largely "output legitimate": its legitimacy was based, for the most part, on providing policy solutions that produced positive outcomes for Europe's citizens (Scharpf 1999). During that era, there was little tension between the *unintended* depoliticization associated with multilingual practices inside the institutions and the *intended* depoliticization of the European project: to succeed, the process of "building Europe" had to escape the suspicions and objections of both the member states and their citizens by avoiding contestation along a great many potentially divisive dimensions, including ideology, identity, culture, tradition, political institutions, models of political economy, and, of course, language. The depoliticizing effects of multilingual practices in the institutions may have been unintended, but they conformed with deliberate, and deliberately institutionalized, efforts to depoliticize the European integration process.

Over time, however, the permissive consensus has given way to an increasingly "constraining dissensus" that forces political elites to "look over their shoulders when negotiating European issues" (Hooghe and Marks 2009, 5). The EU has become politicized as both a political entity and political project (e.g., Hutter and Grande 2014; Hutter, Grande, and Kriesi 2016; de Wilde, Leuphold, and Schmidtke 2016), not least over the course of the past decade and a half, which have seen the French, Dutch, and Irish rejections of the Constitutional and Lisbon Treaties in popular referenda,[8] the euro crisis, and the so-called migrant crisis. EU issues now feature prominently in electoral politics both at the European level and in the member states (e.g., de Vries 2007; Spoon 2012; Senninger and Wagner 2015). Under these circumstances, and to address the so-called "democratic deficit" (Follesdal and Hix 2006), the EU requires more "input legitimacy," or legitimacy based on popular participation and the involvement of the governed (Scharpf 1999).

Multilingualism complicates the EU's efforts to increase its input legitimacy. To start, EU English deviates from standard English, which is a nuisance for native speakers but poses potentially serious problems of comprehension for citizens who are nonnative speakers of standard English. In that sense, the EU's multilingual regime does not only impact who is more or less excluded from EU politics based on foreign language proficiency—which has important implications for social and political disenfranchisement (Gazzola 2016b; Barbier 2018)—there is a more general question of the comprehensibility and accessibility of the EU's language of politics. A language of politics that feels strangely unfamiliar, impassive, oftentimes awkward, and sometimes altogether incomprehensible is unlikely to ease the alienation many ordinary Europeans feel from the transnational polity that affects their lives in ways that are both increasingly consequential and increasingly visible.[9]

Using political language that is simple, utilitarian, neutral, and standardized may not be much of a problem when most citizens ignored or acquiesced to the EU and the integration process, but that is no longer the case today. From the perspective of deliberative or discursive democracy, this is problematic. As Habermas writes, somebody's power of articulation and "precise choice of inspiring sentences" can lend "analytical clarity and sweeping significance to the political thought itself"; speech, therefore,

> can change the public's perception of politics; it can raise the level of discourse and broaden the horizons of public debate. As such, it can improve the quality not just of political opinion and the formation of political will, but of political action itself. (Habermas 2017)

Much of this gets lost in EU politics, as the former Commission official from above notes:

> There is a growing gap [between those who work in the European environments and those who stay home], because very soon the European MEPs forget to use their normal doctrinal and idiosyncratical ways of speaking. . . . They come with an imported language, which restrains their possibility to exchange with the audience. They are inhibited. It is very strange, they all of a sudden develop another language. (#51)

Hence, the EU's language of politics and its depoliticizing effects are directly at odds with the increasing politicization of the EU, which introduces an emotional dimension to EU politics that is not met by the EU's neutral, decultured, and de-ideologized language of politics. Democratic accountability, moreover, is short-chained if constituents are hampered in their ability to distinguish between political actors based on what they say or write.

All this presents a genuine dilemma for the EU, as it pits the functional dimension of language against its symbolic and (especially) its representational dimensions, because the EU's output legitimacy depends on governance that functions reasonably efficiently and effectively. After all, a growing need for participation *by the people* does not negate the reality that producing policy outcomes *for the people* continues to generate legitimacy for the EU. But the very language regime that provides for effective governance, by meeting the linguistic needs of participants in EU policymaking, also presents an obstacle to greater participation of EU citizens in EU politics and, by extension, greater identification with the EU as a polity and political project. In sum, the EU may have found a balance between the symbolic, legal, representational, and functional dimensions of language that works for *internal* purposes; for *external* purposes, however, this balance skews too much toward the legal and functional dimensions.

Contributions

The external dimension of EU multilingualism has not been the focus of this book, however. Its ambition, and its main contribution, has been to relate multilingualism explicitly to politics inside the EU institutions, which previous research—mostly in disciplines other than political science—has not. But the microfoundations of decision making, information exchange, and the social and relational aspects of politics are all fundamentally about substantive and strategic communication and, therefore, about the language(s) of politics. Hence, my book highlights the significance of a key component of the very nature of politics in the EU that political scientists have largely ignored. It also adds a new, previously marginalized dimension to studies of the inner workings of the EU's core institutions, including both intra- and interinstitutional deliberation and negotiation.

EU policymaking and the inner workings of the EU's core institutions have been subjects of a large and growing body of research, in particular in the context of the "comparativist turn" in EU studies (Hix 1994). This turn shifted attention away from the EU as an international organization and the process of European integration toward the study of the EU as a political system that can and should be examined in reference to politics in traditional domestic arenas. The result is a burgeoning literature that contributes immensely to our knowledge of EU politics, but also more generally to our understanding of comparative political institutions. My own research falls squarely in the comparativist camp, and I consider systematic comparison to be the most appropriate and fruitful approach to studying the EU. Yet there is a tendency to focus on those aspects of EU politics that resemble what we observe in "normal" domestic politics, which can lead us to lose sight of what is, in fact, systematically *different* about political dynamics in the EU's supranational institutions. In other words, the emphasis on EU politics as "normal" can distract from what makes the EU different. The reality that politics in the EU take place in a multilingual environment is a case in point. EU scholars recognize and acknowledge it, but this recognition does not inform empirical research either theoretically or empirically. Putting language and politics on the agenda is, therefore, an important and original contribution of my research, with the potential to open up a new line of inquiry in the study of EU politics.

Beyond EU studies, this research contributes to studies of comparative political institutions (including dynamics of institutional stability and change, as discussed in chapter 3), policymaking dynamics and strategic interaction, and politics in other multilingual polities. Moreover, it makes a contribution to research on nationalism, especially in relation to political institutions and their (de)mobilizing and and (de)politicizing potential. My research also speaks to the recent "relational" turn in political science that is reflected in the ascent of social network analysis in the discipline (see Victor, Montgomery, and Lubell 2017). Put simply, this approach recognizes that politics is, by definition, about relationships, communication, and strategic interaction and offers political scientists a new set of tools for capturing social connections and interdependencies between political actors. Language plays a key role in the creation and maintenance of political networks and thus warrants our attention. Finally, the analyses, descriptions, and conclusions of this book provide a theoretical and empirical basis for the use of text-as-data in political science and other fields.

Extensions

Much remains to be learned about language and politics in the EU and beyond. In the first place, the argument that multilingualism depoliticizes EU politics and policymaking was derived inductively. Hence, the key propositions advanced throughout this book ought to be subjected to new evidence and scrutiny. There are also important extensions that future research can address.

One way to think about accounting for language in research on EU politics is as a potential omitted variable, since language is one possible determinant of a wide range of outcomes of interest to political scientists but is generally excluded from both theoretical consideration and empirical models. The inclusion of variables capturing language repertoires or language proficiency may, for example, lead us to reconsider what we know about rapporteurship assignment in the EP (Kaeding 2004; Yoshinaka, McElroy, and Bowler 2010; Häge and Ringe 2019, 2020), the inclusion and placement of candidates on party lists for EP elections (Hobolt and Høyland 2011; Pemstein, Meserve, and Bernhard 2015), political networks in the Council of Ministers and the European Parliament (Huhe, Naurin, and Thomson 2018; Ringe, Victor, and Gross 2013), or EU politicians' career paths (Daniel 2015; Hobolt and Høyland 2011), because previous studies focused on those topics without systematically accounting for language effects. Language might also affect what resonates with legislators in terms of the framing of legislation (Ringe 2010). Coming back to a previously used example, "*service publique*" in French has a different connotation than "public service" does in English and may, therefore, evoke a different reaction for MEPs from different member states. Similarly, German does not make the distinction between sex and gender (although the English word is increasingly used); the word "*Geschlecht*" is thus much more ambiguous, which may affect deliberation and bargaining dynamics (even if lawyer-linguists make sure that the ambiguity is cleared up in the final legislative text). Accounting for the effects of language and multilingualism raises tricky questions related to measurement and data availability, which calls for innovative and creative solutions but promises to shed important new light on EU politics.

The significance of studying the politics of language extends beyond the question of proper model specification, however, because multilingualism affects the nature of EU politics in more profound ways. The previously discussed experimental research in psychology would suggest as much, and my own findings point in similar directions. To give just one example, my interview data suggest that both foreign language use and simultaneous interpretation neutralize those personal attributes we associate with effective political communication: politicians whose eloquence and persuasiveness in their mother tongues give them an edge in traditional bargaining situations face more of a level playing field in a multilingual environment because they are less effective when speaking a nonnative language, because their communication skills are lost on counterparts who are nonnative speakers, or because simultaneous translation distorts communication. The use of EU English also seems to have this neutralizing effect because, in comparison to standard English, it is simple, technical, and "decultured," instead of complex, nuanced, and emotional. In this light, differences in political communication appear to substantially alter the very nature of politics in the EU, and additional research is warranted to test these propositions. Examples of such research would be sentiment analyses of speech in the EU (ideally using natural, spontaneous speech rather than prepared statements) or efforts to predict party affiliation, ideology, or gender based on what EU actors say or write. Jones (2016), for example, investigates how feminine or masculine the language used by Hillary Clinton has been over time. If it is true that language is neutralized and standardized in the EU, as my interview data suggest, making such a distinction should be more difficult for EU actors.

Finally, the EU is an obvious case for comparison to other multilingual political contexts. But how much can one generalize from the case of the EU? To what extent might the argument about the depoliticizing effects of multilingualism on politics and policymaking travel to other multilingual polities? While this is largely an empirical question, one can speculate about what factors may affect my argument's applicability beyond the EU.

For example, all else equal, multilingualism is more likely to be depoliticizing when multilingualism is limited to the level of government and bureaucracy and does not extend into the public sphere. If that is the case, multilingual decision makers will tend to be more insulated from public scrutiny and pressure, factors that would counteract the depoliticizing effect of multilingualism. The types of policies at stake likely also matter. If the policies that are subject to multilingual decision making are technocratic, have no distributional effects, do not activate constituents' social identities, do not cut across social or linguistic cleavages, and/or do not otherwise map onto political or partisan fault lines, multilingualism is more likely to be depoliticizing because the policies at stake are less likely to be politicized. The language context itself ought to be considered as well. Is there an actively contested or otherwise unresolved "language question" at the political or societal level? If so, multilingualism is less likely to be depoliticizing. In contrast, it is more likely to be depoliticizing if the multilingual context involves a greater number of languages and if decision makers tend not to speak a shared lingua franca with high levels of proficiency, since both are the types of foreign language limitations that depoliticize politics and policymaking. Finally, multilingualism is more likely to be depoliticizing if language services are limited (which would result in greater nonnative language use) or low-quality (the output of which is more likely standardized and neutralizing).

Overall, the conditions that provide for the depoliticizing effects of multilingualism are more likely to be present in international organizations than multilingual states, but one should also expect meaningful variation across the latter. I hope for this book to provide the basis for systematic comparison of the EU to other multilingual international organizations and multilingual states, which promises to shed further light on an increasingly common feature of politics today: that consequential political decisions are negotiated between political actors who do not share a common native language.

Conclusion

In the EU, multilingualism affects the language of politics in that political actors use less complex language due to their own foreign language handicaps, to accommodate the foreign language handicaps of others, and to better get their message across when relying on language services. Those language services, in turn, have their own depoliticizing effects, as transla-

Conclusion 203

tion and interpretation inevitably constrict, condense, and transform what is originally expressed. Depoliticization through language does not mean that all political differences and contestation are muted or moot, however. EU actors have diverging ideological, partisan, and national preferences, and those differences do not disappear in a multilingual environment; there is real contestation in EU politics over real differences in political agendas. Political dynamics are different, however, when language serves primarily as a means of communication instead of a political tool used to advance particular policy agendas; when decision makers are less distinguishable based on what they say or write; and when their language is not as indicative of particular national and political backgrounds, preferences, and priorities. The language of politics in EU politics and policymaking tends to be utilitarian, simple, pragmatic, standardized, neutral, decultured, and de-ideologized, and there is reason to suspect that the same may be true in the many international political contexts today in which decision makers do not share a common language. If we take seriously the premise that language is fundamentally political and all politics a function of political communication—as it provides the basis for all political interaction, collaboration, contestation, deliberation, persuasion, negotiation, and transaction—these propositions are of consequence for a great many processes and outcomes of interest to political scientists, and of note to scholars in other disciplines.

Appendix: Multilingual Lawmaking under the Ordinary Legislative Procedure

Laws in the EU are typically created under the so-called ordinary legislative procedure (previously called the codecision procedure, a label that is still widely used), which prescribes that the Commission introduce a legislative proposal that is then jointly considered, revised, and accepted or rejected by the Council of the EU (the Council of Ministers, where the member state government are represented) and the European Parliament (composed of directly elected representatives of the European people). To illustrate the prevalence and importance of language services in the creation of laws, what follows offers a (stylized) description of the ordinary legislative procedure with indications of when translators, lawyer-linguists, and interpreters are involved.[1] Regarding the latter, it is important to emphasize that not all meetings in the Commission, the EP, and the Council feature interpretation, since it is mostly offered on request. I thus indicate when interpretation is always or typically offered in meetings, or when it may be offered depending on the language repertoires of participants. Notably, however, when no interpretation is offered, deliberation and negotiation take place among nonnative speakers or a shared language, which is usually English; hence, the context remains one in which decision making is multilingual. There is, moreover, variation in the number of languages that are actively used, driven in part by the foreign language skills of those who happen to be involved in a given legislative negotiation. The number of actively used languages also varies over the course of the legislative process: the original legislative proposal is issued in all official languages, negotiations generally take place in a more limited number of languages, before the final text is again issued in all.

The ordinary legislative procedure begins with a proposal drafted in one of the Directorates-General in the Commission (which DG depends on the subject area), following consultations with the member states and stakeholders (e.g., nongovernmental organizations and civil society, local authorities, representatives of industry).[2] Preparatory meetings will often not involve interpretation, or only be offered for English and French, although interpretation into other languages may also be provided if national experts are included. For any one text there is not one single drafter, however; instead, "the Commission's proposal is the work of many hands, and minds" (Robinson 2014a, 249). The drafting language is typically English and, to a substantially lesser extent, French, and the drafters in most cases are nonnative speakers of those languages. For this reason, the draft text may be examined and corrected by the editing services of DG Translation, with an eye to grammar, spelling, punctuation, and syntax as well as content and style. This editing option was introduced in 2005 as a pilot project and has since been extended, but it is not mandatory and is often not taken advantage of. In a 2009 survey, 54 percent of Commission drafters reported that they do not have their documents checked by a native speaker of the drafting language (Robinson 2014b, 196).

The ultimate goal of the internal consultation process that follows is not only to pass a clear, high-quality text on to the legislative institutions, but also to help ensure that the translators who become involved in later stages are not confronted with texts that are inaccurate, ambiguous, or difficult to understand. The text must thus meet the standards of the "Joint Practical Guide for persons involved in the drafting of legislation" of the EP, the Council, and the Commission, which stipulates that the original text be simple, clear, and direct. After internal consultation, which also involves other DGs (as applicable given the subject area) and the Legal Service, the text is sent for translation to DG Translation (it can also happen that the text goes through multiple rounds of translation, if additional changes are made during the deliberation process or if translators' comments and questions are taken into account).[3] It is typically submitted to the College of Commissioners for adoption in the Commission's three procedural languages (English, French, and German), with an indication of the original drafting language. Interpretation of those three languages is typically offered in meetings of the Commissioners. Following approval by the Commissioners, DG Translation produces versions of the text in all official languages, which are transmitted to the EP and the Council.

The Commission proposal is simultaneously received by the responsible EP committee and Council working group for the first reading stage of the ordinary legislative procedure. It is usually assigned to one lead committee in the EP, but other committees may be involved (as joint lead, associated, or opinion-giving committees) if the subject area of the proposal cuts across committee jurisdictions. Interpretation is offered at committee meetings based on the needs of committee members and, if applicable, experts who offer testimony. Within the lead committee, a rapporteur is selected and tasked with drafting the EP's report on the legislative proposal and shepherding it through the lawmaking process on behalf of the parliament. The party groups who are not assigned the rapporteurship typically select so-called shadow rapporteurs (Häge and Ringe 2020), who monitor the work of the rapporteur and act as their party groups' main negotiators and spokespersons regarding the proposal. Rapporteur and shadows hold regular meetings (with interpretation as needed) to deliberate and negotiate on behalf of their party groups. They also keep their own party groups apprised of the negotiations in political group meetings, where interpretation is again provided as required by the participants.

Negotiators in the EP are assisted by the committee secretariat as well as by lawyer-linguists, whose task is to improve the quality of the text produced in committee and to facilitate translation down the road. This becomes necessary because most negotiators are, again, nonnative speakers of English, the main negotiation and drafting language in the EP, and because political compromises may introduce substantive ambiguities. The lawyer-linguists' tasks involve the review and editing of amendments (in their original language) and of the committee's draft report, before it is sent to the EP's translation unit for translation into the working languages of the committee (which again depend on the language repertoires of the committee members). It is important to emphasize that lawyer-linguists in the EP (and also in the Council, discussed below) may not change the meaning of the text of a political agreement or reopen discussion on substantive issues; their responsibility is to improve the quality of the text and to ensure its consistency across language versions. Once amendments are voted on and incorporated into the committee's report, that report is again reviewed by lawyer-linguists and then translated into all languages. Lawyer-linguists then review all language versions of the text to ensure consistency before it becomes subject to consideration, amendment, and final decision by the EP plenary, where a full interpretation regime is offered. The text may be amended at the plenary stage, in which case lawyer-linguists and translators become involved to process the newly amended report.

208   *Appendix*

In the meantime, the Commission's proposal is also considered by the relevant working party in the Council, which usually works in the text's source language, which is usually English. National experts, however, may consider the text in their own language versions. About 15 percent of working parties have full interpretation regimes and about 60 percent have interpretation by request;[4] the remainder have no interpretation (for details, see Council of the European Union 2015).[5] Since the legislative text is, again, handled mostly by nonnative speakers of the drafting language, deficiencies and ambiguities may arise. These are subject to review after the working party stage by both lawyer-linguists and advisors from the Council's Legal Service. In case of questions or doubts, the so-called quality team—composed of a legal advisor and a lawyer-linguist who is charged with helping to improve the text and facilitate translation at later stages of the process—may check with the drafter(s) of the text to establish the intended meaning. The text is then translated into all languages before it is transmitted to the higher-level decision-making bodies, the first of which is Coreper (the Committee of the Permanent Representatives of the Governments of the Member States to the European Union). In preparation for Coreper meetings, the member states may become involved in the drafting process by submitting linguistic remarks or by issuing linguistic reservations, if they determine that the different language versions of the text are not aligned. The so-called Antici Group and Mertens Group meetings, which precede the meetings of Coreper, do not have interpretation, while Coreper itself has a standing interpretation regime of English, French, and German. Final political agreements are made at meetings of the ministers from the member states who are responsible for the policy area at hand, which involve full interpretation regimes (all languages). But before adoption of the final text, lawyer-linguists in the Council conduct another legal revision in collaboration with experts of the responsible working party. The text is then translated into all languages before the ministers make the final decision.

It is possible for the EP and the Council to conclude the legislative process in first reading, if they can agree on an identical legislative text. This requires close coordination between political actors in the two institutions, but also between their language services, because lawyer-linguists in the EP and the Council work together when finalizing the text. Both happens in the context of so-called trilogues, which are informal meetings between representatives from the EP, the Council, and the Commission that may be preceded by preparatory technical meetings of experts from the three institutions (both types of meetings have interpretation based on the participants' needs). Trilogues often help pave the way for agreements in first reading, but they may also continue to take place at later stages in the legislative process if there is no agreement. In that case, the ordinary legislative procedure goes into second reading and, if again no agreement is forthcoming, into third reading. In the third reading stage, a conciliation committee is convened, composed of representatives from the EP and the Council, to broker a final compromise. This conciliation committee works in the languages of its members (interpretation is offered accordingly) and is preceded by separate preparatory meetings of the EP and Council delegations as well as several trilogue meetings that involve both (interpretation is offered as needed). The EP and the Council take turns hosting the meetings, and the draft text of the conciliation committee is prepared by the host.

Throughout the second and third reading stages, lawyer-linguists remain involved to help with the production of high-quality texts that are consistent across all language versions, which are prepared at relevant points in time by the EP's and the Council's translation units. And whether an agreement is reached in first, second, or third reading, the drafting and translation processes in the EP and the Council are closely coordinated, an aspect of the process that has been strengthened after the Lisbon Treaty came into effect (Guggeis 2014).

Lawyer-linguists of both institutions also conduct the *legal-linguistic finalization* or *verification* of any provisional agreement between the legislating institutions, be it in first, second, or third reading. This is aimed at ensuring legal certainty and consistency between the language versions of the final legislative text, the substance of which, however, can no longer be altered at this point. The lawyer-linguists in the EP and the Council, under the leadership of the EP's "file coordinator" and the Council's "chef de file," jointly create a consolidated version of the text in the language of the provisional agreement, which is then translated. They then finalize the texts of all language versions on the basis of the original language version of the provisional agreement. The finalization task and the translation of the final agreement into all official languages is shared equally between lawyer-linguists from both institutions. The legal-linguistic revision of the text involves its being sent back and forth between EP and Council lawyer-linguists, which can take six to eight weeks. It culminates in a final "jurist-linguist meeting" that is attended by lawyer-linguists from the EP and the Council, a member of the Council General Secretariat, a Commission representative (usually the person who drafted the original Commission proposal), and representatives of each member state. In the meeting, the English text is carefully reviewed and agreed upon. It is then distributed to the Council lawyer-linguists for each official language, who go through the text in consultation with the member state representatives to produce final versions that then go to the EP lawyer-linguists for one last review. Lastly, the legislative act is published in the Official Journal of the European Union and finally enters into force.[6]

Translation and interpretation also figure prominently when the Court of Justice of the EU adjudicates, but, as previously discussed, the language regime of the Court differs from those of the other institutions: there is a single internal working language; the most important language in the Court is French, not English; and each court action has a "language of procedure," which is the official language in which the case was initiated. So there are two dominant languages for any one case: French and the language of procedure. Hearings before the Court are held in the language of procedure or with interpretation into that language, the language is used by the Court in any correspondence, reports, or decisions addressed to the parties in the case, and both the Advocate General's opinion and the Court's judgment are made available in it.[7] The Advocate General's opinion is drafted in English, French, German, Spanish, Italian, or Polish (McAuliffe 2012, 208). The Court's judgment is drafted in French following the judges' deliberations, which occur in French behind closed doors, without interpreters. The judgment is authentic in the language of the case (Bengoetxea 2016, 103–4). Throughout, member states have the right to use their own official languages in statements, observations, or pleadings and may request any documents in their language. In sum, interpretation and, to an even greater extent, translation also play an important role in court proceedings.

Notes

CHAPTER 1

1. Referencing Pool (1992), Grin distinguishes between languages as "instruments of communication, thought, play, identity/solidarity, and control/domination" (Grin 1994, 32).

2. François Grin and Peter A. Kraus conclude that "in the context of European history, it seems hardly an exaggeration to argue that nation-building and linguistic standardization were basically two sides of the same medal" (Grin and Kraus 2018, 2). Stein Rokkan considered language development more important in nation building than religion (Flora, Kuhnle, and Urwin 1999, 66), but William Safran also reminds us that national identity is not always related to a specific language and points to the Irish expressing their nationalism in English, for example (Safran 2005, 8).

3. http://www.rajbhasha.nic.in/en/languages-included-eighth-schedule-indian-constution, accessed June 3, 2019.

4. https://www.un.org/en/sections/about-un/official-languages/, accessed June 3, 2019.

5. https://www.coe.int/en/web/about-us/did-you-know, accessed June 3, 2019.

6. There are also monolingual international organizations, such as the Association of Southeast Asian Nations, which has about one thousand languages spoken in its territory but only uses English as its official and working language, without translation or interpretation (Lim 2017).

7. The full powers of the Court of Justice are laid out in Article 263 of the Treaty on the Functioning of the European Union (TFEU).

8. To illustrate the prevalence and importance of language services in this process, the appendix offers a stylized description of the ordinary legislative procedure with indications of when and how language service providers are involved.

9. The power of the supranational institutions is restricted in a very small num-

212 *Notes to Pages 6–17*

ber of "intergovernmental" policy areas, most importantly foreign and security policy.

10. In other words, the problem arose because some languages (like French) require the use of a definite article, while there are no definite articles in other languages or, as is the case in English, their use is optional (Ginsburgh and Weber 2011, 3).

11. I am grateful to Tikiri Bandara for pointing me to this example.

12. For a detailed overview of research on the intersection of language and politics outside of political science, see Strani 2020.

13. Indeed, there is a tendency to conflate ethnic and linguistic heterogeneity, for example in the frequent use of ethnolinguistic fractionalization as a measure of diversity (Anderson and Paskeviciute 2006).

14. Some scholars, however, emphasize that the focus on language and conflict can be exaggerated (Laitin 2000; Liu 2015) or find associations of linguistic diversity with desirable outcomes such as greater interest in politics and higher levels of participation in voluntary organizations, at least in weak democracies (Anderson and Paskeviciute 2006).

15. One possible solution is reliance on a "neutral language" that helps generate a sense of fairness, inclusiveness, and equality in heterogeneous multilingual societies, as more than half of the 100+ countries that gained independence since 1945 have done (Liu 2015). Miles (2000) similarly argues that European languages in Africa often serve as neutral tools of communication because they are not identified with and seen as favoring a particular ethnic group.

16. For additional references to these apparent contradictions in EU multilingualism see, for example, Kraus 2008, 127; Wright 2009, 96; Wodak 2009, 96; Phillipson 2003.

17. Wodak interviewed 28 respondents in 1997 (14 MEPs from a single committee, ten Commission officials, and four Austrian delegates to the Council).

18. It is notable, however, that "explicit definitions of the concept [of depoliticization] are extremely rare" (Flinders and Buller 2006, 55).

19. Standardized language also develops in other multilingual contexts, like multinational corporations and academia, but when political actors are less distinguishable from each other it affects perceptions of political and policy differences, the quality of contestation or intensity of debate, and political polarization. Moreover, mass democracy involves a representational dimension that requires communication with an external constituency capable of holding decision makers accountable, which is more difficult if those decision makers are less distinctive.

20. See also Hopkins, Tran, and Fischer Williamson 2014; Sobolewska, Lessard-Phillips, and Galandini 2016.

21. Gal (2006) is another useful review of interdisciplinary work on the intersection of language and politics.

22. The "Antici Group" and "Mertens Group" prepare the meetings of Coreper II (composed of the EU member states' Permanent Representatives to the EU) and Coreper I (composed of the Deputy Permanent Representatives), respectively.

23. Rather than referencing interviews selectively, I list all relevant interviews to support a given point, e.g., #2, 19, 23, 52, 63, 64, 78. When quoting from a par-

Notes to Pages 17–29   213

ticular interview, I indicate when I could have used equivalent quotes from other respondents by using "also," e.g., #22, also 26, 69.

24. This lowest level of agreement was 83.4 percent for the "description of the interpretation process" node. It was the research assistant who coded more extensively in that case, meaning the person who coded the complete set of interviews "over-coded" rather than "under-coded."

25. That much existing research in other fields does not directly connect EU multilingualism to EU politics is of course not meant as a critique. Scholars across disciplines naturally ask different research questions, find meaning and significance in different types of observations, and use different methods and data. I learned a tremendous amount engaging their ideas and findings in my own research for this book, above and beyond their insights related to EU politics.

26. Other political scientists focus exclusively on societal, as opposed to institutional, multilingualism in the EU and EU language policy (e.g., Climent-Ferrando 2016; Lacey 2014). Hence, their work only marginally relates to the focus of this book.

27. By highlighting these particular aspects of multilingualism, I am not taking a position in a debate about the exact meaning of the term, especially as it is used in different disciplines (see Strani 2020). I am merely offering a working definition that captures the particular empirical context at hand and the substantive focus of this book.

CHAPTER 2

1. EU civil servants must fulfill linguistic requirements for recruitment and promotion. For recruitment, they must speak two official languages (one thoroughly and one satisfactorily [van der Jeught 2015, 145]), of which one must be English, French, or German, unless they apply for linguist positions (translators, interpreters, lawyer-linguists), in which case they have to show proficiency in three languages. Between 2003 and 2008, the second language of two-thirds of applicants to EU jobs was English. For their first promotion, civil servants need to demonstrate sufficient command of a third language; there is no requirement that it be one of the three major languages, but for 63 percent of cases that third language was English, French, or German (Gravier and Lundquist 2016).

2. While all language versions of EU *legislation* are equally valid, this is not strictly true for EU *law*, because judgments of the Court of Justice constitute EU law but not all language versions are equally valid. Judgments are always authentic in the language(s) of the case.

3. The EU is not the only multilingual entity in which different language versions of legislative texts are equally authentic (see Leung 2012 for details); the same is true, for example, in Canada, Switzerland, and Belgium. Canadian legislation is equally authentic in English and French, the Swiss Civil Code in German, French, and Italian, and Belgian law in French and Dutch (Šarčević 2012a, 190; Gambaro 2007, 6). In both Switzerland and Belgium, however, laws are *not* equally authentic in the other official languages (Romansh and German, respectively), which are only spoken by less than 1 percent of their populations.

4. This was, in fact, the case for the Treaty of Paris, which established the European Coal and Steel Community as the EU's first predecessor organization.

5. In other multilingual legal contexts, the "distance" between language versions is also partly a function of different legal traditions. In Canada, for example, legislation drafted in French and English reflects traditionally different legal cultures; hence, drafting laws that can be understood in the legal context of civil and common law alike requires special care and effort. In contrast, legal concepts in both Belgium and Switzerland are expressed in different languages but have common roots in the civil law tradition, which facilitates multilingual legal drafting (Gambaro 2007, 6–7).

6. In the Stauder case, the Court argued that the intention of the drafter could only be determined by comparing all language versions (four at the time), writing in its judgment of November 12, 1969, that "when a single decision is addressed to all the Member States the necessity of uniform application and, accordingly, for uniform interpretation, makes it impossible to consider one version of the text in isolation but requires that it be interpreted on the basis of both the real intention of its author and the aim he seeks to achieve, in the light in particular of the version in all four languages." Baaij (2012a) identifies 170 judgments by the Court of Justice between 1960 and 2010 in which divergences between language versions were observed. In 75 of those judgments, the Court took a teleological approach in dealing with those divergences, meaning that it let its interpretation "be guided by the function, purpose, or objective of the provision or legislative instrument" (Baaij 2012a, 220). In 95 cases, it relied on a literal approach, or the comparison of the meaning of various language versions. In approximately one-third of those cases, the Court gave preference to the language versions that it considered clearer and less ambiguous; in the other two-thirds, it favored the meaning conveyed in the majority of language versions. A literal interpretation was more likely than the teleological approach when the case text at hand was of a more technical nature or when only one or a small number of language versions deviated from the others. It was also more likely when the discrepancy was likely caused by "a translation error or textual imperfection" (Baaij 2012a, 231), in which case the Court may (at least implicitly) consider the meaning of the presumed source text (see also Ginsburgh and Weber 2011).

7. Trilogues are informal tripartite meetings between the EU institutions involved in the legislative process and aimed at facilitating interinstitutional agreement. Provisional agreements reached in trilogues are subject to approval by the Council and the EP. The basis for negotiations are so-called "four-column documents" that specify, respectively, the Commission proposal, the EP position, the Council position, and the proposed compromise. They are almost always drafted and made available in English (#10). One respondent estimates that "90 percent" of trilogues rely on English as the main language (#10); another recalled only a single trilogue in French even when France last held the Council's rotating presidency (#4).

8. Reference withheld to ensure anonymity.

9. Code switching in the EU institutions thus ranges from the low-level phenomenon of "borrowing" certain terms from other language to the high-level phenomena of "code mixing" and "code switching" (Bhatia and Ritchie 2008, 13).

10. Wright (2000, 177) also highlights that monolingual speakers of languages of lesser diffusion are more disadvantaged than monolingual speakers of a "big" language.

11. It is important to emphasize, however, that the use of languages can also vary within a given institution, "from unit to unit as well as from working context to working context" (Gravier and Lundquist 2016, 80).

12. There is also some variation in the languages used in EP committees, depending on their composition, although perhaps less than there used to be (#79). One respondent, for example, suggests that a proportionally greater number of members from Portugal and Spain on the Fisheries committee gives that committee "a more Mediterranean favor" and leads to a greater use of southern European languages, including in the languages in which amendments are submitted (#4, also #79).

13. The Council's "Presidency Handbook" from 2015 lists a maximum of 20 preparatory body meetings with a full interpretation regime (Council of the European Union 2015).

14. References withheld to ensure anonymity.

15. This amount is about EUR 1.9 million for each language (Council of the European Union 2015). Unused funds may be used to help cover delegates' travel expenses (SCIC.02—Strategic Communication and Outreach, DG Interpretation, European Commission, personal communication, March 22, 2019).

16. One respondent suggested that this provision may at times be used as a less directly confrontational way of postponing a decision or to signal disagreement (#20).

17. Language "sizes" are from Special Eurobarometer 386 (2012), Europeans and their Languages (http://ec.europa.eu/commfrontoffice/publicopinion/archives/ebs/ebs_386_sum_en.pdf).

18. https://curia.europa.eu/jcms/jcms/Jo2_6999/, accessed March 2, 2018.

19. Since the deliberations of the judges are not open to the public, this information is anecdotal.

20. For detailed treatments of the Court's institutional development and its languages, see Arnull 2018; 2019.

21. Unless otherwise indicated, all figures and estimates are from "Interpreting and Translating for Europe" (European Union 2017).

22. Information about necessary qualifications is available at https://epso.europa.eu/career-profiles/languages_en, accessed October 28, 2020.

23. The numbers are rough estimates calculated by adding up the estimated or actual numbers of interpreters and translators listed in the body of the text and dividing them by estimates of the total number of staff in each institution, which is about 32,000 in the Commission, about 3,500 in the Council (https://europa.eu/european-union/about-eu/figures/administration_en, accessed October 28, 2020), about 7,000 in the EP (excluding political group staff; http://www.europarl.europa.eu/news/en/faq/22/how-many-people-work-in-the-parliament, accessed October 28, 2020), and about 2,200 in the Court of Justice (https://curia.europa.eu/jcms/jcms/P_80908/en/, accessed October 28, 2020).

24. As a point of comparison, the whole United Nations only employs about 120 interpreters (Kraus 2008, 115).

216   *Notes to Pages 47–53*

25. In general, the more high profile a meeting in the Commission and the Council, the more likely it is to be covered by staff interpreters; the same does not seem to be true in the EP (Duflou 2016, 105), where interpretation is based on the language profiles of participants.

26. For meetings with interpretation involving more than 6 active and/or passive languages (where an active language is one *into which* and a passive language one *from which* interpretation is provided), 3 interpreters are required per language. For meetings with fewer than 6 languages, the minimum is 2. Therefore, the size of simultaneous interpreting teams ranges from 4 interpreters in meetings with 2 active and passive languages to 69 in meetings with 23 active and passive languages, that is, those with a full language regime excluding Irish. Irish, which is only interpreted passively, adds two more interpreters for a total of 71 (Duflou 2016, 108–9).

27. Numbers are from http://europa.eu/whoiswho/whoiswho.html, accessed March 1, 2019.

28. http://www.europarl.europa.eu/interpretation/en/the-interpreter.html, accessed March 1, 2019.

29. One implication of these rules is that when a new political group is created, especially in the middle of a legislative term, it has all kinds of implications for the scheduling of meetings with interpretation (#10).

30. The EP has staff shortages for Maltese, Croatian, and Irish, in particular (DG LINC, European Parliament, personal communication, February 4, 2019).

31. In the Commission, it is also possible for a meeting for which there is a last-minute request to be sufficiently important to warrant the cancelation of interpretation in another meeting (SCIC.02—Strategic communication and Outreach, DG Interpretation, European Commission, personal communication, March 22, 2019).

32. The EP's rapporteur is responsible for drafting the EP's report on a particular legislative proposal and for guiding it through the lawmaking process on behalf of the parliament. The party groups who are not assigned the rapporteurship typically select so-called shadow rapporteurs (Häge and Ringe 2020), who monitor the work of the rapporteur and act as their party groups' main negotiators and spokespersons regarding the proposal.

33. The figures and discussion in this section focus on active translation only, which indicates the language *into* which interpretation is provided (whereas passive interpretation indicates the language *from* which interpretation is offered). This distinction is meaningful in practice because there are meetings, for example, in which participants are comfortable listening in English but prefer speaking in their own native language. The correlation between active and passive translation over the course of a year, however, is quite high; for more than two-thirds of the languages, it is above 0.95, and for another five languages it is above 0.92. Only English (0.85) and German (0.81) have lower correlations.

34. These numbers do not add up to 100 percent because interpretation is sometimes offered from and into non-EU languages, for example when foreign dignitaries visit the institutions.

35. These numbers (again) do not add up to 100 percent because interpretation is sometimes offered from and into non-EU languages, for example when foreign dignitaries visit the institutions.

36. These variables are based on Special Eurobarometer 386 (2012) for the

2007–2011 period and Eurobarometer 243 (2006) for 2012–2016, questions D48a ("Thinking about the languages that you speak, which language is your mother tongue?") and D48T1 ("Languages that you speak well enough in order to be able to have a conversation").

37. Note that some languages are associated with more than one member state (e.g., German with Germany and Austria or Greek with Greece and Cyprus) and some member states with more than one language (e.g., French and Dutch in Belgium or French and German in Luxembourg). The variable was coded accordingly. Relay languages in the Council are English and French (Baaij 2018, 63) and in the Commission English, French, German, Italian, Spanish, Dutch, and Portuguese (Duflou 2016, 111).

38. In those analyses in which the proportion of staff i-slots is the dependent variable, the proportion of freelancer i-slots is included as a control variable, and vice versa.

39. But note that much of the variance for each model is explained by the fixed effects.

40. While freelancers cover between 20–30 percent of translations in the Commission, the EP, and the Court of Justice, freelance translation is rare in the Council (less than 1 percent of total workload; all figures from 2009) (Wagner, Bech, and Martínez 2014, 16–20).

41. Numbers are from http://europa.eu/whoiswho/whoiswho.html, accessed March 1, 2019.

42. See https://www.consilium.europa.eu/media/30482/qc-32-11-696_en_web.pdf, accessed October 28, 2020.

43. See http://publications.europa.eu/webpub/eca/special-reports/court-of-justice-14-2017/en/, accessed October 28, 2020.

44. The European Personnel Selection Office, which is responsible for selecting staff to work in EU institutions and agencies, highlights that "the job requires capable lawyers with outstanding linguistic abilities, who are experienced in drafting or translating, checking or revising legal texts. Lawyer-linguists must be able to discern precisely what EU legislation is intended to convey, and faithfully reflect that intention in their own native language." To this end, they "must have a perfect command of one EU language and a thorough command of at least 2 others and a law degree. Previous experience of translating legal texts and additional languages are an asset." (https://epso.europa.eu/career-profiles/languages_en, accessed April 12, 2018).

45. Robertson (2010a) offers a detailed account of this process.

46. See Guggeis and Robinson (2012) for further details on the legal-linguistic revision and finalization processes.

47. https://curia.europa.eu, accessed September 18, 2020.

48. Much media coverage is also often ill-informed, tends to strongly reflect national standpoints (Kraus 2008, 125), and is always eager to invoke "the tired myth of Babel" (Phillipson 2016, 58).

49. Commission press release of September 26, 2013, "Frequently asked questions on languages in Europe" (http://europa.eu/rapid/press-release_MEMO-13-825_en.htm).

50. Directorate-General for Translation, European Parliament, personal communication, February 27, 2019.

218 *Notes to Pages 63–71*

51. In an interview, François Grin describes informally surveying his students to see how much they would be willing to pay in additional taxes to ensure that their language remains an official and working language of the EU. The average amount his students indicate is "vastly higher than the cost of translation and interpretation in the European institutions. Always. Year in, year out" (Directorate-General for Translation, European Commission 2011).

52. Special Eurobarometer 386 (2012), Europeans and their Languages (http://ec.europa.eu/commfrontoffice/publicopinion/archives/ebs/ebs_386_sum_en.pdf).

53. The privileged position of national versus minority languages is observed by some commentators (e.g., Caviedes 2003) and explicitly criticized by others (e.g., Climent-Ferrando 2016; House 2003; Phillipson 2016; Strubell 2007).

54. That changing the language rules requires unanimous agreement of the member states is, of course, explicitly recognized by most research on the topic (Ammon 2010; Ammon and Kruse 2013; Fidrmuc 2011; Ginsburgh and Weber 2011; Horspool 2006; Phillipson 2003; van Els 2005), as is the reality that language issues are particularly politically sensitive (Ammon 2006; Ban 2013; Gazzola 2006; Loos 2000; Mamadouh 1999, 2002; Phillipson 2003, 2016; Wright 2000, 2013; van Els 2005). This recognition does not prevent many of the same observers from proposing alternatives that are politically highly unlikely. The value of their approach lies in identifying alternatives that may be optimal given a particular set of solution criteria, which helps articulate appropriate policy solutions independent of what may be feasible at a given time (Pool 1996, 164).

55. Tosi emphasizes that "the EU institutions should not naively assume that after several linguistic transactions the final version of a text will preserve the same content as the original" (Tosi 2013); my conversations with both policymakers and language service providers suggest that he would be hard-pressed to find people in the institutions who would, in fact, "naively assume" as much. My respondents were quite aware of the challenges Tosi highlights.

56. European Court of Justice website (curia.europa.eu), accessed June 20, 2018.

57. EUR-Lex (eur-lex.europa.eu), accessed June 20, 2018.

58. Concerns about the potentially dire effects of poorly executed translations on legal certainty for EU citizens are not new (e.g., Pool 1996; Xanthaki 2001), but the expected crisis has not materialized, at least to this day.

59. Corrigenda are a common practice used to realign the published legislative text with the original "will of the legislator." They can affect legal meaning by narrowing or broadening notions in the text, turning positive statements into negative statements, or even plainly rewriting substantive parts of a piece of EC legislation (Bobek 2016, 128). Such "meaning changing" corrigenda are not usually the consequence of typing or typesetting, but of incorrect translations prior to adoption of the legal act (Bobek 2016, 128). When an act contains an error, the incorrect text applies until a corrected version is published, at which point the new version applies retrospectively from the date of adoption (Robinson 2012).

60. Some apparent "misunderstandings" are not actual mistakes, but attempts by policymakers to shift blame onto language providers (#13, 16, 22, 24, 79, 81). Such instances are described as very rare (#24, 79, 81), but they do occur on occasion. Political actors may also use language services strategically in other ways. They may, for example, use even the short time lag that comes with interpretation to

Notes to Pages 71–81   219

prepare a better response (#3, 13, 24) or use interpretation for clarification if they did not fully understand an intervention in its original (#24).

61. This interpretation is in line with previous research on vote choice in the European Parliament (e.g., Ringe 2010).

62. It is notable that evaluations of how EU multilingualism works in practice tend to highlight problems, when a closer look at previous work that takes the voices of actors inside the EU institutions seriously tends to confirm my more positive takeaway (e.g., Abélès 1999; Bellier 1997; Horspool 2006; Stritar and Stabej 2013; McAuliffe 2008). It was even the "commonly held view that multilingualism is not an obstacle" among Wodak's respondents (Wodak 2009, 89, 128). This conclusion is also confirmed in "customer satisfaction surveys" conducted in both 2015 and 2016 by the Commission's Directorate-General for Translation and in March 2014 by the EP's DG INTE. The results of these internal surveys must be taken with a grain of salt, due to the fairly low response rates and likely nonrepresentative samples of respondents, but they also point to broadly positive views of EU language services. The Commission surveys find that respondents—810 total in 2015 and 481 in 2016—are generally quite satisfied with the quality of the language services. On a 1–5 scale, where 1 indicates "very dissatisfied" and 5 "very satisfied," the mean score is a 4.17. They are slightly less satisfied with the timeliness of the services provided (3.95), but the average user also indicates that s/he "rarely (just once or twice)" experienced problems (DG Translation, European Commission, Customer Satisfaction Survey, 2015 and 2016). In the EP survey, 38.4 percent of respondents indicate being "very satisfied" with the overall quality of interpretation in the EP, 41.6 percent report being "satisfied," and another 16.8 percent are "fairly satisfied"; only 2.4 percent of respondents report being dissatisfied (DG Interpretation and Conferences, Satisfaction Survey of MEPs, March 2014). The EU Courts of Auditor's report on interpretation similarly highlights that "[t]he users are generally satisfied with the quality of the interpretation services provided" (Court of Auditors 2005, 15).

63. I sought this information from the European Parliament, which uses MEPs' "language profiles" for administrative purposes, for example to better anticipate the language needs of participants in different meetings and thus the required interpretation regime. Unfortunately, these data were not made available to me, citing privacy concerns. I thus had to rely on my qualitative data for analytical leverage.

64. It was not possible to unequivocally categorize the answers of some respondents to this question, for example if they discussed in general terms the factors that would allow policymakers with limited language skills to participate successfully in EU decision making as well as those that would inhibit their effectiveness, without taking a definitive stance. Rather than (mis-)interpret such responses, I only report those that were unambiguous.

65. The "family photo" is EU jargon for the joint photo of all participants taken at the conclusion of a meeting, especially of the EU heads of state and government.

CHAPTER 3

1. One contribution of this chapter is that it is adds to a small but growing body of work on "the practice of language planning, that is, the development, implemen-

220 *Notes to Pages 81–92*

tation, and evaluation of specific language policies" (Ricento 2006, 18; for other important examples, see especially Cardinal and Sonntag 2015; Royles and Lewis 2019).

2. Mamadouh recognizes that "the present settlement has been very successful in achieving linguistic peace" (Mamadouh 1999, 142).

3. For the EU, in other words, as is also the case "for many postcolonial states, multilingual outcomes for individuals is a powerful equilibrium" (Laitin 1993, 227).

4. Available at https://eur-lex.europa.eu/content/techleg/KB0213228ENN.pdf.

5. Gazzola (2006), Athanassiou (2006), Nißl (2011), and van der Jeught (2015) offer detailed descriptions of the evolution of EU multilingualism, among others.

6. Horspool (2006, 180) maintains that the four official languages were "used equally in meetings" of the ECSC, yet French seems to have quickly established itself as dominant.

7. The "official language" of an applicant country is the one the country itself indicates during the accession negotiations; the choice is not dictated by the EU. The member states then decide unanimously to amend Regulation No. 1 to add another language.

8. A small number of other languages that are recognized by the constitution of a member state may also be used in formal EU meetings and documents, for example in Council formations that include regional representatives, as well as plenary meetings of the Committee of the Regions and the European Economic and Social Committee. Agreements on the use of Basque, Calalan, and Galician were concluded with Spain, which has to cover the costs associated with the use of these languages; similar agreements also existed regarding Welsh and Scottish (Climent-Ferrando 2016, 3). These languages are sometimes referred to as "quasi-official."

9. The principles laid out in Articles 2 and 3 have been confirmed in various treaty revisions (Ammon and Kruse 2013, 16), e.g., Article 24 of the Lisbon Treaty.

10. The ECSC language protocol did allow the Assembly to decide on the practical question of language use, but not the other institutions.

11. The symbolic (associated with cultural and political traits) and functional or communicative (about the transmission of information in a broad sense) dimensions of language are well-recognized (Edwards 1985; Gazzola 2006, 394). The representational and legal dimension are also crucial in the context of EU multilingualism, however.

12. In 2013, for example, the Bundestag raised concerns about a disadvantaging of the German language in the EU and requested that the German government take up the issue (Der Spiegel 2015).

13. Some Germans were particularly keen to insist on the equal use of French and German—or that the two languages be equal in *not* being used—as former EP Secretary-General Julian Priestley describes: "One MEP in particular, Michael Gahler, himself a former diplomat and excellent linguist, made it his personal mission to track down any administrative use of French (even signs in lifts), insisting that they be replaced by English, or, if not, complemented by German" (Clark and Priestley 2012, 161).

14. Opinion of Advocate General Maduro in Case C-160/03 (Spain v Eurojust) of December 16, 2004.

15. The Civil Service Tribunal has also validated that "an EU institution has the

Notes to Pages 92–101   221

right, even without taking a formal decision to that effect, to choose a limited number of languages of internal communication, provided that that choice is based on objective considerations relating to its operational needs" (Van der Jeught 2015, 132–33).

16. Case C-566/10 P Italy vs. Commission, June 21, 2012; Case T-124/13, Italy vs. Commission and Case T-191/13 Spain vs. Commission, September 24, 2015; Decision of the European Ombudsman on complaint 259/2005(PB)GG against the European Commission, April 30, 2008; see also the Court's judgments of March 26, 2019, in Case C-621/16 and Case C-377/16.

17. See, for example, Fidrmuc 2011.

18. This proposal mirrors the so-called "Priestley Rule" (named after former EP Secretary-General Julian Priestley, who introduced it), whereby EP civil servants were only allowed to use nonnative languages in internal meetings in the 2000s. According to my respondents, the rule worked reasonably well until the 2004 enlargement, but too few of the incoming officials from the new member states understood enough French for it to be sustainable (#78, 79, 81). Anecdotally, a similar rule is still used in some Council working groups when interpretation is not available, for example during meetings in the early morning or evening (#74).

19. Formal requests for information were made to the interpretation and translation services in the Commission, the Council of the EU, and the EP to ask explicitly if there was any consideration of changing Regulation No. 1 in the run-up to the 2004 enlargement. Each response emphasized that relevant discussions focused on making necessary adjustments to EU multilingualism within the confines of the existing rules and that changing Regulation No. 1 was not considered an option. Unit SCIC.02 (Strategic Communication and Outreach) in the Commission's Directorate-General for Interpretation, for example, responded that "Regulation 1/58 is one of the basic legislative texts in the EU and there has been no discussion about modifying it in its substance," while the EP's Directorate-General for Logistics and Interpretation for Conferences emphasized that "the aim was to safeguard the equivalence of all languages while introducing measures to contain cost increases." Moreover, none of my respondents suggested that changing the EU's primary language rules was discussed in preparation for the 2004 enlargement. I was thus unable to find any support for claims that the 2004 enlargement "triggered debates whether (i) each of the acceding states should bring their official language into the EU . . . and (ii) whether the 'new' languages should have the same rights as enjoyed by the 'old' member states" (Wodak and Krzyżanowski 2011, 623–24), at least among political actors in positions to meaningfully advocate or potentially pursue such changes.

20. One of my respondents similarly explained that one of the reasons why the system continues to work is that languages were "gradually, gradually, gradually" introduced, allowing for adjustments and refinements to be made "incrementally" (#58).

21. For a discussion of quality assurance initiatives taken by DG Translation over time, including in the context of the 2004 enlargement, see Strandvik 2018.

22. Information provided by different services of DG Interpretation by unit SCIC.02—Strategic Communication and Outreach, personal communication, March 22, 2019.

23. Wagner, Bech, and Martinez (2014) offer a detailed description of EU enlargement and its impact on translation.

24. Information provided by different services of DG Interpretation by unit SCIC.02—Strategic Communication and Outreach, personal communication, March 22, 2019.

25. "The profession of translator in the European Parliament" (http://www.europarl.europa.eu/multilingualism/trade_of_translator_en.htm), accessed February 25, 2019.

26. McAuliffe (2008, 810) suggests that direct translation is used whenever possible.

27. There are no formal pivot languages in the Commission; the use of English and French is the logical consequence of those being the two working languages that all translators can use (DG Translation, European Commission, personal communication, July 5, 2019).

28. Translation Service, General Secretariat of the Council, personal communication, July 3, 2019.

29. DG Translation, European Parliament, personal communication, February 27, 2019.

30. Gravier and Lundquist (2016) suggest that about one-quarter of translations in 2007 were done by external staff, while Wagner, Bech, and Martinez (2014) put the number of external translation after the 2004 enlargement at 40 percent.

31. Reforms aimed at containing the costs of language services continue to be implemented. In 2012, for example, the EP cut part of its translation budget in an effort to decrease its general budget by 8.6 million euros per year, which meant that it no longer required the translation of recordings of its plenary sessions into all official languages (Hall 2012).

32. Hence, the EU institutions, and the language services themselves, played an active role in the preservation of the language regime by adjusting their practices to new realities.

33. One might ask if the factors discussed in this section truly are quasi-parameters that change endogenously over time, or if they are in fact gradually changing parameters that are exogenous to the EU language regime. Societal foreign language capacity or advances in machine translation, for example, at first glance appear to be unrelated, and thus exogenous, to EU multilingualism. Each of the factors considered here is at least partially impacted by the EU's language regime, however, and thus best conceived of as a quasi-parameter, because any parameter that is affected by the institution itself such that long-term change ensues should be classified as such (Greif and Laitin 2004, 634). And indeed, EU policies aimed at supporting foreign language learning in the member states are explicitly grounded in the EU's commitment to multilingualism and influence societal foreign language capacity (see Article 165(1) of the Treaty on the Functioning of the European Union (TFEU), which provides that "Union action shall be aimed at developing the European dimension in education, particularly through the teaching and dissemination of the languages of the Member States"). Similarly, advances in machine translation and interpretation are in part a function of EU multilingualism not only because the EU invests in the development of its own machine translation programs, but also because developers elsewhere use readily available, human-translated EU texts to create and advance machine translation

Notes to Pages 106–18   223

processes. For example, translations of European Parliament proceedings featured prominently in the development of Google Translate (Adams 2010).

34. Notably, some of the reforms of the EU's secondary language rules that have been adopted to make EU multilingualism more efficient have already taken advantage of an improvement in foreign language proficiency, first and foremost the provision of language services on a "real needs" basis.

35. Laitin (1994) argues that a single language may result from market forces (a critical mass of people speak English so that the efficiency gains sufficiently outweigh identity concerns).

36. Wodak (2013, 93) confirms that "multilingualism is perceived as an inherent part of Europe's and the EU's identity, as constitutive for European democracies" by her interview respondents, while Longman maintains that attempts to give one language any kind of privileged position is contrary to the very spirit of European integration (Longman 2007, 185).

37. Wright (2000, 156) offers some evidence to suggest that language proficiency is taken into account in some countries/parties when electoral lists for EP elections are drawn up, but it is unclear even two decades later to what extent and how systematically this happens.

38. In total, 41,123,000 e-pages were processed in eTranslation in 2018, more than double the volume of 2017 (18,874,000) (Information provided by different services of DG Interpretation by unit SCIC.02—Strategic Communication and Outreach, personal communication, March 22, 2019).

39. Christopher Manning, professor of machine learning, linguistics, and computer science at Stanford University, considers this scenario to be conceivable (Lustig 2018).

40. I am grateful to Professors Yulia Tsvetsov and Graham Neubig at Carnegie Mellon University for taking the time to share their knowledge of these matters with me.

41. In 2018, Microsoft announced that it had created the first machine translation system that achieves "human parity" in the quality of its translations (https://blogs.microsoft.com/ai/chinese-to-english-translator-milestone/).

42. Brown commented almost 30 years ago on the Court's "remarkable skill in solving the problems raised by the linguistic regime" (Brown 1981, 341).

43. Laitin emphasizes that rulers of new states "have needed to be far more sensitive to the linguistic repertoires of their citizens than were rulers of consolidated states in earlier centuries. Imposing a specific language as the sole language for rule on a population that does not speak it will more likely mobilize the population" (Laitin 1997, 284). After all, "any decision on the question of national or official language . . . can have broad resonance for the wider issues of democratic participation and political equality" (Laitin 1977, 4). While the EU is not a new state, similar advice seems warranted.

CHAPTER 4

1. See Costa, Vives, and Corey (2017) for a review of this research.

2. The original German reads, "Meine deutschen Wörter haben keine Kindheit." I am grateful for Boaz Keysar for making me aware of this quote.

3. Costa, Duñabeitia, and Keysar (2019, 1–2) emphasize that there is, of course,

large variability of individual experiences with foreign languages in terms of "how and when a foreign language has been acquired (in a social vs. an academic context; early or late in life), its current use (immersed or not), the proficiency attained, and so on. All of these factors can modulate the variables that are likely to be behind the foreign language effect (e.g., cognitive load, cognitive fluency, emotional reactivity, etc.)."

4. Kruse and Ammon (2013, 166) suggest that MEPs whose languages are most often interpreted via relay have a greater incentive to speak English (see also Wright 2007, 157–58).

5. Wodak, Krzyżanowski, and Forchtner would interpret such examples to be indicative of the "the perceived larger symbolic capital of English" and thus as supportive of their concept of "hegemonic multilingualism" (Wodak, Krzyżanowski, and Forchtner 2012, 177), when in fact they simply reflect speakers' concerns about being understood correctly by others.

6. There is, however, no obligation to stay with the same language over the course of the legislative process. For example, "the Commission may work in one language, say French, and the Council presidency may choose to work on the English translation as base" (Robertson 2012b, 7), or the language used to prepare the base text may change when the Council Presidency switches from an anglophone to a francophone member state.

7. McAuliffe finds that référendaires in the Court of Justice who are native speakers of French, the Court's primary drafting language, were more likely than nonnative French speakers to express problems or difficulties drafting "in the formulaic style of Court of Justice judgments" (McAuliffe 2011, 104). This raises the interesting question if something similar might be true for native English drafters in the other institutions.

8. More than half the drafters in the Commission reported rarely or never having their documents checked by native speakers (Robinson 2012, 9).

9. See Strandvik (2014) and Guggeis and Robinson (2012) for detailed discussions of these guidelines.

10. A reminder: codecision is what is today known as the ordinary legislative procedure.

11. This was also evident in the Spitzenkandidaten debate on May 15, 2014, in which three candidates (Martin Schulz, Ska Keller, and Guy Verhofstadt) spoke English (Jean-Claude Juncker spoke French and Alexis Tsipras Greek). According to the *Economist*, the three who chose to speak English "showed remarkable fortitude in trying to reach out to voters in what was often their second language," but "inevitably, it made for a stiff and stilted exchange. . . . language barriers added to a sense of strange remoteness" (The Economist 2014).

12. One handicap that many native English speakers share is their own limited command of languages other than English (#46, 54, 73). It can also lead to some discontent when monolingual native English speakers "never make an effort" and then "complain about a person who speaks three of four languages . . . some of them don't even know how to say hello in another language; it's horrible" (#54).

13. Ban (2013) and Wright (2007) also discuss how nonnative speakers often find native speakers of English difficult to understand, for similar reasons as those highlighted by my respondents, while Bugarski (2009, 115) emphasizes that "careful

Notes to Pages 129–35 225

and competent non-native English is more readily comprehended, along with the messages it carries, than carefree, even irresponsibly used native English." See also Longman 2007.

14. It is not just a joke. Wright (2007) offers the example of "a meeting where a German MEP spoke first, using English. His delivery was slow, with heavy emphasis, his sentences were short and mostly SVO [subject-verb-object] and his lexis plain. Only a dozen of the one hundred twenty or so members of the audience (with a mixture of first languages) put on head phones. An Irish MEP then gave an address, in English. After a few sentences, 55 more people had put on their head phones" (Wright 2007, 153).

15. Van Els (2001, 337–38) explains that nonnative speakers are more confident when interacting with only nonnative speakers and are better able to concentrate on the message they want to convey because they feel less pressure to speak the foreign language flawlessly.

16. Wright rightly emphasizes that particular influence lies not with native speakers per se, but with those whose language repertoires allow them to function efficiently (Wright 2007, 164).

17. Wagner, Bech, and Martinez (2014, 75) highlight that native speakers adjusting their native language "risks some erosion of their ability to speak and write their mother tongue. This is because of interference from other languages: the invasion of foreign vocabulary and syntax; exposure to the frequent misuse of their mother tongue; the effects of fatigue and compromise; and the desire not to appear pedantic."

18. Wright discusses similar efforts by native speakers to use simple English (Wright 2007, 152–53).

19. Respondents in the Court of Justice, where French remains the main procedural language, made similar arguments regarding native French speakers (#35).

20. I referred to Martin Schulz in my interviews for illustration but invited respondents to think of other examples. Conversations thus revolved mostly around Schulz, but some respondents brought up others, such as Commission President Jean-Claude Juncker, MEP and former Belgian prime minister Guy Verhofstadt, former Belgium prime minister Leo Tindemans, Commission Vice-President Frans Timmermans, or former MEP and Finnish prime minister Alexander Stubb. Hence, policymakers' assessment that it "does not matter as much as one might think" is based on their consideration of Schulz and others *like* Schulz.

21. Doerr observes that actors in another multilingual context—the preparatory assemblies for the European Social Forum—are awarded the time they need to express themselves (Doerr 2009, 2012).

22. Regarding Martin Schulz, for example, the assistant to an MEP—a native French speaker—acknowledged that Schulz is "not as convincing as a French politician" in that language, but emphasized that just the effort of speaking another language can buy good will; Martin Schulz "is perceived very positively in France" because of that (#37; also 55, 71, 81).

23. Doerr's analyses of another multilingual environment (preparatory meetings for the European Social Form) reveal not only that that speakers are awarded the time they need to express themselves, but also a greater tendency of participants to "listen attentively" than their counterparts in monolingual assemblies at the national level (Doerr 2009, 2012).

226   *Notes to Pages 137–50*

24. I am grateful to Art Goldhammer for pointing me to this example.

25. Online Etymology Dictionary (https://www.etymonline.com), accessed September 22, 2020.

26. Reference withheld to ensure anonymity.

27. Other examples of partisan language in the United States include "estate taxes" vs. "death taxes," "comprehensive health reform" vs. "Washington takeover of health care," and "tax breaks for the wealthy" vs. "tax reform" (Thompson 2016).

CHAPTER 5

1. Gardner (2016) assembled a long list of "Misused English words and expressions in EU publications," published by the EU Court of Auditors.

2. Gazzola and Grin (2013) also explicitly reject the use of "English as a lingua franca" in reference to the EU's institutional context.

3. Thirty-four respondents offered detailed substantive insights into the use and nature of EU English (#1, 15, 16, 27, 33, 35, 41, 42, 45, 46, 49, 51, 55, 56, 57, 58, 59, 60, 61, 62, 64, 66, 67, 68, 70, 71, 72, 73, 74, 75, 76, 78, 82, 83).

4. Similarly, 81.5 percent of Balič's respondents (and competent English speakers more so than less competent ones) believe that EU English differs from standard English (Balič 2016b, 122).

5. One respondent, a former high-ranking official in the EP, emphasized that the challenge of adjusting to hearing and using EU English is not limited to policymakers, but that new translators and interpreters have to get "tuned to what is the Euro language, the institutional language" in the EU (#81), because interpretation and translation from and into EU English can be tricky (#17). This conforms with Vuorikoski's observation that "mastering EU concepts requires time and exposure to the EU genre" even for new interpreters (Vuorikoski 2004, 174).

6. Spirling (2016) shows that politicians adjust how they speak to changing circumstances, such as an extension of the franchise.

7. In some circumstances, EU English may travel outside the EU institutions and into the homes of EU officials, as one Commission official explained: "a lot of the people here, including me by the way, are in binational, bilingual marriages or relationships. You get a lot of mixed marriages, so a lot of people go home and carry on speaking a foreign language or funny English" (#56).

8. Biel (2007) makes the point that in Brussels, English speakers have to learn to say subsidiarity instead of the UK-specific term devolution.

9. One Mertens counselor, for example, emphasized that "we spend entire days, sometimes twelve, fourteen hours together. There are meetings of the Council and European Council that continue for almost 24 hours. So these people spend all their time together in this very closely tied group. So this creates also the links between them and this feeling that you know, 'we speak the language that . . . everybody in the group understands'" (#75).

10. Tosi (2003, 56) highlights that the subordination of spoken language in the EU is "exactly the opposite of what happens in a monolingual situation in the national communities where changes are generally adopted in writing long after they have been used and accepted in the spoken language."

11. A similar story has been told about the "Geneva language" prevalent in the

League of Nations, where the language services "created a lingua franca suited to the technical terminology of the League, smooth translation from French to English (or vice versa), and taking diplomatic tact into consideration." (Ikonomou 2017).

12. Mollin (2006) also relies on the "Europarl" corpus, but since her focus is explicitly on Euro-English (i.e., the English of nonnative speakers across Europe), rather than EU English (i.e., the English of actors inside the EU institutions), she complements the EU data with radio samples from English-language channels from several EU countries. As a result, her results do not offer insights into the subject at hand.

13. Token counts are higher than word counts because punctuation marks also count as tokens.

14. I am indebted and grateful to Anna Meier for her assistance with these text analyses.

15. The Flesch Reading Ease test, a more common measure, assesses the difficulty of a text on a 0–100 scale, with lower numbers indicating greater reading difficulty (Flesch 1948). The FRE was developed for elementary educators and has therefore received criticism when applied to political texts (e.g., Benoit, Munger, and Spirling 2019). Flesch-Kincaid scores, which build on the FRE and thus are subject to similar critiques (though they use different weights), were developed for the U.S. Navy and thus may be more valid for assessing the complexity of political documents.

16. In very literal terms, this means that sentences in the non-EU transcripts are longer and that words have more syllables. These measures accord with the conventional wisdom about how to represent complexity of language, yet they may also mask important variation in particular vocabulary used and ignore dimensions, such as word rarity, that are divorced from syllable counts.

17. The spaCy algorithm is selected over alternatives, such as Natural Language Toolkit or CoreNLP, because it is highly accurate and was trained on a wide range of texts that make it more likely to correctly identify parts of speech in a variety of documents (Choi, Tetreault, and Stent 2015). For example, it is common to train NLP algorithms on newspaper texts only, limiting their validity for other types of texts.

18. I added to this one additional disfluency mentioned in my interviews: "badger" (the person who issues visitor's badges in an EU institutions).

19. Wordfish was developed to measure the left-right positions of German political parties over time but has since been used more widely to estimate the positions of political texts.

20. For a detailed discussion of this topic, see also *World Englishes* Volume 36, Issue 3, a special "Forum on English in a Post-Brexit European Union."

21. In personal communications, both DG Interpretation (on March 22, 2019) and DG LINC in the European Parliament (February 4, 2019) stated that they fully expect English to remain an official language and that it will continue to be paid for out of the EU budget. In what might be interpreted as a first step toward ensuring the continued financing of interpretation from and into English, in December 2018 the Council created a "technical interpreting envelope" aimed at funding the languages currently used as "pivot languages," most importantly Eng-

lish. This "technical envelope" will be financed through unused funds for delegates' travel expenses. EC Interpretation (personal communication, SCIC.02—Strategic Communication and Outreach, DG Interpretation, European Commission, March 22, 2019).

22. Even senior MEP Danuta Hübner, who made a splash in Brussels in June 2016 by suggesting that English might be dropped after Brexit, was ultimately confident that English would remain an official language (Nielsen 2016).

23. Mac Giolla Chriost and Bonotti (2018) present a normative case for English as the lingua franca of a post-Brexit EU.

24. Over time, reliance on a "third party's language" may even lead to the development of "a sense of collective community," as Liu suggests in reference to non-EU cases (Liu 2015, 16).

25. This proposition relates to the debate among academic commentators about the "ownership" of English in multilingual contexts. Proponents of the concept of "English as a lingua franca," for example, maintain that "if 'English' in the EU were conceptualized not as ENL (English as a native language) and therefore the 'property' of the British and the Irish, but as ELF and thus the property of all its users, English native speakers would lose their privilege in ELF communication, and EU citizens would not need to feel that they are disadvantaged by succumbing to the 'owners' of the language (Seidlhofer 2011, 55). Others question this premise and the utility of "re-labeling" English as ELF (Gazzola and Grin 2013).

26. McAuliffe, in fact, suggests that there exists a "Court French" in the Court of Justice (McAuliffe 2011, 2013a, 2013b).

CHAPTER 6

1. Creech (2005) offers a discussion of challenges in the interpretation process, which reflects many of the points highlighted by my respondents.

2. Differences not only exist between speakers of different nationalities, however, but also between speakers with different functions. One counselor in a Permanent Representation finds members of the EP to be more expressive and less straightforward than people in the Council, which creates different challenges for the interpreter (#61).

3. The respondent appears to be right in assuming that users of interpretation services seem to care less about interpreters accurately conveying the tone and feelings of a speaker, which just over 50 percent of MEPs who responded to an internal customer satisfaction survey conducted in March 2014 in the EP considered to be "important" or "very important," compared to well over 90 percent of respondents who said the same about conveying the speaker's message clearly and accurately and about using correct and appropriate terminology. The sample of respondents of this internal survey was likely nonrepresentative, however, so its findings have to be taken as indicative at best.

4. Other examples are that the French word "*délai*" means deadline, not delay; "*adéquat*" means suitable, not adequate; "*actuel*" means current, not actual; and "*compléter*" means supplement, not complete (Wagner, Bech, and Martínez 2014).

5. What the respondent said in the original German is "da werden Sachen einfach ein bißchen abgeschliffen."

Notes to Pages 167–72 229

6. It helps that prepared statements are sometimes made available to interpreters in advance (#44), often at their explicit request (#18). One counselor in a Permanent Representation, for example, acknowledged that "if you want to have good interpreters you have to work with them" (#62). Another respondent in the Council described how: "I try to talk to the interpreters before the meeting, to give them my papers in which I have our national position, or simply tell them which direction we are going . . . [And] I try to speak slowly" (#61, also 67, 74). But frequently notes are not shared in advance, because some people are less sensitive than others to the needs of the interpreters, or because an interpretation assignment is changed at the last minute (#6, 44).

7. The problem was recognized by the former Secretary-General of the EP, Klaus Welle, who urged MEPs to slow down for the sake of interpreters (BBC 2016). Interpreters can also hit a button in the plenary that indicates to the EP President or whoever else is chairing the meeting that they have difficulty following (#14).

8. Wagner, Bech, and Martínez (2014, 64) emphasize that the use of puns also creates difficulties for translators, not just interpreters.

9. A good case in point, in this regard, is one of the most (in)famous moments in the history of the EP. In 2003, the then prime minister of Italy, Silvio Berlusconi, likened Martin Schulz to a concentration camp guard during a speech before the EP. Schulz likely would not have appreciated only finding out about the insult afterwards. One of my respondents suggested, however, that more was made of the incident than Berlusconi's words merited. "I remember that very well," he recounted, "you needed to know Italian really well, you needed to know Italian culture because I don't think they were referring to concentration camp guards. Actually, he was referring to a TV series. He was referring to a character in a TV series who was a concentration camp guard, and he actually said the name. So that is very difficult. If Italian is not your first language and you heard it, and you say 'you remind me of a concentration camp guard,' that is very different than what he intended to say" (#13).

10. See also Robinson (2014b) and Wagner, Bech, and Martínez (2014) for discussions of difficulties with translation in the EU, which highlight some of the same problems as those emphasized by my respondents.

11. A translation job that seems especially difficult a priori, however, can have the positive effect of making translators more careful and conscious, and the resulting translation more reliable, according to a French translator who maintained that "when we translate from Hungarian, we really pay more attention because the language is perhaps more demanding" (#33).

12. An interesting side note, in this regard, is that translation can also be used to create the opposite effect: rather than establish similarities, it has been used to create "difference where there is none to be found" in the former Yugoslavia (Longinovic 2011, 288).

13. Robertson (2010c, 4) also discusses words changing their meaning over time. Robertson (2011, 63–64) emphasizes that it can be particularly confusing when a new term is used in one language but terminology stays the same in others.

14. But it is not only translators who use Latin or Greek terms; policymakers may also prefer the use of a Latin term if it avoids confusion (#61).

230 *Notes to Pages 172–83*

15. When in doubt, language service providers likely err on the side of caution. In the Court of Justice, for example, "the person that makes the revisions of the text thinks, 'oh, no, no, they didn't want to innovate on language.' They will assume that you want to say the same that was said in the previous judgment. And so they will replace what might have intended to be something innovative by the same formula that has always been used" (#84).

16. Another respondent discussed the difficulty of translating "microeconomic conditionality" into one of the southern European languages, a term that not only lacks an obvious equivalent but which, on top of it, became highly politically charged during the euro crisis. She explained, "We've actually discussed this in the terminology group, because the word 'conditionality' means nothing, does not exist, so we had to find a way to decide on a fixed translation of the word. . . . What is it? Is it a condition? Is it something that means that you have to choose? . . . It's a made-up English word that would not really mean anything outside of the EU." (#19)

17. McAuliffe (2013b) and Robertson (2010c) make similar observations, while Tosi (2003, 2005, 2013)—taking a linguistic rather than a legal perspective in evaluating the quality of EU translation—offers a critical account.

18. Van Els similarly explains that "people who . . . are aware of the horrendously difficult task that confronts the translator . . . modify their linguistic usage, consciously or subconsciously, in order to oblige the translator. For example, they speak in short sentences, avoid metaphorical expressions and jokes, and tend towards less oblique forms of linguistic usage, all of which often leads to a lack of essential nuances" (van Els 2003, 336).

19. Some newcomers in Brussels may not yet recognize the need to speak for interpretation. One respondent described that "you have some people who are inexperienced, who come for the first time. . . . They speak very fast and then it gets lost a little bit in translation" (#73).

20. In the end, the texts that are created reflect their "multiple permutations" (McAuliffe 2011, 97), having been written and translated into and out of up to 24 different languages by those who draft the original proposal, the lawmakers who negotiate it (with the help of interpreters, as needed), the lawyer-linguists who offer assistance, and the translators who help create the different language versions. The final language versions of EU legislation are thus simply not the product of monolingual drafting and subsequent translation, but of multilingual conception, deliberation, contestation, negotiation, revision, translation, and legal-linguistic finalization.

21. One respondent in the EP suggested that policymakers were initially reluctant to accept the presence of lawyer-linguists in meetings (#79).

22. Others similarly highlight that the "contradictions and ambiguities that legislative bargaining and compromise create" are routinely left to be resolved at the administrative level (Brodkin 2013, 144), and that passing on "intractable problems" constitutes "a typical mechanism of legislative conflict resolution" (Lipsky 1980, 41).

23. Wright (2000, 172) offers an example of purposeful constructive ambiguity, namely a circumstance in which the French "*droits*" was translated as "worker's involvement" instead of "worker's rights" to appease the UK Conservatives. The anecdote also appears to date back about 40 years, however.

24. Calculated intentional ambiguity may be more likely to occur when we look beyond the creation of legislation, however. One EP official, for example, indicated that "maybe I can be a bit more open to [the] suggestion [of calculated intended ambiguity] if you think of resolutions. . . . It is easier in that context to leave a grey zone in many languages" (#39). Respondents in the Council discussed how European Council documents, especially the Conclusions of meetings of the heads of state and government, are carefully calibrated (#70) and may include calculated intentional ambiguities (#61). The situation may also differ across policy areas, according to a Council official, who suggested that in a field like foreign affairs, which remains largely under the control of the member states, ambiguous language is more common than in matter relating to the EU single market. Regarding the latter, "member states want it to be crystal clear, they want it to be very specific, because they don't want any kind of market advantage to go to their fellow member state next door. So they will pay attention to how things are translated and they will spend a lot of time making sure that the terms are the right ones and that expressions are not ambiguous" (#20).

CHAPTER 7

1. McAuliffe (2013b) makes a similar argument about a single EU legal language being a fiction.
2. Public Information Service, General Secretariat of the Council of the EU, personal communication, April 5, 2019.
3. DG Translation, European Commission, personal communication, March 1, 2019.
4. DG for Translation, European Parliament, personal communication, February 27, 2019; Public Information Service, General Secretariat of the Council of the European Union, personal communication, April 5, 2019.
5. Rule 169.6 of the EP's Rules of Procedures stipulates that "Amendments shall be put to the vote only after they have been made available in all the official languages, unless Parliament decides otherwise. Parliament may not decide otherwise if at least 40 Members object. Parliament shall avoid taking decisions which would place Members who use a particular language at an unacceptable disadvantage." One long-time participant in EP lawmaking explained that although the rule specifies that 40 MEPs must object, in practice a single objection would likely suffice because speakers of the "smaller" languages and those who happen to be opposed to the relevant provision would eagerly support the blocking of the vote (#39).
6. Boroditsky, Schmidt, and Phillips (2003, 71–72) provide a useful discussion of language and culture.
7. These conclusions challenge Wright's suggestion that multilingualism makes compromise less likely because it "prohibits quiet negotiation and deal making" (Wright 2007, 160).
8. The Irish ultimately signed off on the Lisbon Treaty in a second referendum.
9. As Arturo Tosi puts it, the prevailing "lexical vagueness and weak logical connections" in EU communications "spread a sense of mechanistic virtuality that makes the voice of Europe sound awkward, abstract, and completely distant from any language spoken in everyday life" (Tosi 2005, 385).

APPENDIX

1. This section relies extensively on European Parliament 2017, European Commission 2010a, and Stefaniak 2013.

2. See Robinson 2014a for a detailed description of the drafting process in the Commission.

3. In the translation process, "previous translations of identical sentences, passages, etc. are without exception followed verbatim in legal texts" (Dollerup 2001, 281).

4. Member states can request active or passive interpretation for their official languages for these preparatory meetings. The costs are offset against annual "envelopes" for each language in the Council budget. If the costs exceed the allocated amount, member states can choose to request interpretation at their own expense. If the allocated amount is not used up, 66 percent of the unused funds are transferred to the member states' travel expense budget, or the funds can be used toward interpretation in the subsequent budget period.

5. The Commission provides interpretation for a small number of committees in the Council.

6. This description of the finalization process draws heavily from Robinson (2012).

7. Any judge or Advocate General may also request that "anything said or written in the course of the proceedings before the Court" be translated into any official language (Rules of Procedure of the Court of Justice, Article 39), but that choice has effectively been waived so as not to overwhelm the workload of the translation services; "the judges must work solely in French" (McAuliffe 2013a, 485).

Bibliography

Abélès, Marc. 1999. "Multiculturalism and Multilingualism in the European Institutions." In *Which Languages for Europe? Report of the Conference Held in Oegstgeest, The Netherlands, 9–11 October, 1999*, edited by Nikki Bos, 111–17. Amsterdam: European Cultural Foundation.

Adams, Tim. 2010. "Can Google Break the Computer Language Barriers." *The Guardian*, December 18.

Addis, Adeno. 2001. "Cultural Integrity and Political Unity: The Politics of Language in Multilingual States." *Arizona State Law Journal* 33: 719–89.

Adida, Claire L., Karen E. Ferree, Daniel N. Posner, and Amanda L. Robinson. 2016. "Who's Asking? Interviewer Coethnicity Effects in African Survey Data." *Comparative Political Studies* 49, no. 12: 1630–60.

Almond, Gabriel A. 1956. "Comparative Political Systems." *Journal of Politics* 18: 391–409.

Alesina, Alberto F., Arnaud Devleeschauwer, William Easterly, Sergio Kurlat, and Romain T. Wacziarg. 2003. "Fractionalization." *Journal of Economic Growth* 8, no. 2: 155–94.

Ammon, Ulrich. 2006. "Language Conflicts in the European Union." *International Journal of Applied Linguistics* 16, no. 3: 319–38.

Ammon, Ulrich. 2010. "Why Accepting One Common Language plus Preserving All the Other Languages as National or Minority Languages Would Not Solve the European Language Conflicts." In *Diskurs—Politik—Identität/ Discourse—Politics—Identity. Festschrift Für Ruth Wodak*, edited by Rudolf de Cillia, Helmut Gruber, Michał Krzyżanowski, and Florian Menz, 229–34. Tübingen: Stauffenburg.

Ammon, Ulrich, and Jan Kruse. 2013. "Does Translation Support Multilingualism in the EU? Promises and Reality—the Example of German." *International Journal of Applied Linguistics* 23, no. 1: 15–30.

Anderson, Benedict. 1983. *Imagined Communities: Reflections on the Origin and Spread of Nationalism*. London: Verso.

Bibliography

Anderson, Benedict R O'G. 1990. *Language and Power: Exploring Political Cultures in Indonesia*. Ithaca: Cornell University Press.

Anderson, Christopher J., and Aida Paskeviciute. 2006. "How Ethnic and Linguistic Heterogeneity Influence the Prospects for Civil Society: A Comparative Study of Citizenship Behavior." *Journal of Politics* 68, no. 4: 783–802.

Archibugi, Daniele. 2005. "The Language of Democracy: Vernacular or Esperanto? A Comparison between the Multiculturalist and Cosmopolitan Perspectives." *Political Studies* 53, no. 3: 537–55.

Arnull, Anthony. 2018. "The Court of Justice Then, Now and Tomorrow." In *The Court of Justice of the European Union: Multidisciplinary Perspectives*, edited by Matthias Derlen and Johan Lindholm, 1–16. Oxford: Hart Publishing.

Arnull, Anthony. 2019. "The Working Language of the CJEU: Time for a Change?" Institute of European Law Working Paper 01/2019.

Athanassiou, Phoebus. 2006. "The Application of Multilingualism in the European Union Context." European Central Bank, Legal Working Paper Series, No. 2, February.

Aziz, Anealka, Chan Yuen Fook, and Zubaida Alsree. 2010. "Computational Text Analysis: A More Comprehensive Approach to Determine the Readability of Reading Materials." *Advances in Language and Literary Studies* 1, no. 2: 200–219.

Baaij, Cornelis J. W. 2012a. "Fifty Years of Multilingual Interpretation in the European Union." In *The Oxford Handbook of Language and Law*, edited by Lawrence M. Solan and Peter M. Tiersma. Oxford: Oxford University Press.

Baaij, Cornelis J. W. 2012b. *The Role of Legal Translation in Legal Harmonization*. Alphen aan den Rijn: Wolters Kluwer.

Baaij, Cornelis J. W. 2018. *Legal Integration and Language Diversity: Rethinking Translation in EU Lawmaking*. Oxford: Oxford University Press.

Balič, Tina. 2016a. "Attitudes towards Euro-English in a European Union Institution." *ELOPE: English Language Overseas Perspectives and Enquiries* 13, no. 2: 131–52.

Balič, Tina. 2016b. "Euro-English in the European Commission: Language Use and Attitudes." Doctoral dissertation, Univerza v Mariboru, Slovenia.

Ban, Carolyn. 2009. "'Sorry, I Don't Speak French': The Impact of Enlargement on Language Use within the European Commission." In *Walk the Talk: Integrating Languages and Cultures in the Professions*, edited by Michel Gueldry. Lewiston, NY: Edward Mellen Press.

Ban, Carolyn. 2013. *Management and Culture in an Enlarged European Commission*. London: Palgrave Macmillan.

Bánhegyi, Mátyás. 2014. "Translation and Political Discourse." *Acta Universitatis Sapientiae, Philologica* 6, no. 2: 139–58.

Barbier, Jean-Claude. 2015. "English Speaking, a Hidden Political Factor of European Politics and European Integration." *Politiche Sociali/Social Policies* 2: 185–218.

Barbier, Jean-Claude. 2018. "European Integration and the Variety of Languages." In *The Politics of Multilingualism: Europeanisation, Globalisation and Linguistic Governance*, edited by François Grin and Peter A. Kraus, 333–57. Amsterdam: John Benjamins Publishing.

Baumgartner, Frank R., and Bryan D. Jones. 2009. *Agendas and Instability in American Politics*. Chicago: University of Chicago Press.

BBC. 2016. "Fast-Talking MEPs Urged to Slow down for Interpreters." February 5.

BBC. 2017. "Brexit: English Language 'Losing Importance'—EU's Juncker." May 5.

Beaton, Morven. 2007. "Interpreted Ideologies in Institutional Discourse: The Case of the European Parliament." *The Translator* 13, no. 2: 271–96.

Bellier, Irene. 1997. "The Commission as an Actor: An Anthropologists's View." In *Participation and Policy-Making in the European Union*, edited by Helen Wallace and Alasdair R. Young, 91–115. Oxford: Clarendon.

Bellier, Irene. 2002. "European Identity, Institutions and Languages in the Context of the Enlargement." *Journal of Language and Politics* 1: 85–114.

Bengoetxea, Joxerramom. 2016. "Multilingual and Multicultural Legal Reasoning: The European Court of Justice." In *Linguistic Diversity and European Democracy*, edited by Anne Lise Kjær and Silvia Adamo, 97–122. New York: Routledge.

Benoit, Kenneth, Kevin Munger, and Arthur Spirling. 2019. "Measuring and Explaining Political Sophistication Through Textual Complexity." *American Journal of Political Science* 63, no. 2: 491–508.

Bereby-Meyer, Yoella, Sayuri Hayakawa, Shaul Shalvi, Joanna D. Corey, Albert Costa, and Boaz Keysar. 2018. "Honesty Speaks a Second Language." *Topics in Cognitive Science*, 1–12.

Bernhofer, Juliana, Francesco Constantini, and Matija Kovacic. 2015. "Risk Attitudes, Investment Behavior and Linguistic Variation." University Ca' Foscari of Venice, Dept. of Economics Research Paper Series No. 34/15.

Berns, Margie. 1995. "English in the European Union." *English Today* 11, no. 3: 3–11.

Berns, Margie. 2017. "Breaking Away and Building Anew." *World Englishes* 36, no. 3: 328–29.

Berthoud, Anne-Claude, François Grin, and Georges Lüdi. 2013. "Conclusion." In *Exploring the Dynamics of Multilingualism: The DYLAN Project*, edited by Anne-Claude Berthoud, François Grin, and Georges Lüdi, 429–36. Amsterdam: John Benjamins Publishing.

Beveridge, Ross. 2017. "The (Ontological) Politics in Depoliticisation Debates: Three Lenses on the Decline of the Political." *Political Studies Review* 15, no. 4: 589–600.

Bhatia, Tej K., and William C. Ritchie. 2008. "The Bilingual Mind and Linguistic Creativity." *Journal of Creative Communications* 3, no. 1: 5–21.

Biel, Łucja. 2007. "Translation of Multilingual EU Law as a Sub-Genre of Legal-Translation." In *Court Interpreting and Legal Translation in the Enlarged Europe*, edited by Danuta Kierzkowska, 144–63. Warsaw: Translegis.

Bilaniuk, Laada. 1994. *Contested Tongues: Language Politics and Cultural Correction in Ukraine*. Ithaca: Cornell University Press.

Black, Ian. 2004. "Euro Babble." *The Guardian*, April 22, 2004.

Bobek, Michal. 2009. "Corrigenda in the Official Journal of the European Union: Community Law as Quicksand." *European Law Review* 34, no. 6: 950–62.

Bobek. Michal. 2016. "The Multilingualism of the European Union Law in the

National Courts: Beyond the Textbooks." In *Linguistic Diversity and European Democracy*, edited by Anne Lise Kjær and Silvia Adamo, 123–42. New York: Routledge.

Bormann, Nils-Christian, Lars-Erik Cederman, and Manuel Vogt. 2017. "Language, Religion, and Ethnic Civil War." *Journal of Conflict Resolution* 61, no. 4: 744–71.

Boroditsky, Lera. 2001. "Does Language Shape Thought? Mandarin and English Speakers' Conception of Time." *Cognitive Psychology* 43, no. 1: 1–22.

Boroditsky, Lera, Lauren Schmidt, and Webb Phillips. 2003. "Sex, Syntax, and Semantics." In *Language in Mind: Advances in the Study of Language and Thought*, edited by Dedre Gentner and Susan Goldin-Meadow, 61–79. Cambridge, MA: MIT Press.

Bourdieu, Pierre. 1992. *Language and Symbolic Power*. Cambridge: Polity Press.

Bresnahan, Mary Jiang, Rie Ohashi, Reiko Nebashi, Wen Ying Liu, and Sachiyo Morinaga Shearmana Sherman. 2002. "Attitudinal and Affective Response toward Accented English." *Language & Communication* 22: 171–85.

Brock, William A., and Steven N. Durlauf. 2001. "Growth Empirics and Reality." *World Bank Economic Review* 15: 229–72.

Brodkin, Evelyn Z. 2013. "Commodification, Inclusion, or What? Workfare in Everyday Organizational Life." In *Work and the Welfare State*, edited by Evelyn Z. Brodkin and Gregory Marston. Washington, DC: Georgetown University Press.

Brown, L. Neville. 1981. "The Linguistic Regime of the European Communities: Some Problems of Law and Language." *Valparaiso University Law Review* 15, no. 2: 319–41.

Bugarski, Ranko. 2009. "English in European Institutions: Some Observations." *Belgrade English Language and Literature Studies* 1: 109–17.

Buller, Jim, Pinar Dönmez, Adam Standring, and Matthew Wood, eds. 2019. *Comparing Strategies of (De)Politicisation in Europe: Governance, Resistance and Anti-Politics*. London: Palgrave Macmillan.

Calster, Geert van. 1997. "The EU's Tower of Babel—The Interpretation by the European Court of Justice of Equally Authentic Texts Drafted in More than One Official Language." *Yearbook of European Law* 17, no. 1: 363–93.

Capoccia, Giovanni. 2016. "Critical Junctures." In *The Oxford Handbook of Historical Institutionalism*, edited by Orfeo Fioretos, Tulia G. Falleti, and Adam Sheingate, 89–106. Oxford: Oxford University Press.

Cardinal, Linda, and Selma K. Sonntag, eds. 2015. *State Traditions and Language Regimes*. Montreal: McGill–Queen's University Press.

Catalinac, Amy. 2016. "From Pork to Policy: The Rise of Programmatic Campaigning in Japanese Elections." *Journal of Politics* 78, no. 1: 1–18.

Caviedes, Alexander. 2003. "The Role of Language in Nation-Building within the European Union." *Dialectical Anthropology* 27: 249–68.

Chaudenson, Robert. 2001. "Rapport de Synthèse." In *L'Europe Parlera-t-Elle Anglais Demain?*, edited by Robert Chaudenson, 139–57. Paris: L'Harmattan.

Chen, M. Keith. 2013. "The Effect of Language on Economic Behavior: Evidence from Savings Rates, Health Behaviors, and Retirement Assets." *American Economic Review* 103, no. 2: 690–731.

Bibliography

Chilton, Stephen. 1988. "Defining Political Culture." *Western Political Quarterly* 41, no. 3: 419–45.

Choi, Jinho D., Joel Tetreault, and Amanda Stent. 2015. "It Depends: Dependency Parser Comparison Using a Web-Based Evaluation Tool." In Proceedings of the 53rd Annual Meeting of the Association for Computational Linguistics and the 7th International Joint Conference on Natural Language Processing, 387–96.

Christiansen, Pia Vanting. 2006. "Language Policy in the European Union: European/English/Elite/Equal/Esperanto Union?" *Language Problems and Language Planning* 30, no. 1: 21–44.

Cipolletti, Heather, Steven McFarlane, and Christine Weissglass. 2016. "The Moral Foreign-Language Effect." *Philosophical Psychology* 29, no. 1: 23–40.

Clark, Stephen, and Julian Priestley. 2012. *Europe's Parliament: People, Places, Politics.* London: John Harper.

Climent-Ferrando, Vicent. 2016. "Linguistic Neoliberalism in the European Union. Politics and Policies of the EU's Approach to Multilingualism." *Revista de Llengua i Dret/Journal of Lanuguage and Law*, no. 66: 1–14.

Cogo, Alessia, and Jennifer Jenkins. 2010. "English as a Lingua Franca in Europe: A Mismatch between Policy and Practice." *European Journal of Language Policy* 2, no. 2: 271–94.

Corey, Joanna D., Sayuri Hayakawa, Alice Foucart, Melina Aparici, Juan Botella, Albert Costa, and Boaz Keysar. 2017. "Our Moral Choices Are Foreign to Us." *Journal of Experimental Psychology: Learning, Memory, and Cognition* 43, no. 7: 1109–28.

Cosmidou, Olga. 2011. "The European Parliament: A Temple of Multilingualism, a Pioneer in Interpreting 'Exploits.'" *Gamma: Journal of Theory and Criticism* 19: 129–32.

Costa, Albert, Jon Andoni Duñabeitia, and Boaz Keysar. 2019. "Language Context and Decision-Making: Challenges and Advances." *Quarterly Journal of Experimental Psychology* 72, no. 1: 1–2.

Costa, Albert, Alice Foucart, Inbal Arnon, Melina Aparici, and Jose Apesteguia. 2014a. "'Piensa' Twice: On the Foreign Language Effect in Decision Making." *Cognition* 130, no. 2: 236–54.

Costa, Albert, Alice Foucart, Sayuri Hayakawa, Melina Aparici, Jose Apesteguia, Joy Heafner, and Boaz Keysar. 2014b. "Your Morals Depend on Language." *PLoS ONE* 9, no. 4: 1–7.

Costa, Albert, Marc-Lluís Vives, and Joanna D. Corey. 2017. "On Language Processing Shaping Decision Making." *Current Directions in Psychological Science* 26, no. 2: 146–51.

Council of the European Union. 2015. *Handbook of the Presidency of the Council of the European Union.* Luxembourg: Publications Office of the European Union.

Court of Auditors. 2005. "Court of Auditors Special Report No. 5/2005: Interpretation Expenditure Incurred by the Parliament, the Commission and the Council, Together with the Institutions' Replies." Luxembourg: Court of Auditors.

Creech, Richard L. 2005. *Law and Language in the European Union: The Paradox of a Babel "United in Diversity."* Groningen: Europa Law Publishing.

Crystal, David. 1999. "The Future of Englishes." *English Today* 15, no. 2: 10–20.

Daniel, William T. 2015. *Career Behaviour and the European Parliament*. Oxford: Oxford University Press.

Daniel, William T., and Shawna K. Metzger. 2018. "Within or between Jobs? Determinants of Membership Volatility in the European Parliament, 1979–2014." *Journal of Legislative Studies* 24, no. 1: 90–108.

Danziger, Shai, and Robert Ward. 2010. "Language Changes Implicit Associations Between Ethnic Groups and Evaluation in Bilinguals." *Psychological Science* 21, no. 6: 799–800.

De Clerq, Orphéé, and Véronique Hoste. 2016. "All Mixed up? Finding the Optimal Feature Set for General Readability Prediction and Its Application to English and Dutch." *Computational Linguistics* 42, no. 3: 457–90.

De Groot, Gerard-René, and Conrad J. P. Laer. 2006. "The Dubious Quality of Legal Dictionaries." *International Journal of Legal Information* 34, no. 1: 65–86.

De Swaan, Abram. 1999. "The European Language Constellation." In *Which Languages for Europe? Report of the Conference Held in Oegstgeest, The Netherlands, 9–11 October, 1999*, edited by Nikki Bos, 13–23. Amsterdam: European Cultural Foundation.

De Swaan, Abram. 2001. *Words of the World: The Global Language System*. Cambridge: Polity.

De Swaan, Abram. 2007. "The Language Predicament of the EU Since the Enlargements." *Sociolinguistica* 21, no. 1: 1–21.

de Vries, Catherine E. 2007. "Sleeping Giant: Fact or Fairytale? How European Integration Affects National Elections." *European Union Politics* 8, no. 3: 363–85.

de Wilde, Peter, Anna Leuphold, and Henning Schmidtke. 2016. "Introduction: The Differentiated Politicisation of European Governance." *West European Politics* 39, no. 1: 3–22.

Der Spiegel. 2015. "Bundestagsabgeordnete Wollen Dokumente Auf Deutsch," August 7.

Deutsch, Karl W. 1942. "The Trend of European Nationalism: The Language Aspect." *American Political Science Review* 36, no. 3: 533–41.

Deutsch, Karl. W. 1953. *Nationalism and Social Communication: An Inquiry into the Foundations of Nationality*. New York: Wiley & Sons.

Díaz-Lago, Marcos, and Helena Matute. 2019. "Thinking in a Foreign Language Reduces the Causality Bias." *Quarterly Journal of Experimental Psychology* 72, no. 1: 41–51.

Directorate-General for Translation, European Commission. 2011. *Lingua Franca: Chimera or Reality? Dictus, 2011*. Riga: Dictus.

Doczekalska, Agnieszka. 2009. "Drafting or Translation—Production of Multilingual Legal Texts." In *Translation Issues in Language and Law*, edited by Frances Olsen, Alexander Lorz, and Dieter Stein, 116–35. Basingstoke: Palgrave Macmillan.

Doerr, Nicole. 2009. "Language and Democracy 'in Movement': Multilingualism and the Case of the European Social Forum Process." *Social Movement Studies* 8, no. 2: 149–65.

Doerr, Nicole. 2012. "Translating Democracy: How Activists in the European Social Forum Practice Multilingual Deliberation." *European Political Science Review* 4, no. 3: 361–84.

Dollerup, Cay. 2001. "Complexities of EU Language Work." *Perspectives: Studies in Translatology* 9, no. 4: 271–92. https://doi.org/10.1080/0907676X.2001.9961424

Duflou, Veerle. 2016. *Be(Com)Ing a Conference Interpreter: An Ethnography of EU Interpreters as a Professional Community.* Amsterdam: John Benjamins Publishing.

Easterly, William, and Ross Levine. 1997. "Africa's Growth Tragedy: Policies and Ethnic Divisions." *Quarterly Journal of Economics* 112: 1203–50.

The Economist. 2013. "Languages of Diplomacy: Towards a Fairer Distribution." April 2.

The Economist. 2014. "Charlemagne: The Globish-Speaking Union." May 24.

The Economist. 2016. "Of Two Minds." April 9.

The Economist. 2017. "Britain Is Leaving the EU, but Its Language Will Stay." May 13.

Edwards, John. 1985. *Language, Society and Identity.* Oxford: Basil Blackwell.

Esman, Milton J. 1992. "The State and Language Policy." *International Political Science Review* 13, no. 4: 381–96.

European Commission. 2005. "A New Framework Strategy for Multilingualism." Commission of the European Communities, Brussels, Belgium.

European Commission. 2010a. *Study on Lawmaking in the EU Multilingual Environment.* Luxembourg: Publication Office of the European Union.

European Commission. 2010b. *Translation at the European Commission: A History.* Luxembourg: Office for Official Publications of the European Communities.

European Commission. 2016a. "2016 Annual Activity Report, Directorate-General for Interpretation." Brussels: European Commission.

European Commission. 2016b. "2016 Annual Activity Report, Directorate-General for Translation." Brussels: European Commission.

European Parliament. 2004. "Code of Conduct on Multilingualism." Adopted by the Bureau on April 19; Brussels: European Parliament.

European Parliament. 2014. "Code of Conduct on Multilingualism." Adopted by the Bureau on June 16; Brussels: European Parliament.

European Parliament. 2017. "Handbook on the Ordinary Legislative Procedure." Brussels: European Parliament. http://www.epgenpro.europarl.europa.eu/static/ordinary-legislative-procedure/en/ordinary-legislative-procedure/handbook-on-the-ordinary-legislative-procedure.html

European Union. 2017. "Interpreting and Translating for Europe." Luxembourg: Publications Office of the European Union.

Fan, Samantha P., Zoe Liberman, Boaz Keysar, and Katherine D. Kinzler. 2015. "The Exposure Advantage: Early Exposure to a Multilingual Environment Promotes Effective Communication." *Psychological Science* 26, no. 7: 1–8.

Fausey, Caitlin M., and Lera Boroditsky. 2011. "Who Dunnit? Cross-Linguistic Differences in Eye-Witness Memory." *Psychonomic Bulletin Review* 18, no. 1: 150–57.

Fausey, Caitlin M., Bria L. Long, Aya Inamori, and Lera Boroditsky. 2010. "Constructing Agency: The Role of Language." *Frontiers in Cultural Psychology* 1: 1–11.

Fearon, James D., and David D. Laitin. 1996. "Explaining Interethnic Cooperation." *American Political Science Review* 90, no. 4: 715–35.

Fenno, Richard F. 1978. *Homestyle: House Members in Their Districts.* Boston: Little, Brown.

Bibliography

Fidrmuc, Jan. 2011. "The Economics of Multilingualism in the EU." Economics and Finance Working Paper Series, Brunel University, Working Paper No. 11-04.

Fidrmuc, Jan, and Victor Ginsburgh. 2007. "Languages in the European Union: The Quest for Equality and Its Cost." *European Economic Review* 51, no. 6: 1351–69.

Fidrmuc, Jan, Victor Ginsburgh, and Shlomo Weber. 2006. "Economic Challenges of Multilingual Societies." Paper presented at Panel Meeting of Economic Policy. Vienna.

Fidrmuc, Jan, Victor Ginsburgh, and Shlomo Weber. 2009. "Voting on the Choice of Core Languages in the European Union." *European Journal of Political Economy* 25, no. 1: 56–62.

Flesch, Rudolf. 1948. "A New Readability Yardstick." *American Journal of Political Science* 32, no. 3: 221–33.

Flinders, Matthew, and Jim Buller. 2006. "Depoliticization, Democracy, and Arena Shifting." In *Autonomy and Regulation: Coping with Agencies in the Modern State*, edited by Tom Christensen and Per Lægreid, 53–80. Northampton, MA: Edward Elgar.

Flora, Peter, Stein Kuhnle, and Derek Urwin, eds. 1999. *State Formation, Nation-Building, and Mass Politics in Europe: The Theory of Stein Rokkan*. Oxford: Oxford University Press.

Follesdal, Andreas, and Simon Hix. 2006. "Why There Is a Democratic Deficit in the EU: A Response to Majone and Moravcsik." *Journal of Common Market Studies* 44, no. 3: 533–62.

Forchtner, Bernhard. 2014. "Multilingualism in the European Commission: Combining an Observer and a Participant Perspective." In *Multilingual Encounters in Europe's Institutional Spaces: Advances in Sociolinguistics*, edited by Johann W. Unger, Michał Krzyżanowski, and Ruth Wodak, 147–69. London: Bloomsbury.

Fuhrman, Orly, Kelly McCormich, Eva Chen, Heidi Jiang, Dingfang Shu, Shuaimei Mao, and Lera Boroditsky. 2011. "How Linguistic and Cultural Forces Shape Conceptions of Time: English and Mandarin Time in 3D." *Cognitive Science* 35: 1305–28.

Gal, Susan. 2006. "Language, Its Stakes, and Its Effects." In *Oxford Handbook of Contextual Political Analysis*, edited by Robert E. Goodin and Charles Tilly, 376–91. Oxford: Oxford University Press.

Gambaro, Antonio. 2007. "Interpretation of Multilingual Legislative Texts." *Electronic Journal of Comparative Law* 11, no. 3: 1–20.

Gao, Shan, Ondrej Zika, Robert D. Rogers, and Guillaume Thierry. 2015. "Second Language Feedback Abolishes the 'Hot Hand' Effect during Even-Probability Gambling." *Journal of Neuroscience* 35, no. 15: 5983–89.

Gardner, Jeremy. 2016. "Misused English Words and Expressions in EU Publications." European Court of Auditors.

Gazzola, Michele. 2006. "Managing Multilingualism in the European Union: Language Policy Evaluation for the European Parliament." *Language Policy* 5, no. 4: 393–417.

Gazzola, Michele. 2016a. "Is the European Commission's de Facto Language Regime Effective? An Empirical Assessment." Paper presented to the 24th World Congress of Political Science, Poznań, Poland.

Gazzola, Michele. 2016b. "Multilingual Communication for Whom? Language Policy and Fairness in the European Union." *European Union Politics* 17, no. 4: 546–69.

Gazzola, Michele, and François Grin. 2013. "Is ELF More Effective and Fair than Translation? An Evaluation of the EU's Multilingual Regime." *International Journal of Applied Linguistics* 23, no. 1: 93–107.

Geipel, Janet, Constantinos Hadjichristidis, and Luca Surian. 2015a. "How Foreign Language Shapes Moral Judgment." *Journal of Experimental Social Psychology* 59: 8–17.

Geipel, Janet, Constantinos Hadjichristidis, and Luca Surian. 2015b. "The Foreign Language Effect on Moral Judgment: The Role of Emotions and Norms." *PLoS ONE* 10, no. 7: 1–17.

Geipel, Janet, Constantinos Hadjichristidis, and Luca Surian. 2016. "Foreign Language Affects the Contribution of Intentions and Outcomes to Moral Judgment." *Cognition* 154: 34–39.

Gibová, Klaudia. 2009. "EU Translation as the Language of a Reunited Europe Reconsidered." In *Language, Literature and Culture in a Changing Transatlantic World: International Conference Proceedings*, edited by Milan Ferenčík and Juraj Horvath, 145–53. Prešov: Institute of British and American Studies, Faculty of Arts, University of Prešov, Slovak Association for the Study of English.

Ginsburgh, Victor, Ignacio Ortuno-Ortin, and Shlomo Weber. 2005. "Disenfranchisement in Linguistically Diverse Societies: The Case of the European Union." *Journal of the European Economic Association* 3: 946–65.

Ginsburgh, Victor, and Shlomo Weber. 2005. "Language Disenfranchisement in the European Union." *Journal of Common Market Studies* 43, no. 2: 273–86.

Ginsburgh, Victor, and Shlomo Weber. 2011. *How Many Languages Do We Really Need? The Economics of Linguistic Diversity*. Princeton: Princeton University Press.

Gobbo, Federico. 2005. "The European Union's Need for an International Auxiliary Language." *Journal of Universal Language* 6, no. 1: 1–28.

Gravier, Magali, and Lita Lundquist. 2016. "Getting Ready for a New Tower of Babel." In *Linguistic Diversity and European Democracy*, edited by Anne Lise Kjær and Silvia Adamo, 75–96. New York: Routledge.

Greif, Avner, and David D. Laitin. 2004. "A Theory of Endogenous Institutional Change." *American Political Science Review* 98, no. 4: 633–52.

Grimmer, Justin, and Brandon M. Stewart. 2013. "Text as Data: The Promise and Pitfalls of Automatic Content Analysis Methods for Political Texts." *Political Analysis* 21, no. 3: 267–97.

Grin, François. 1994. "The Economics of Language: Match or Mismatch?" *International Political Science Review* 15, no. 1: 25–42.

Grin, François. 1997. "Gérer Le Plurilinguisme Européen: Approche Économique Au Problème de Choix. [Managing European Multilingualism: An Economic Approach to the Problem of Choice]." *Sociolinguistica* 11: 1–15.

Grin, François, and Peter A. Kraus. 2018. "The Politics of Multilingualism: General Introduction and Overview." In *The Politics of Multilingualism: Europeanisation, Globalisation and Linguistic Governance*, edited by François Grin and Peter A. Kraus, 1–18. Amsterdam: John Benjamins Publishing.

Grin, François, and François Vaillancourt. 1997. "The Economics of Multilingualism: Overview and Analytical Framework." *Annual Review of Applied Linguistics* 17: 43–65.

Grynaviski, Eric. 2014. *Constructive Illusions: Misperceiving the Origins of International Cooperation*. Ithaca: Cornell University Press.

Grzega, Joachim. 2005. "Reflections on Concepts of English for Europe." *Journal for EuroLinguistix* 2: 44–64.

Gubbins, Paul. 2002. "Lost in Translation: EU Language Policy in an Expanded Europe." In *Beyond Boundaries: Language and Identity in Contemporary Europe*, edited by Paul Gubbins and Mike Holt, 46–58. Clevedon: Multilingual Matters.

Guggeis, Manuela. 2014. "The Role of the Council Lawyer-Linguists in Improving the Formal Quality of EU Legislation." *Theory and Practice of Legislation* 2, no. 3: 273–81.

Guggeis, Manuela, and William Robinson. 2012. "'Co-Revision': Legal-Linguistic Revision in the European Union 'Co-Decision' Process." In *The Role of Legal Translation in Legal Harmonization*, edited by Cornelis J.W. Baaij, 51–82. Alphen aan den Rijn: Wolters Kluwer.

Habermas, Jürgen. 1998. *The Inclusion of the Other*. Cambridge, MA: MIT Press.

Habermas, Jürgen. 2017. "How Much Will the Germans Have to Pay? What Macron Means for Europe." *Der Spiegel*, October 26.

Hadjichristidis, Constantinos, Janet Geipel, and Lucia Savadori. 2015. "The Effect of Foreign Language in Judgments of Risk and Benefit: The Role of Affect." *Journal of Experimental Psychology: Applied* 21, no. 2: 117–29.

Hadjichristidis, Constantinos, Janet Geipel, and Luca Surian. 2017. "How Foreign Language Affects Decisions: Rethinking the Brain-Drain Model." *Journal of International Business Studies* 48: 645–51.

Hadjichristidis, Constantinos, Janet Geipel, and Luca Surian. 2019. "Breaking Magic: Foreign Language Suppresses Superstition." *Quarterly Journal of Experimental Psychology* 72, no. 1: 18–28.

Häge, Frank M., and Nils Ringe. 2019. "Rapporteur–Shadow Rapporteur Networks in the European Parliament: The Strength of Small Numbers." *European Journal of Political Research* 58, no. 1: 209–35.

Häge, Frank M., and Nils Ringe. 2020. "Top-Down or Bottom-Up? The Selection of Shadow Rapporteurs in the European Parliament." *European Union Politics* 21, no. 4: 706–27.

Hall, Marc. 2012. "EU Parliament Makes Cuts to Translation Budget." *Euractiv. Com*, November 22, 2012.

Haselhuber, Jakob. 1991. "Erste Ergebnisse Einer Empirischen Untersuchung Zur Sprachensituation in Der EG-Kommission (Februar 1990)." *Sociolinguistica* 5, no. 1: 37–50.

Hay, Colin. 2007. *Why We Hate Politics*. Malden, MA: Polity Press.

Hayakawa, Sayuri, Albert Costa, Alice Foucart, and Boaz Keysar. 2016. "Using a Foreign Language Changes Our Choices." *Trends in Cognitive Sciences* 20, no. 11: 791–93.

Hayakawa, Sayuri, Becky Ka Ying Lau, Sophie Holtzmann, Albert Costa, and Boaz Keysar. 2019. "On the Reliability of the Foreign Language Effect on Risk-Taking." *Quarterly Journal of Experimental Psychology* 72, no. 1: 29–40.

Hayakawa, Sayuri, David Tannenbaum, Albert Costa, Joanna D. Corey, and

Boaz Keysar. 2017. "Thinking More or Feeling Less? Explaining the Foreign-Language Effect on Moral Judgment." *Psychological Science* 28, no. 10: 1387–97.

Hayes-Renshaw, Fiona, Wim van Aken, and Helen Wallace. 2006. "When and Why the EU Council of Ministers Votes Explicitly." *Journal of Common Market Studies* 44, no. 1: 161–94.

Heine, Matthias. 2015. "Dieses Wort lässt die globale Linke vor Wut beben." *Die Welt*, October 20.

Heisenberg, Dorothee. 2005. "The Institution of 'Consensus' in the European Union: Formal versus Informal Decision-Making in the Council." *European Journal of Political Research* 44, no. 1: 65–90.

Hiebert, Theodore. 2007. "The Tower of Babel and the Origin of the World's Cultures." *Journal of Biblical Literature* 126, no. 1: 29–58.

Hix, Simon. 1994. "The Study of the European Community: The Challenge to Comparative Politics." *West European Politics* 17, no. 1: 1–30.

Hix, Simon, Abdul G. Noury, and Gérard Roland. 2007. *Democratic Politics in the European Parliament.* New York: Cambridge University Press.

Hobolt, Sara B., and Bjørn Høyland. 2011. "Selection and Sanctioning in European Parliamentary Elections." *British Journal of Political Science* 41, no. 3: 477–98.

Hooghe, Liesbet, and Gary Marks. 2009. "A Postfunctionalist Theory of European Integration: From Permissive Consensus to Constraining Dissensus." *British Journal of Political Science* 39, no. 1: 1–23.

Hopkins, Daniel. 2014. "One Language, Two Meanings: Partisanship and Responses to Spanish." *Political Communication* 31, no. 3: 421–45.

Hopkins, Daniel. 2015. "The Upside of Accents: Language, Inter-Group Difference, and Attitudes toward Immigration." *British Journal of Political Science* 45, no. 3: 531–57.

Hopkins, Daniel, Van C. Tran, and Abigail Fischer Williamson. 2014. "See No Spanish: Language, Local Context, and Attitudes toward Immigration." *Politics, Groups, and Identities* 2, no. 1: 35–51.

Horspool, Margot. 2006. "Over the Rainbow: Languages and Law in the Future of the European Union." *Futures* 38, no. 2: 158–68.

House, Juliane. 2001. "A Stateless Language That Europe Must Embrace." *The Guardian*, April 19, 2001.

House, Juliane. 2003. "English as a Lingua Franca: A Threat to Multilingualism?" *Journal of Sociolinguistics* 7, no. 4: 556–78.

Huhe, Narisong, Daniel Naurin, and Robert Thomson. 2018. "The Evolution of Political Networks: Evidence from the Council of the European Union." *European Union Politics* 18, no. 1: 25–51.

Hülmbauer, Cornelia. 2011. "English as a Lingua France (ELF): A Mode and Its Implications." In *A Toolkit for Transnational Communication in Europe*, edited by J. Normann Jørgensen, 43–68. Copenhagen: University of Copenhagen.

Hülmbauer, Cornelia, and Barbara Seidlhofer. 2013. "English as a Lingua Franca in European Multilingualism." In *Exploring the Dynamics of Multilingualism: The DYLAN Project*, edited by Anne-Claude Berthoud, François Grin, and Georges Lüdi, 387–406. Amsterdam: John Benjamins Publishing.

Hutter, Swen, and Edgar Grande. 2014. "Politicizing Europe in the National Electoral Arena: A Comparative Analysis of Five West European Countries, 1970–2010." *Journal of Common Market Studies* 52, no. 5: 1000–1018.

Hutter, Swen, Edgar Grande, and Hanspeter Kriesi. 2016. *Politicising Europe: Integration and Mass Politics*. Cambridge: Cambridge University Press.

Ikonomou, Haakon A. 2017. "An International Language: The Translation and Interpretation Service." *The Invention of International Bureaucracy, Aarhus University* (blog). March 30. http://projects.au.dk/inventingbureaucracy/blog/show/artikel/an-international-language-the-translation-and-interpretation-service/

Jablonkai, Réka. 2009. "'In the Light Of': A Corpus-Based Analysis of Lexical Bundles in Two EU-Related Registers." *Working Papers in Language Pedagogy* 3: 1–27.

Jayakody, Y. 2018. "Explained: The Constitutional Crisis in Sri Lanka." *The Wire*, November 5. https://thewire.in/south-asia/explained-the-constitutional-crisis-in-sri-lanka

Jenkins, Jennifer, Marko Modiano, and Barbara Seidlhofer. 2001. "Euro-English." *English Today* 17, no. 4: 13–19.

Jones, Jennifer J. 2016. "Talk 'Like a Man': The Linguistic Styles of Hillary Clinton, 1992–2013." *Perspectives on Politics* 14, no. 3: 625–42.

Kaduczak, Marek. 2005. "Legal Drafting and Translation under Constraints of Multilingualism." In *Language and the Law: East Meets West*, edited by Stanisław Goźdź-Roszkowski and Krzysztof Kredens, 38–39. Łodź: Łodź University Press.

Kaeding, Michael. 2004. "Rapporteurship Allocation in the European Parliament: Information or Distribution?" *European Union Politics* 5, no. 3: 353–71.

Kashima, Emiko S., and Yoshihisa Kashima. 2003. "Individualism, GNP, Climate, And Pronoun Drop: Is Individualism Determined by Affluence and Climate, or Does Language Use Play a Role?" *Journal of Cross-Cultural Psychology* 34, no. 1: 125–34.

Keysar, Boaz, Sayuri L. Hayakawa, and Sun Gyu An. 2012. "The Foreign-Language Effect: Thinking in a Foreign Tongue Reduces Decision Biases." *Psychological Science* 23, no. 6: 661–68.

Kincaid, J. Peter, Robert Fishburne, Richard Rogers, and Brad Chissom. 1975. "Derivation of New Readability Formulas (Automated Readability Index, Fog Count, and Flesch Reading Ease Formula) for Navy Enlisted Personnel." Tech. rept. Vol. Research Branch Report 8–75 Naval Air Station Memphis: Chief of Naval Technical Training.

Kjær, Anne Lise. 2015. "Theoretical Aspects of Legal Translation in the EU: The Paradoxical Relationship between Language, Translation, and the Autonomy of EU Law." In *Language and Culture in EU Law: Multidisciplinary Perspectives*, edited by Susan Šarčević, 91–108. New York: Routledge.

Kjær, Anne Lise, and Silvia Adamo. 2016. "Linguistic Diversity and European Democracy: Introduction and Overview." In *Linguistic Diversity and European Democracy*, edited by Anne Lise Kjær and Silvia Adamo, 1–16. New York: Routledge.

Klüver, Heike. 2009. "Measuring Interest Group Influence Using Quantitative Text Analysis." *European Union Politics* 10, no. 4: 535–49.

Koehn, Philipp. 2005. "Europarl: A Parallel Corpus for Statistical Machine Translation." Proceedings of the Machine Translation Summit In Proceedings of Machine Translation Summit X, Phuket, Thailand.

Koskinen, Kaisa. 2008. *Translating Institutions: An Ethnographic Study of EU Translation*. Kinderhook, NY: InTrans Publications.

Kraus, Peter A. 2008. *A Union of Diversity: Language, Identity and Polity-Building in Europe*. Cambridge: Cambridge University Press.

Kraus, Peter, and Rūta Kazlauskaitė-Gürbüz. 2014. "Addressing Linguistic Diversity in the European Union: Strategies and Dilemmas." *Ethnicities* 14, no. 4: 517–38.

Kruse, Jan, and Ulrich Ammon. 2013. "Language Competence and Language Choice within EU Institutions and Their Effects on National Legislative Authorities." In *Exploring the Dynamics of Multilingualism: The DYLAN Project*, edited by Anne-Claude Berthoud, François Grin, and Georges Lüdi, 157–78. Amsterdam: John Benjamins Publishing.

Krzyżanowski, Michał. 2014. "Multilingual Communication in Europe's Supranational Spaces: Developments and Challenges in European Union Institutions." In *Multilingual Encounters in Europe's Institutional Spaces: Advances in Sociolinguistics*, edited by Johann W. Unger, Michał Krzyżanowski, and Ruth Wodak, 105–23. London: Bloomsbury.

Krzyżanowski, Michał, and Ruth Wodak. 2010. "Hegemonic Multilingualism in/of the EU Institutions: An Inside-Outside Perspective on European Language Policies and Practices." In *Mehrsprachigkeit aus der Perspektive zweier EU-Projekte: DYLAN Meets LINEE*, edited by Cornelia Hülmbauer, Eva Vetter, and Heike Böhringer, 115–35. Frankfurt: Peter Lang. https://doi.org/10.3726/978-3-653-02153-0

Labrie, Normand. 1992. *La Construction Linguistique de La Communauté Européenne*. Paris: Champion.

Lacey, Joseph. 2014. "Must Europe Be Swiss? On the Idea of a Voting Space and the Possibility of a Multilingual Demos." *British Journal of Political Science* 44, no. 1: 61–82.

Laitin, David D. 1977. *Politics, Language, and Thought: The Somali Experience*. Chicago: University of Chicago Press.

Laitin, David D. 1993. "The Game Theory of Language Regimes." *International Political Science Review* 14, no. 3: 227–39.

Laitin, David D. 1994. "The Tower of Babel as a Coordination Game: Political Linguistics in Ghana." *American Political Science Review* 88, no. 3: 622–34.

Laitin, David D. 1997. "The Cultural Identities of a European State." *Politics & Society* 25, no. 3: 277–302.

Laitin, David D. 1998. *Identity in Formation*. Ithaca: Cornell University Press.

Laitin, David D. 2000. "Language Conflict and Violence: The Straw That Strengthens the Camel's Back." *European Journal of Sociology* 41, no. 1: 97–137.

Laitin, David D., Joachim Moortgat, and Amanda Lea Robinson. 2012. "Geographic Axes and the Persistence of Cultural Diversity." *Proceedings of the National Academy of Sciences* 109, no. 26: 10263–68.

Lakoff, Robin Tolmach. 1992. *Talking Power: The Politics of Language*. New York: Basic Books.

Laponce, Jean A. 1987. *Languages and Their Territories*. Toronto: University of Toronto Press.

Laponce, Jean A. 2004. "Language and Politics." In *Encyclopedia of Government and Politics*, edited by Mary Hawkesworth and Maurice Kogan, 2nd ed., 587–602. London: Routledge.

Lee, Taeku, and Efrén O. Pérez. 2014. "The Persistent Connection between Language-of-Interview and Latino Political Opinion." *Political Behavior* 36, no. 2: 401–25.

Leung, Janny. 2012. "Statutory Interpretation in Multilingual Jurisdictions: Typology and Trends." *Journal of Multilingual and Multicultural Development* 33, no. 5: 481–95.

Lev-Ari, Shiri, and Boaz Keysar. 2012. "Less-Detailed Representation of Non-Native Language: Why Non-Native Speakers' Stories Seem More Vague." *Discourse Processes* 49, no. 7: 523–38.

Lewis, Jeffrey. 1998. "Is the 'Hard-Bargaining' Image of the Council Misleading? The Committee of Permanent Representatives and the Local Elections Directive." *Journal of Common Market Studies* 36, no. 4: 479–504.

Lien, Pei-te, M. Margaret Conway, and Janelle Wong. 2004. *The Politics of Asian Americans*. New York: Routledge.

Lim, Lisa. 2017. "Speaking in Tongues: Why Asean Members Stick to English." *South China Morning Post*, August 6.

Lippi-Green, Rosina. 2012. *English with an Accent: Language, Ideology, and Discrimination in the United States*. London: Routledge.

Lipsky, Michael. 1980. *Street-Level Bureaucracy: Dilemmas of the Individual in Public Services*. New York: Russell Sage Foundation.

Liu, Amy H. 2011. "Linguistic Effects of Political Institutions." *Journal of Politics* 73, no. 1: 125–39.

Liu, Amy H. 2015. *Standardizing Diversity: The Political Economy of Language Regimes*. Philadelphia: University of Pennsylvania Press.

Liu, Amy H., and Vanessa A. Baird. 2012. "Linguistic Recognition as a Source of Confidence in the Justice System." *Comparative Political Studies* 45, no. 10: 1203–29.

Longinovic, T. Z. 2011. "Serbo-Croatian: Translating the Non-Identical Twins." In *Translation and Opposition*, 283–95. Bristol, UK: Multilingual Matters.

Longman, Chris. 2007. "English as Lingua Franca: A Challenge to the Doctrine of Multilingualism." In *The Language Question in Europe and Diverse Societies: Political, Legal and Social Perspectives*, edited by Dario Castiglione and Chris Longman, 185–215. Oxford: Hart Publishing.

Loos, Eugène. 2000. "Language Choice, Linguistic Capital and Symbolic Domination in the European Union." *Language Problems and Language Planning* 24, no. 1: 37–53.

Loos, Eugène. 2004. "Composing 'Panacea Texts' at the European Parliament: An Intertextual Perspective on Text Production in a Multilingual Community." *Journal of Language and Politics* 3, no. 1: 3–25.

Lu, Chao, Bu Yi, Jie Wang, Ying Ding, Vetle Ingvald Torvik, Matthew Schnaars, and Chengzhi Zhang. 2019. "Examining Scientific Writing Styles from the Perspective of Linguistic Complexity." *Journal of the Association for Information Science and Technology* 70, no. 5: 462–75.

Lu, Xiaofei. 2011. "A Corpus-Based Evaluation of Syntactic Complexity Measures as Indices of College-Level ESL Writers' Language Development." *TESOL Quarterly* 45, no. 1: 36–62.

Lustig, Robin. 2018. "Can English Remain the 'World's Favourite' Language?" *BBC*, May 22.

Mac Giolla Chriost, Diarmait, and Matteo Bonotti. 2018. *Brexit, Language Policy and Linguistic Diversity.* New York: Palgrave.

Magistro, Elena. 2013. "The Challenges of 'Translating' Polite Discourse for the EU Multilingual Community." *International Journal of Applied Linguistics* 23, no. 1: 60–79.

Mamadouh, Virginie. 1999. "Beyond Nationalism: Three Visions of the European Union and Their Implications for the Linguistic Regime of Its Institutions." *GeoJournal* 48: 133–44.

Mamadouh, Virginie. 2002. "Dealing with Multilingualism in the European Union: Cultural Theory Rationalities and Language Policies." *Journal of Comparative Policy Analysis: Research and Practice* 4: 327–45.

March, James G., and Johan P. Olsen. 2006. "The Logic of Appropriateness." In *The Oxford Handbook of Public Policy*, edited by Michael Moran, Martin Rein, and Robert E. Goodin. Oxford: Oxford University Press.

McArthur, Tom. 2003. "World English, Euro-English, Nordic English?" *English Today* 19, no. 1: 54–58.

McAuliffe, Karen. 2008. "Enlargement at the European Court of Justice: Law, Language and Translation." *European Law Journal* 14, no. 6: 806–18.

McAuliffe, Karen. 2009. "Translation at the Court of Justice of the European Communities." In *Translation Issues in Language and Law*, edited by Frances Olsen, Alexander Lorz, and Dieter Stein, 99–115. New York: Palgrave MacMillan.

McAuliffe, Karen. 2010. "Languages and the Institutional Dynamics of the Court of Justice of the European Commission: A Changing Role for Lawyer-Linguists?" In *How Globalizing Professions Deal With National Languages: Studies in Cultural Conflict and Cooperation*, edited by Michel Gueldry, 239–62. Lewiston, NY: Edwin Mellen Press.

McAuliffe, Karen. 2011. "Hybrid Texts and Uniform Law? The Multilingual Case Law of the Court of Justice of the European Union." *International Journal for the Semiotics of Law—Revue Internationale de Sémiotique Juridique* 24: 97–115. https://doi.org/10.1007/s11196-010-9188-3

McAuliffe, Karen. 2012. "Language and Law in the European Union: The Multilingual Jurisprudence of the ECJ." In *The Oxford Handbook of Language and Law*, edited by Lawrence M. Solan and Peter M. Tiersma. Oxford: Oxford University Press.

McAuliffe, Karen. 2013a. "Precedent at the ECJ: The Linguistic Aspect." *Current Legal Issues* 15: 483–92.

McAuliffe, Karen. 2013b. "The Limitations of a Multilingual Legal System." *International Journal for the Semiotics of Law—Revue Internationale de Sémiotique Juridique* 26: 861–82. https://doi.org/10.1007/s11196-013-9314-0

McAuliffe, Karen. 2015. "Translating Ambiguity." *Journal of Comparative Law* 9, no. 2: 65–87.

McCluskey, Brian. 2002. "English as a Lingua Franca for Europe." *European English Messenger* 11, no. 2: 40–45.

Meyer-Schwarzenberger, Matthias. 2015. "Grammatik Und Sozialkapital: Sprachliche Relativität in Wirtschaft and Gesellschaft." Doctoral dissertation, University of St. Gallen.

Miles, William F. S. 2000. "The Politics of Language Equilibrium in a Multilingual Society: Mauritius." *Comparative Politics* 32, no. 2: 215–30.

Modiano, Marko. 2000. "Euro-English: Educational Standards in a Cross-Cultural Context." *European English Messenger* 9, no. 1: 33–37.

Modiano, Marko. 2017. "English in a Post-Brexit European Union." *World Englishes* 36, no. 3: 313–27.

Mollin, Sandra. 2006. "Evidence for the Formal Independence of Euro-English?" *Language in Performance* 33: 88–157.

Morgan, Sam. 2018. "Translations of British Brexit Plan Provoke Ridicule." *EURACTIV*, July 19. https://www.euractiv.com/section/uk-europe/news/translations-of-british-brexit-plan-provoke-ridicule/

Nic Craith, Máiréad. 2006. *Europe and the Politics of Language*. New York: Palgrave.

Nielsen, Nikolaj. 2016. "English at Risk as Official EU Language." *EU Observer*, June 27.

Nißl, Sandra. 2011. *Die Sprachenfrage in Der Europäischen Union. Möglichkeiten Und Grenzen Einer Sprachenpolitik Für Europa*. München: Herbert Utz.

Nordland, Rasmus. 2002. "Equality and Power in EU Language Work." *Perspectives* 10, no. 1: 31–53.

Novak, Stéphanie. 2013. "The Silence of Ministers: Consensus and Blame Avoidance in the Council of the European Union." *Journal of Common Market Studies* 51, no. 6: 1091–1107.

Oganian, Yulia, Hauke R. Heekeren, and Christoph W. Korn. 2019. "Low Foreign Language Proficiency Reduces Optimism about the Personal Future." *Quarterly Journal of Experimental Psychology* 72, no. 1: 60–75.

Özdamar, Emine Sevgi. 2001. *Der Hof Im Spiegel*. Cologne: Verlag Kiepenheuer & Witsch.

Paunio, Elina. 2007. "The Tower of Babel and the Interpretation of EU Law." In *Private Law and the Many Cultures of Europe*, edited by Thomas Wilhelmson, Elina Paunio, and Annika Pohjolainen, 385–402. Alphen aan den Rijn: Kluwer Law International.

Paunio, Elina. 2013. *Legal Certainty in Multilingual EU Law: Language, Discourse and Reasoning at the European Court of Justice*. New York: Routledge.

Pavlenko, Aneta. 2005. *Emotions and Multilingualism*. Cambridge: Cambridge University Press.

Pavlenko, Aneta. 2012. "Affective Processing in Bilingual Speakers: Disembodied Cognition?" *International Journal of Psychology* 47, no. 6: 405–28.

Pemstein, Daniel, Stephen A. Meserve, and William T. Bernhard. 2015. "Brussels Bound: Policy Experience and Candidate Selection in European Elections." *Comparative Political Studies* 48, no. 11: 1421–53.

Pérez, Efrén O. 2016. "Rolling off the Tongue into the Top-of-the-Head: Explaining Language Effects on Public Opinion." *Political Behavior* 38, no. 3: 603–34.

Pérez, Efrén O., and Margit Tavits. 2017. "Language Shapes People's Time Perspective and Support for Future-Oriented Policies." *American Journal of Political Science* 61, no. 3: 715–27.

Pérez, Efrén O., and Margit Tavits. 2019. "Language Influences Public Attitudes Toward Gender Equality." *Journal of Politics* 81, no. 1: 81–93.

Peters, B. Guy. 2005. *Institutional Theory in Political Science: The "New Institutionalism."* 2nd ed. New York: Continuum.

Phillipson, Robert. 2003. *English-Only Europe? Challenging Language Policy.* New York: Routledge.

Phillipson, Robert. 2016. "The EU and Languages: Diversity in What Unity." In *Linguistic Diversity and European Democracy*, edited by Anne Lise Kjær and Silvia Adamo, 57–74. New York: Routledge.

Piris, Jean-Claude. 2005. "The Legal Orders of the European Community and of the Member States: Peculiarities and Influences in Drafting." *Amicus Curiae* (March/April): 21–28.

Polizzotti, Mark. 2018. "Why Mistranslation Matters." *New York Times*, July 28.

Pool, Jonathan. 1991. "The Official Language Problem." *American Political Science Review* 85, no. 2: 495–514.

Pool, Jonathan. 1992. "Come Let Us Speak Together: The Rational Choice of Official Languages." Unpublished. University of Washington.

Pool, Jonathan. 1996. "Optimal Language Regimes for the European Union." *International Journal of the Sociology of Language* 121, no. 1: 159–79.

Posner, Daniel N. 2005. *Institutions and Ethnic Politics in Africa.* New York: Cambridge University Press.

Pozzo, Barbara. 2012. "English as a Legal Lingua Franca in the EU Multilingual Context." In *The Role of Legal Translation in Legal Harmonization*, edited by Cornelis J. W. Baaij, 183–202. Alphen aan den Rijn: Wolters Kluwer.

Proksch, Sven-Oliver, and Jonathan B. Slapin. 2015. *Politics of Parliamentary Debate: Parties, Rebels, and Representation.* Cambridge: Cambridge University Press.

Pütter, Uwe. 2012. "Europe's Deliberative Intergovernmentalism: The Role of the Council and European Council in EU Economic Governance." *Journal of European Public Policy* 19, no. 2: 161–78.

Pym, Anthony. 2000. "The European Union and Its Future Languages: Questions for Language Policies and Translation Theories." *Across Languages and Cultures* 1, no. 1: 1–17.

Pym, Anthony. 2014. "Translation Studies in Europe—Reasons for It, and Problems to Work On." *Target* 26, no. 2: 185–205.

Pym, Anthony, François Grin, Claudio Sfreddo, and Andy L. J. Chan. 2013. *The Status of the Translation Profession in the European Union.* London: Anthem.

Quell, Carston. 1997. "Language Choice in Multilingual Institutions: A Case Study at the European Commission with Particular Reference to the Role of English, French, and German as Working Languages." *Multilingua* 16, no. 1: 57–76.

Rabinovich, Ella, Sergiu Nisioi, Noam Ordan, and Shuly Wintner. 2016. "On the Similarities Between Native, Non-Native and Translated Texts." *Proceedings of the 54th Annual Meeting of the Association for Computational Linguistics*, 1870–81.

Radulescu, Adina. 2012. "Preserving Conceptual Concordance in the Multilingual Translations of EU Legislation." *Contemporary Readings in Law and Social Justice* 4, no. 2: 318–23.

Reh, Christine, Adrienne Héritier, Edoardo Bressanelli, and Christel Koop. 2013.

"The Informal Politics of Legislation: Explaining Secluded Decision Making in the European Union." *Comparative Political Studies* 46, no. 9: 1112–42.

Reilly, Gavan. 2012. "Brussels Made 17 Errors Translating the ESM Treaty into Irish." *TheJournal.Ie*, June 22.

Ricento, Thomas. 2006. "Language Policy: Theory and Practice—An Introduction." In *An Introduction to Language Policy: Theory and Method*, edited by Thomas Ricento, 10–23. Malden, MA: Blackwell Publishing.

Ringe, Nils. 2010. *Who Decides and How? Preferences, Uncertainty, and Policy Choice in the European Parliament*. Oxford: Oxford University Press.

Ringe, Nils, and Jennifer N. Victor. 2013. *Bridging the Information Gap: Legislative Member Organizations as Social Networks in the United States and the European Union*. Ann Arbor: University of Michigan Press.

Ringe, Nils, Jennifer N. Victor, and Justin H. Gross. 2013. "Keeping Your Friends Close and Your Enemies Closer? Information Networks in Legislative Politics." *British Journal of Political Science* 43, no. 3: 601–28.

Roberts, Richard H. 2006. "Gaia and Europa: Religion and Legitimation Crisis in the 'New Europe.'" In *The Shape of the New Europe*, edited by Ralf Rogowski and Charles Turner. Cambridge: Cambridge University Press.

Robertson, Colin. 2010a. "Legal-Linguistic Revision of EU Legislative Texts." In *Legal Discourse across Languages and Cultures*, edited by Maurizio Gotti and Christopher Williams, 51–73. Bern: Peter Lang.

Robertson, Colin. 2010b. "Legislative Drafting in English for Non-Native Speakers: Some Do's and Dont's (With Reference to EU Legislation)." *ESP Across Cultures* 7: 147–67.

Robertson, Colin. 2010c. "LSP and EU Legal Language." In *Reconceptualizing LSP: Online Proceedings of the XVII European LSP Symposium 2009*, edited by Carmen Heine and Jan Engberg. Aarhus: Aarhus School of Business, Aarhus University.

Robertson, Colin. 2011. "Multilingual Legislation in the European Union. EU and National Legislative-Language Styles and Terminology." *Research in Language* 9, no. 1: 51–67.

Robertson, Colin. 2012a. "EU Legal English: Common Law, Civil Law, or a New Genre?" *European Review of Private Law* 20, no. 5–6: 1215–39.

Robertson, Colin. 2012b. "The Problem of Meaning in Multilingual EU Legal Texts." *International Journal of Law, Language & Discourse* 2, no. 1: 1–30.

Robinson, William. 2012. "Drafting European Union Legislation." Brussels: European Parliament.

Robinson, William. 2014a. "Drafting EU Legislation in the European Commission: A Collaborative Process." *Theory and Practice of Legislation* 2, no. 3: 249–72.

Robinson, William. 2014b. "Translating Legislation: The European Union Experience." *Theory and Practice of Legislation* 2, no. 2: 185–210.

Rodrik, Dani. 1999. "Where Did All the Growth Go? External Shocks, Social Conflict and Growth Collapses." *Journal of Economic Growth* 4: 385–412.

Rokkan, Stein, and Derek Urwin. 1983. *Economy, Territory, Identity: Politics of West European Peripheries*. Beverly Hills, CA: Sage.

Rose, Richard. 2008. "Political Communication in a European Public Space: Language, the Internet and Understanding as Soft Power." *Journal of Common Market Studies* 46, no. 2: 451–75.

Bibliography

Ross, George. 1995. *Jacques Delors and European Integration*. London: Oxford University Press.

Royles, Elin, and Huw Lewis. 2019. "Language Policy in Multi-Level Systems: A Historical Institutionalist Analysis." *British Journal of Politics and International Relations* 21, no. 4: 709–27.

Runions, Erin. 2014. *The Babylon Complex: Theopolitical Fantasies of War, Sex, and Sovereignty*. New York: Fordham University Press.

Safran, William. 2005. "Introduction: The Political Aspects of Language." In *Language, Ethnic Identity, and the State*, edited by William Safran and Jean A. Laponce, 1–14. New York: Routledge.

Safran, William, and Amy H. Liu. 2012. "Nation-Building, Collective Identity, and Language Choices: Between Instrumental and Value Rationalities." *Nationalism and Ethnic Politics* 18, no. 3: 269–92.

Šarčević, Susan. 2007. "Making Multilingualism Work in the Enlarged European Union." In *Language and the Law: International Outlooks*, edited by Krzysztof Kredens and Stanislaw Gozdz-Roszkowski, 35–56. Frankfurt: Peter Lang.

Šarčević, Susan. 2012a. "Challenges to the Legal Translator." In *The Oxford Handbook of Language and Law*, edited by Lawrence M. Solan and Peter M. Tiersma, 187–99. Oxford: Oxford University Press.

Šarčević, Susan. 2012b. "Coping with the Challenges of Legal Translation in Harmonization." In *The Role of Legal Translation in Legal Harmonization*, edited by Cornelis J. W. Baaij, 83–108. Alphen aan den Rijn: Wolters Kluwer.

Šarčević, Susan. 2013. "Multilingual Lawmaking and Legal (Un)Certainty in the European Union." *International Journal of Law, Language & Discourse* 3: 1–29.

Šarčević, Susan. 2015. "Language and Culture in EU Law: Introduction and Overview." In *Language and Culture in EU Law: Multidisciplinary Perspectives*, edited by Susan Šarčević, 1–16. New York: Routledge.

Šarčević, Susan, and Colin Robertson. 2013. "The Work of Lawyer-Linguists in the EU Institutions." In *Legal Translation in Context: Professional Issues and Prospects*, edited by Anabel Borja Albi and Fernando Prieto Ramos, 181–202. Bern: Peter Lang.

Schäffner, Christina. 1998. "Parallel Texts in Translation." In *Unity or Diversity? Current Trends in Translation Studies*, edited by Lynne Bowker, 83–90. Manchester: St. Jerome Publishing.

Schäffner, Christina, and Beverly Adab. 1997. "Translation as Intercultural Communication—Contact as Conflict." In *Translation as Intercultural Communication*, edited by Mary Snell-Hornby, Zuzana Jettmarová, and Klaus Kaindl, 325–38. Amsterdam: John Benjamins Publishing.

Scharpf, Fritz W. 1999. *Governing in Europe. Effective and Democratic?* Oxford: Oxford University Press.

Schlossmacher, Michael. 1994. "Die Arbeitssprachen in Den Organen Der Europäischen Gemeinschaft. Methoden Und Ergebnisse Einer Empirischen Untersuchung." *Sociolinguistica* 8: 101–22.

Seidlhofer, Barbara. 2011. *Understanding English as a Lingua Franca*. Oxford: Oxford University Press.

Seidlhofer, Barbara, and Henry G. Widdowson. 2006. "Creative Incompetence." In *Ach!Texte—Didak-Tick Der (Modernen, Unmodernen Und Außerirdischen)*

Sprachen, edited by Frauke Intemann and Frank G. Königs, 143–54. Bochum: AKS-Verlag.

Senninger, Roman, and Markus Wagner. 2015. "Political Parties and the EU in National Election Campaigns: Who Talks about Europe, and How?" *Journal of Common Market Studies* 53, no. 6: 1336–51.

Sharkansky, Ira. 1999. *Ambiguity, Coping, and Governance: Israeli Experiences in Politics, Religion, and Policymaking.* Westport, CT: Praeger.

Sharpston, Eleanor. 2014. "Language Law and the (Golden) Towers of Babel." Lecture presented at the Chartered Institute of Linguists, Threlford Memorial Lecture.

Simon, Frédéric. 2012. "Commission Denies English Language Favouritism." *Euractiv.Com*, July 4.

Slapin, Jonathan B., and Sven-Oliver Proksch. 2008. "A Scaling Model for Estimating Time-Series Party Positions from Texts." *American Journal of Political Science* 52, no. 3: 705–22.

Slobin, Dan. 1996. "From 'Thought and Language' to 'Thinking for Speaking.'" In *Rethinking Linguistic Relativity*, edited by John J. Gumperz and Stephen C. Levinson. Cambridge: Cambridge University Press.

Sobolewska, Maria, Laurence Lessard-Phillips, and Silvia Galandini. 2016. "Exploring Public Opinion on Immigrant Integration with Survey Experiments." *Migration and Citizenship* 4, no. 1: 18–23.

Solan, Lawrence M. 2009. "Statutory Interpretation in the EU: The Augustinian Approach." In *Translation Issues in Language and Law*, edited by Frances Olsen, Alexander Lorz, and Dieter Stein, 35–54. Basingstoke: Palgrave Macmillan.

Spirling, Arthur. 2016. "Democratization and Linguistic Complexity: The Effect of Franchise Extension on Parliamentary Discourse, 1832–1915." *Journal of Politics* 78, no. 1: 120–36.

Spoon, Jae-Jae. 2012. "How Salient Is Europe? An Analysis of European Election Manifestos, 1979–2004." *European Union Politics* 13, no. 4: 558–79.

Standring, Adam. 2018. "Depoliticising Austerity: Narratives of the Portuguese Debt Crisis 2011–15." *Policy & Politics* 46, no. 1: 149–64.

Stefaniak, Karolina. 2013. "Multilingual Legal Drafting, Translators' Choices and the Principle of Lesser Evil." *Meta* 58, no. 1: 58–65.

Strandvik, Ingemar. 2014. "Is There Scope for a More Professional Approach to EU Multlingual Lawmaking?" *Theory and Practice of Legislation* 2, no. 2: 211–28.

Strandvik, Ingemar. 2018. "Towards a More Structured Approach to Quality Assurance: DGT's Quality Journey." In *Institutional Translation for International Governance: Enhancing Quality in Multilingual Legal Communication*, edited by Fernando Prieto Ramos. New York: Bloomsbury.

Strani, Katerina. 2020. "Multilingualism and Politics Revisited: The State of the Art." In *Multilingualism and Politics*, edited by Katerina Strani, 17–45. London: Palgrave Macmillan.

Strawn, Brent A. 2011. "Focus on Tower of Babel." *Oxford Biblical Studies Online* (blog). 2011. https://global.oup.com/obso/focus/focus_on_towerbabel/

Stritar, Mojca, and Marko Stabej. 2013. "EU and Lesser-Used Languages: Slovene Language in EU Institutions." In *Exploring the Dynamics of Multilingualism: The*

Bibliography 253

DYLAN Project, edited by Anne-Claude Berthoud, François Grin, and Georges Lüdi, 179–204. Amsterdam: John Benjamins Publishing.

Strubell, Miquel. 2007. "The Political Discourse on Multilingualism in the European Union." In *The Language Question in Europe and Diverse Societies: Political, Legal and Social Perspectives*, edited by Dario Castiglione and Chris Longman, 149–83. Oxford: Hart Publishing.

Sunstein, Cass R. 2019. "Is Cost–Benefit Analysis a Foreign Language?" *Quarterly Journal of Experimental Psychology* 72, no. 1: 3–7.

Szabó, Péter K. 2020. "The Grilling: An Ethnographic Language Policy Analysis of Multilingualism Performed in the European Parliament." In *Multilingualism and Politics*, edited by Katerina Strani, 77–104. London: Palgrave Macmillan.

Thelen, Kathleen. 1994. "Beyond Corporatism: Toward a New Framework for the Study of Labor in Advanced Capitalism." *Comparative Politics* 27, no. 1: 107–24.

Thelen, Kathleen. 2004. *How Institutions Evolve: The Political Economy of Skills in Germany, Britain, the United States, and Japan*. New York: Cambridge University Press.

Thompson, Derek. 2016. "Why Democrats and Republicans Literally Speak Different Languages." *The Atlantic*, July 22, 2016.

Tocqueville, Alexis de. 1839. *Democracy in America*. New York: George Adlard.

Tosi, Arturo. 2003. "The Writer, the Translator and the Reader." In *Crossing Barriers and Bridging Cultures*, edited by Arturo Tosi, 45–66. Bristol: Multilingual Matters.

Tosi, Arturo. 2005. "EU Translation Problems and the Danger of Linguistic Devaluation." *International Journal of Applied Linguistics* 15, no. 3: 384–88.

Tosi, Arturo. 2013. "Translation as a Test of Language Vitality." *International Journal of Applied Linguistics* 23, no. 1: 1–14.

Translation Centre for the Bodies of the European Union. 2017. "Highlights of the Year 2016." Luxembourg: Translation Centre for the Bodies of the European Union.

Trebits, Anna. 2008. "English Lexis in the Documents of the European Union—A Corpus-Based Exploratory Study." *Working Papers in Language Pedagogy* 2: 38–54.

Trebits, Anna. 2009a. "Conjunctive Cohesion in English Language EU Documents—A Corpus-Based Analysis and Its Implications." *English for Specific Purposes* 28: 199–210.

Trebits, Anna. 2009b. "The Most Frequent Phrasal Verbs in English Language EU Documents—A Corpus-Based Analysis and Its Implications." *System* 37: 470–81.

Trosborg, Anna. 1997. "Translating Hybrid Political Texts." In *Text Typology and Translation*, edited by Anna Trosborg, 145–59. Amsterdam: John Benjamins Publishing.

Truchot, Claude. 1994. *Le Plurilinguisme Européen, Théories et Pratiques En Politique Linguistique*. Paris: Champion.

van Els, Theo J. M. 2001. "The European Union, Its Institutions and Its Languages: Some Language Political Observations." *Current Issues in Language Planning* 2, no. 4: 311–60.

Bibliography

van Els, Theo J. M. 2003. "Language Policy of and for the European Union: Consequences for Foreign Language Teaching in the Member States. In *Europäische Sprachenpolitik/European Language Policy*, edited by Rüdiger Ahrens, 45–56. Heidelberg: Universitätsverlag Winter.

van Els, Theo J. M. 2005. "Multilingualism in the European Union." *International Journal of Applied Linguistics* 15, no. 3: 263–81.

van der Jeught, Stefaan. 2015. *EU Language Law*. Amsterdam: Europa Law Publishing.

van Parijs, Phillippe. 2011. *Linguistic Justice for Europe and for the World*. Oxford: Oxford University Press.

Victor, Jennifer N., Alexander H. Montgomery, and Mark Lubell, eds. 2017. *The Oxford Handbook of Political Networks*. Oxford: Oxford University Press.

Visconti, Jacqueline. 2013. "European Integration: Connectives in EU Legislation: European Integration: Connectives in EU Legislation." *International Journal of Applied Linguistics* 23, no. 1: 44–59.

Volk, Stefan, Tine Köhler, and Markus Pudelko. 2014. "Brain Drain: The Cognitive Neuroscience of Foreign Language Processing in Multinational Corporations." *Journal of International Business Studies* 45, no. 7: 862–85.

Vuorikoski, Anna-Riita. 2004. "A Voice of Its Citizens or a Modern Tower of Babel? The Quality of Interpreting as a Function of Political Rhetoric in the European Parliament." Tampere: Tampere University Press.

Vuorikoski, Anna-Riita. 2005. "A Voice of Its Citizens or a Modern Tower of Babel?" *Neuphilologische Mitteilungen* 106, no. 3: 229–33.

Wagner, Emma, Svend Bech, and Jesús M. Martínez. 2014. *Translating for the European Union Institutions*. New York: Routledge.

Wodak, Ruth. 2009. *The Discourse of Politics in Action: Politics as Usual*. London: Palgrave Macmillan.

Wodak, Ruth. 2013. "Multilingualism in EU Institutions: Between Policy Making and Implementation." In *Multilingualism and Multimodality: Current Challengers for Educational Studies*, edited by Ingrid de Saint-Georges and Jean-Jacques Weber, 81–99. Rotterdam: Sense Publishers. https://doi. org/10.1007/978-94-6209-266-2_5

Wodak, Ruth. 2014. "The European Parliament: Multilingual Experiences in the Everyday Life of MEPs." In *Multilingual Encounters in Europe's Institutional Spaces: Advances in Sociolinguistics*, edited by Johann W. Unger, Michał Krzyżanowski, and Ruth Wodak, 125–46. London: Bloomsbury.

Wodak, Ruth, and Michał Krzyżanowski. 2011. "Language in Political Institutions of Multilingual States and the European Union." In *The Languages and Linguistics of Europe: A Comprehensive Guide*, edited by Bernd Kortmann and Johan van der Auwera, 621–37. Berlin: Mouton de Gruyter.

Wodak, Ruth, Michał Krzyżanowski, and Bernhard Forchtner. 2012. "The Interplay of Language Ideologies and Contextual Cues in Multilingual Interactions: Language Choice and Code-Switching in European Union Institutions." *Language in Society* 41, no. 2: 157–86.

Wong, Janelle, S. Karthick Ramakrishnan, Taeku Lee, and Jane Junn. 2011. *Asian American Political Participation: Emerging Constituents and Their Political Identities*. New York: Russell Sage Foundation.

Wood, Matthew, and Matthew Flinders. 2014. "Rethinking Depoliticization: Beyond the Governmental." *Policy & Politics* 42, no. 2: 151–70.

Wright, Sue. 2000. *Community and Communication: The Role of Language in Nation State Building and European Integration*. Bristol: Multilingual Matters.

Wright, Sue. 2007. "English in the European Parliament: MEPs and Their Language Repertoires." *Sociolinguistica* 21: 151–65.

Wright, Sue. 2009. "The Elephant in the Room: Language Issues in the European Union." *European Journal of Language Policy* 1, no. 2: 93–120.

Wright, Sue. 2013. "Why Isn't EU Language Policy Working?" In *Vielfalt, Variation Und Stellung Der Deutschen Sprache*, edited by Karina Schneider-Wiejowski, Birte Kellermeier-Rehbein, and Jakob Haselhuber, 259–73. Berlin: De Gruyter.

Wu, Yan Jing, and Guillaume Thierry. 2012. "How Reading in a Second Language Protects Your Heart." *Journal of Neuroscience* 32: 6485–89.

Xanthaki, Helen. 2001. "The Problem of Quality in EU Legislation: What on Earth Is Really Wrong?" *Common Market Law Review* 3: 651–76.

Yoshinaka, Antoine, Gail McElroy, and Shaun Bowler. 2010. "The Appointment of Rapporteurs in the European Parliament." *Legislative Studies Quarterly* 35, no. 4: 457–86.

Zaretsky, Robert. 2017. "France Is Debating Whether French Is Sexist." *Foreign Affairs*, November 20.

Index

ambiguous language: accidental ambiguity, 169, 179–82, 185; ambiguous terms, 137, 201; calculated intentional ambiguity, 162; 180–85, 230nn22–23, 231n24; consequential, 31; limiting ambiguity, 12, 25, 125–26, 179, 194; post hoc intentional ambiguity, 181–85; room for, 73, 161; 177, 179; in text, 57–60, 63, 108–9; 144, 183–85, 206–8; translation and interpretation of, 31, 175–76
Ammon, Ulrich, 21, 37, 41, 88, 191, 224n4
Anderson, Benedict, 13
anticipation of translation or interpretation (*see also* speaking for interpretation; writing for translation), 12, 24, 161, 167–69, 186
asymmetric interpretation, 101–2
austerity, 11, 136–39, 166
Austria, 1, 39, 71, 95, 174, 217n37

Babel. *See* Tower of Babel
Belgium, 2, 4, 16, 84, 174, 213n3, 214n5
big languages (English, German, French, and Italian), 41–42, 51–52
body language, 163–65
Brexit, 7, 83, 105, 143, 156–58, 228nn22–23
Brussels, 16, 24, 34, 47, 67, 72, 119, 133–

34, 139–43, 147–49, 157, 193
budget: constraints, 99–101; Council budget, 38–39, 232; cuts, 324–25; EU budget, 47, 62–63, 94, 97, 190–92, 222n31, 227n21
Bulgarian (language), 85
Bundestag (lower chamber of German Parliament), 191, 220n12
bureaucratic language, 127, 152

Canada, 2, 4, 16, 122, 152, 213n3, 214n5
charisma, 130–32, 163–65, 169
Clinton, Hillary, 201
Code of Conduct on Multilingualism (of the EP), 40, 48, 101, 104
code switching, 34
co-drafting, 5, 122, 124
Commission. *See* European Commission
Committee of the Regions, 51, 55, 220n8
communication: between EU and its citizens (*see also* link between EU and its citizens), 21, 28–30, 39, 56, 63–64, 86–87, 92–93, 104, 172; communicative intent, 11–12, 24–25, 113–14, 135, 139, 161, 166–67, 172, 186; getting the message across, 12, 80, 120, 126–28, 130, 133, 164, 188, 195, 202; informal, 1, 20, 32, 61, 75, 77, 108
competences (of the EU), 66, 82, 96–100

258   *Index*

complex speech, 11–12, 23–24, 114, 143,
 151–58, 189, 201–2
compromise amendments, 58, 192
computer translation. *See* machine translation and interpretation
consensus norm, 13, 118, 194
constraining dissensus, 197
controlled full multilingualism. *See*
 resource-efficient full multilingualism
Coreper (Committee of Permanent
 Representatives), 38, 120, 164, 193,
 208, 212n22
corrigendum, 70, 218n59
costs of multilingualism, 9, 22–23, 27,
 48, 62–64, 81, 88–89, 93, 96, 100–
 103, 105, 108–9, 188, 220n8, 222n31,
 232n4; costs of errors and misunderstandings, 6, 63, 67–73
Council of Ministers. *See* Council of the
 European Union
Council of the European Union, 5,
 26–28, 35, 38–40, 58–59, 79, 95, 102,
 193, 205–10; Legal Service (JUR), 58,
 124, 149, 206–8; Translation Service
 (LING), 55–56, 191
Council Presidency, 33, 35, 39, 54–55,
 95, 120–21, 182, 214n7, 215n13,
 224n6
Council Regulation No. 1 (1958), 68, 82,
 85–88, 91–99, 220n7, 221n19; Article
 6, 68, 83–93, 104
Council Secretariat, 35, 59
Court of Justice of the EU, 5, 18, 26,
 31–32, 35–36, 44–47, 56, 59–60, 69,
 85–86, 91–93, 97–98, 168, 171–72,
 210, 211n7, 213n2, 214n6, 215n23,
 217n40, 224n7, 228n26, 230n15,
 232n7; translation service, 55–56
Croatian (language), 47, 85, 216n30
Cyprus, 174, 217n37
Czech (language), 37, 85

Danish (language), 36, 47, 53, 75, 84,
 96
De Swaan, Abram, 20, 66, 94
decultured language, 11, 127, 198, 201,
 203
democratic accountability, 28, 198
democratic legitimacy (of the EU) (*see*

also input legitimacy; output legitimacy), 25–28, 107, 196–98
Denmark, 65, 85–86, 96
depersonalizing effect (of interpretation), 161, 164
depoliticization, 4, 9–16, 22–25, 81–83,
 111–12, 113–39, 140–59, 160–86,
 187–89, 194–203, 212n18
dimensions of language, 22, 81–82, 86–
 87, 94, 96, 110, 198; functional, 88, 94;
 legal, 36, 98, 220n11; representational,
 36, 40, 98, 212n19, 220n11; symbolic,
 98–99
direct effect (principle of), 30, 97–98
Directorate for Interpretation (EP), 71
Directorate for Legislative Acts (EP), 58
Directorate for Legislative Quality
 (Council), 58
Directorate-General for Interpretation
 (SCIC) (Commission), 17, 27, 46–47,
 49, 52–53, 55, 221n19
Directorate-General for the Presidency
 (PRES) (EP), 58
Directorate-General for Translation
 (DGT) (Commission), 60, 191, 206,
 219n62
Directorate-General Human Resources
 and Security (HR) (Commission), 38
Directorate-General Logistics and
 Interpretation for Conferences
 (LINC) (EP), 47, 50–51
disfluencies, 154–55
divergences in meaning, 31, 68–69, 109–
 10, 173, 190, 214n6
draft text (of legislation), 58, 122, 178,
 181–82, 206, 209
drafting language, 33, 84, 122–24, 178,
 180, 206–7, 224n7
Dutch (language), 4, 31–32, 41, 84,
 213n3, 217n37
dysfunction (institutional or systemic),
 31, 67, 83, 93, 105, 109

emotions, 115, 137, 163–66, 176, 198,
 224n3; language and, 11, 117–18,
 127–28, 189, 201
empathy, 11, 24, 80, 114–15, 133–36, 188
English (language): as a lingua franca,
 18, 21, 138, 141, 226n2, 228n23,

228n25; as a shared language, 22–24, 35, 88, 106, 139, 189, 205; as a vehicular language, 33, 86, 113, 158, 189; as a working language, 8, 61, 80, 95, 144, 157–58, 211n6; as an official language, 4–5, 84–85, 96, 105, 227n21, 228n22; dominance of, 19, 32–35, 39, 58, 87, 144, 156–57, 159; pushback against, 35; reliance on, 22, 61, 109, 115; standard English, 11, 23–25, 82, 124–26, 139, 144–46, 149–50, 153–59, 189, 197, 201–3; trend toward greater usage, 41–43, 49, 86, 167

enlargement, 82, 96–99, 103, 222n23; eastward enlargement (2004 and 2007), 9, 37, 45, 49, 51, 69, 86, 96, 99–101, 104, 221nn18–21, 222n30; 1973 enlargement, 84–86, 96; 1980s enlargements, 100

equal authenticity, 21, 29–31, 38, 81, 87, 96–98, 110, 122–24, 144, 161, 180, 192, 213nn2–3

equality of all official languages. *See* language equality

Estonian (language), 14, 47, 85, 102

eTranslation, 107, 223n38

EU citizens: equality before the law of, 31, 44, 67, 86–87, 98, 101, 109; foreign language proficiency of, 29, 64, 83, 106–7, 222n33; representation and participation, 21, 28–31, 39, 56, 198

EU English: as a shared non-native language, 11, 24, 189, 197; as a working language, 80; as distinguishable from standard English, 17, 24, 82, 139, 142–45, 150–56, 158–59, 189, 226nn3–7; decultured and neutral nature of, 147, 155, 158–59, 189; depoliticizing effect of, 158–59, 201; learning and adoption of, 143, 147–49; native English speakers' use of, 24, 148; reliance on; 61, 189; simplicity of, 24, 140–46; vocabulary of, 140–46, 150–51

EU-isms (*see also* EU English), 196

EU-sceptics, 106

Euramis, 60

Eurobarometer, 63, 216–17n36

Euro crisis, 136–38, 197, 230n16

Euro-English, 141, 227n12

EUROPARL7 corpus, 150–51, 227n12

European Central Bank, 48, 55

European Coal and Steel Community (ECSC), 9, 29, 83–85, 214n4, 220n6, 220n10

European Commission, 5, 20–21, 31–38, 46–47, 55–56, 92, 95, 102–4, 145, 172, 205–10, 216n31, 222n27, 232n5; legal service (SJ), 38, 126; translation services, 55–56

European Economic and Social Committee, 46, 51, 55, 62, 220n8

European Economic Community (EEC), 84; EEC Treaty, 92

European Investment Bank, 46, 51, 55

European Parliament, 1, 5, 40–44, 57–59, 142–43, 195–96, 205–10; direct election of, 5, 26, 36–37, 40, 98, 155, 205; empowerment of, 82, 94–99; plenary, 41–43, 48, 79, 102, 167, 170, 207, 222n31, 229n7; translation service, 55, 207, 209

European Social Forum, 136, 225n21

Eurospeak (*see also* EU English), 141

exogenous shocks (that catalyze institutional change), 89–93, 97, 105

false friends, 166

federalism, 16

Finland, 4, 79, 95

Finnish (language), 4, 36, 47, 85

Flemish (language), 84

Flesch-Kincaid scores, 153–54, 227n15

foreign language detachment effect, 117–18

foreign language handicap. *See* language handicaps

France, 29, 84, 87, 174, 225n22

French (language): as a language of multilingual states, 4; 213n3, 214n5; continued usage of, 5, 21, 33–47, 54–55, 100–102, 109, 131, 193, 206, 208, 213n1, 222n27; decline in use, 40–43, 122, 157; divergences in meaning and language rules of, 6, 32, 67–73, 134, 137, 166, 168, 171–74, 200, 212n10, 225n22, 228n4, 230n23; historical usage of, 8, 22, 84–86, 92, 95–96; influence of, 144, 147; language of the

Index

French (language) (*continued*)
Court, 32, 44–46, 150, 210, 224n7, 225n19, 228n26, 232n7; replacement of, 82, 84–88

gap between the EU and its citizens. *See* link between the EU and its citizens
Gazzola, Michele, 64, 103, 220n5, 226n2
General Court of the EU, 47, 92, 95
German (language): as a big language, 21, 34, 37–39, 41–43, 55, 65, 92, 101–2, 109, 206–10; as a language of multilingual states, 4; compared to English and French, 34–35; divergences in meaning and language rules of, 31–32, 68, 72, 136–38, 163, 171, 174, 182, 200–201; historical usage of, 92, 95; usage of, 1–2, 35, 47, 84, 131–32, 157, 167
Germanic language, 162
Germany, 29, 34, 84, 87, 117, 174, 217n37
Greece, 174, 217n37
Greek (language), 36–37, 84, 100, 165, 172, 217n37, 224n11, 229n14
Grin, François, 2–3, 211nn1–2, 218n51, 226n2

harmonization of laws, 30, 144
heavyweight politicians, 73–75
heuristic biases (accounting biases, ambiguity aversion, causality bias, intuition bias, loss aversion, positivity bias) (*see also* psychology), 115–18, 195
Hong Kong, 122
House of Lords, 152
humor, 1–2, 25, 71, 127–28, 161, 168–69

i-slots. *See* interpretation slots
identity: ethnic, 2; European, 65, 194, 197; language and, 7–8, 13, 15, 19, 107, 111, 211n1; national, 27, 87, 211n2; social, 87
ideologically neutral language, 11, 23–25, 113–14, 127–28, 143–48, 155, 158–59, 160–61, 176–78, 185–86, 189, 197–203
idiomatic speech, 25, 108, 113–14, 127–29, 151, 161–62, 170, 188

immigration, 5, 11, 14, 139, 197
India, 2, 4, 18
Indonesia, 13
informal communication. *See* communication
informal meetings, 40, 95, 121, 151, 208, 214n7
informal rules, 22, 33, 82, 90, 99, 110
information loss, 128, 164
input legitimacy, 197
institutional design, 9, 84, 94
institutionalism, 88–90, 110
insults, 25, 168–69, 229n9
intent: communicative (*see* communication); of law, 32; of the legislator, 25, 59, 109, 166–67, 174–75, 180–86, 214n6
Inter-Active Terminology for Europe (IATE), 60–61, 173
International Monetary Fund, 2
interpretation: availability of, 35, 46–54, 73, 76–77, 100–104, 190, 205–10, 216n29; costs of, 62–64, 66, 103, 232n4; effects of, 12, 25, 113–15, 160–65, 176–77, 185–86, 188–89, 201; errors and misunderstandings, 67, 71–73; of law, 32, 44–45, 69; need for, 24, 39, 46–54, 97, 106; relay interpretation (*see also* pivot languages), 54–55, 101–2, 165, 169; request for, 17, 39, 48–51, 102, 205–10, 221n19, 232n4; retour interpretation, 101–2
Interpretation Directorate (Court of Justice), 47
interpretation slots, 53–56, 217n38
interpreter days, 17, 47–53
interpreters. *See* language service providers
Ireland, 85–86, 105, 131, 152
Irish (language), 55, 67, 85, 105, 216n26, 216n30
Irish Parliament, 152
Israel, 6
Italian (language), 4, 32, 35, 37, 41, 45, 47, 65, 84, 102, 163, 210
Italy, 92, 131–32

Joint Practical Guide for drafting legislation, 82, 93, 125, 177, 180, 206

Index

jokes. *See* humor
Juncker, Jean-Claude, 122, 157, 224n11, 225n20

Keysar, Boaz, 115, 135, 223–24n3
Kik v OHIM (2001), 91
Kraus, Peter A., 19, 211n2
Krushchev, Nikita, 6

Laitin, David, 3, 13, 18, 28, 89–90, 223n35
language as an instrument; of communication, 2–4, 10, 113; of control and domination, 2; of identity and solidarity, 2; of thought, 2
language capacity. *See* language proficiency
language competence. *See* language proficiency
language diversity, 8, 91, 104, 142; commitment to, 38, 92
language equality (*see also* veil of formal language equality), 8–9, 36, 62, 97–100, 188; commitment to, 23, 87, 91, 99, 109; tension between uneven multilingualism and, 18, 86–88, 103–6, 110–11
language handicaps, 11, 27, 61, 73–79, 108, 114, 119, 133–35, 186, 202
language of the case, 44–45, 210, 213n2
language proficiency: advantages of, 27, 73–78, 108, 134, 192–93, 223n37; of EU citizens, 29, 64, 83, 106–7, 222n33; of EU officials, 29, 34, 36, 94, 98, 106–7, 114, 119, 132, 176, 192–93, 197, 213n1; improvement of, 107, 223n34; North-South split in, 119
language question, 7–9, 16, 19, 23, 67–68, 81, 95–96, 111, 188, 202
language regime: design of the, 7–10, 16, 19–23; effect of the, 23, 194, 197–98; functioning of the, 21, 27–28, 36–39, 61–80, 143–47, 205–10; limited language regime, 38–39, 164; stability and change in the, 9, 81–112, 188
language service providers: availability of, 40, 46–53, 85, 191, 215n23; as communicators and actors, 46–61, 109, 170–75, 184–85, 205–10; free-

lancers, 47–49, 53–56, 103, 191; as language "teachers" for incoming EU actors, 12, 24, 143, 148–50; quality of, 70, 78; reliance on, 2–4, 15, 109, 160; training and recruitment of, 48–49, 85, 100–102, 213n1
language services (of the EU): availability of, 29, 46–53, 88, 118–19; collaboration of, 60, 175; demand for, 82–84, 97, 100; effect of, 6, 12, 160–62, 176–86; funding, resources, and costs of, 16, 22, 62–64, 66, 94, 101–6, 188, 191–92, 222n31; quality of, 61, 188, 219n62; reliance on, 12, 24, 26, 76–80, 94, 107–8, 189
language skills. *See* language proficiency
Latin, 65, 172, 229n14
Latvia, 59
Latvian (language), 59, 85
lawmaking process. *See* legislative process
lawyer-linguists (*see also* language service providers), 26, 46, 56–61, 79, 89, 141, 149, 168–85, 201, 205–10, 217n44, 230n20; file coordinator, 209; jurist-linguist (or legal-linguistic expert), 57; legal reviser, 57; quality advisor, 58
legal effect, 56, 59, 161
legal equivalence. *See* equal authenticity
legal-linguistic verification, 59–61, 209
legal system, 31, 47, 60, 83, 178, 184
legal terminology, 68, 174–75
legislative process, 32, 39, 56–58, 123, 183, 205–10, 214n7, 224n6
Legislative Quality Units (of the EP), 58
level playing field, 65, 77–78, 159, 193, 201
limited multilingualism, 65–66, 81, 86–92, 104, 106, 109
lingua franca, 18, 21–22, 138, 141–42, 147, 202, 226n2, 227n11, 228n223, 228n25
linguistic disenfranchisement, 64, 66, 109
linguistic revision, 57, 59, 209, 217n46
link between the EU and its citizens, 13, 25, 159, 196
Lisbon Treaty, 93, 104, 197, 209, 220n9, 231n8

Lithuanian (language), 85
Luxembourg, 16, 33, 35, 45, 47, 55, 84, 91, 174, 217n37

machine translation and interpretation, 83, 107–9, 222n3, 223nn39–41
Macron, Emmanuel, 87
Malta, 105, 119
Maltese (language), 47, 85, 102, 105, 216n30
McAuliffe, Karen, 60, 122, 124, 171, 222n26, 224n7, 228n26, 230n17, 231n1
medium-sized languages (Spanish, Polish, Romanian, Dutch, and Hungarian), 41–42, 49–52
Member of the European Parliament (MEP), 1, 17, 40–43, 57–58, 66, 76–77, 86, 101, 119, 155, 184, 191–92, 195, 198, 224n4, 229n7, 231n5
migrant crisis, 197
minority languages. *See* regional and minority languages
mistakes, misunderstandings, and uncertainties, 6–7, 27, 62, 67–73, 80, 108–9, 190, 218n60
mother tongue. *See* native language
multilingual states/polities, 2–4, 6, 16, 199, 202

nation building. *See* state-building
nationalism (*see also* identity), 2, 15–16, 43, 200, 211n2
native: English speaker, 19, 24, 96, 114, 119, 122, 125, 128–30, 143, 146–52, 155, 158, 180, 197, 224–25nn12–13, 228n25; language, 1–3, 15, 23, 33, 37, 41, 76, 78, 100–102, 106, 115–17, 122, 126–27, 134, 159, 169–70, 176–77, 181, 189–93, 202, 216n33, 217n44; speaker (general), 11, 20, 23, 53–55, 92, 102, 123, 136, 144, 157, 206, 224nn7–8, 225nn17–19
natural language processing (NLP) algorithms (*see also* text-as-data), 154, 227n17
Netherlands, 174
networks. *See* social networks
nonnative: English speaker, 114, 119,

123–24, 129, 139, 141, 146–51, 166, 171, 197, 225n13, 227n12; language, 4, 11, 14, 20, 23, 26, 101, 112, 113–19, 131, 134, 144, 170, 170, 195, 221n18; speaker (general), 2, 11–12, 23, 54–55, 58, 64–65, 113–19, 125–31, 134–39, 160, 169, 179–80, 184–86, 201, 205–8, 224n7, 225n15
number of languages: changes to the, 88–89, 95–103, 190–91; considerations of the "right," 62, 65; as a critique of the language regime, 65–67; proposals for changing the, 92, 96, 109

official languages, 1–2, 4–5, 8, 16, 18, 21–22, 27–31, 38–41, 44–45, 54–58, 61–64, 84–88, 91–107, 122, 172, 180, 184, 191, 206, 209–10, 210, 213n1, 213n3, 220nn6–8, 222n31
ordinary legislative procedure, 5, 48, 58, 205–10, 211n8, 224n10
Organization for Security and Cooperation in Europe, 4
Organization of American States, 4
original language version. *See* source document; *see also* drafting language
output legitimacy, 196, 198

party groups. *See* political groups
permissive consensus, 196–97
Piris, Jean-Claude, 124
pivot languages, 45, 54, 60, 89, 102, 171, 178, 222n27, 227n21
plurilingualism, 20
Podesta, Guido, 100
Polish (language), 37, 45, 65, 85, 102, 123, 129, 210
political culture (of the EU), 13, 25, 194
political groups, 43, 48, 71, 207, 216n32
political networks. *See* social networks
politically charged language, 11–12, 23, 114–15, 127, 136–39, 166, 189, 230n16
politicization, 83, 105–6, 169, 198
Portugal, 215n12
Portuguese (language), 4, 36, 84, 100, 123, 180, 217n37
pragmatic language (*see also* simple lan-

guage; utilitarian language), 9–11, 80, 113, 124–30, 134, 189, 203
Priestley, Julian, 63, 100–101, 220n13, 221n18
primary language rules, 21, 82–83, 88, 91–94, 98–99, 103, 110, 221n19
procedural languages, 21, 37, 64, 82, 88, 93, 95, 206
proper English. *See* standard English
psychology (*see also* heuristic biases), 14–15, 115–18, 201
public opinion, 14, 93, 105, 196

Quality of Legislation teams, 57–58
quasi-parameters, 89–91, 93, 97, 105, 222n33

rapporteur, 58, 72, 76–77, 151, 182, 193, 200, 207, 216n32
rapporteur-shadow rapporteur meetings, 49, 76–77
rational decision making, 15, 115–18, 195
regional and minority languages, 7–8, 18–19, 65, 106, 218n53
relay interpretation. *See* interpretation
resource-efficient full multilingualism, 40, 101, 104
retour interpretation. *See* interpretation
right to work in one's own language, 40–41, 101
risk assessment, 14–15, 89, 115–17, 195
Robertson, Colin, 31, 68, 144, 149–50, 178, 217n45, 229n13, 230n17
Robinson, William, 122–26, 142, 175, 217n46, 224n9, 229n10, 232n2, 232n6
Romance language, 162
Romanian (language), 41, 85

Sacconi, Guido, 76
SALT (Speak All, Listen Three), 102
Šarčević, Susan, 68–69, 110, 174–79
Schulz, Martin, 130–33, 163–64, 224n11, 225nn20–22, 229n9
secondary language rules, 82–83, 93, 110, 223n34
Secretariat General (Commission), 38
sentence length, 24, 129, 143, 153, 227n16, 230n18

shadow rapporteur, 77, 151, 193, 207, 216n32
Sharpston, Eleanor, 176
simple language (*see also* pragmatic language; utilitarian language), 10–12, 23–25, 113–34, 124–30, 138, 143–46, 158–59, 161, 170–71, 178, 180, 188–89, 197, 201, 203, 206, 225n18
simultaneous interpretation. *See* interpretation
Single European Act, 97
Slovak (language), 85
Slovakia, 35
Slovenian (language), 54, 85
small languages (Bulgarian, Croatian, Czech, Danish, Estonian, Finnish, Greek, Irish, Latvian, Lithuanian, Maltese, Portuguese, Slovak, Slovenian, Swedish), 41–42, 49–52, 100
social networks, 75, 192, 200
Somalia, 13
source text, 30, 122–26, 144, 161–62, 171, 177–79, 214n6
South Africa, 4, 16
Southern African Development Community, 4
sovereignty, 5, 27
Spain, 215n12, 220n8
Spanish (language), 4–5, 14, 35–37, 41, 45, 47, 65, 72, 84, 100, 102, 121, 123, 129, 132, 157, 182, 210, 217n37
speaking for interpretation (*see also* anticipation of translation or interpretation), 12, 161, 176–79, 189, 230n19
spontaneous meetings. *See* informal meetings
Sri Lanka, 6
standard English. *See* English
standardization of language, 8, 10, 23–24, 114, 124–28, 159, 160–61, 176, 186, 193–94, 211n2
state-building, 2, 9, 18, 27, 32, 196, 211n2
Stauder v City of Ulm (1969), 31–32, 214n6
straightforward language. *See* simple language
subsidiarity principle, 140

264   *Index*

supranational institutions, 5, 19, 38, 82, 99, 199, 211n9
supremacy (doctrine of), 30, 97–98
Sweden, 36
Swedish (language), 4, 37, 54, 85, 165
Switzerland, 4, 122, 213n3, 214n5
symbolic power, 3, 81, 87–88, 95, 111, 224n5
Syria, 6

text-as-data, 13, 200
tolerance, 11, 61, 80, 115, 132–35, 188
tone of voice, 127, 163–65, 169
Tower of Babel, 73, 100, 217n48
translation: availability of, 16, 64, 103, 191–92, 217n40; costs of, 62–66, 103, 218n51, 222n31; effects of, 12, 24–25, 124–26, 151, 160–86, 188–89, 201, 229n12; errors and misunderstandings, 6–7, 31, 67–68, 71–72, 137, 176, 181, 214n6, 218nn58–59; logistics of, 26, 44–45, 55–56, 83, 89, 96–97, 102–4, 107–8, 206–10, 222–23nn30–33, 230n20; need for, 106–7, 171, 178, 189; of text and law, 29–30, 39, 57, 161, 170–76, 179, 196
Translation Centre for the Bodies of the European Union, 55, 61
Translation Units, 55, 209
translators. *See* language service providers
transposition (of EU legislation), 30, 59, 141
Treaty of Paris, 83, 214n4
Treaty of Rome. *See* European Economic Community Treaty
type-token ratio (TTR), 153

unanimity rule, 94, 96
uneven multilingualism, 9, 22–23, 110–11, 188
united in diversity, 27
United Kingdom, 7, 45, 85–86, 105,

129, 148–49, 152, 156–57, 171, 226n8, 230n23
United Nations, 2, 4, 6, 215n24
utilitarian language (*see also* pragmatic language; simple language), 11–12, 15, 23–24, 113, 116–18, 124, 127, 143–44, 158–59, 189, 195, 197, 203

value markers, 126
Van der Vecht case (1967), 110
varieties (of a language), 40, 136, 142–43, 146
vehicular language, 22, 33–35, 86, 113, 119, 158, 189
veil of formal language equality, 9, 22, 81, 88, 110–11, 188
veto, 94, 99
victims of multilingualism, 69, 110
vocabulary, 24, 47, 68, 113, 125, 140–46, 149–51, 158, 162, 168, 171, 180, 225n17, 227n16
Vuorikoski, Anna-Riita, 142, 162, 170, 226n5

war and conflict, 2–3, 6–9, 13, 15, 212n14; Cold War, 6; Six Day War, 6
Wodak, Ruth, 8, 212, 219, 223n36, 224n5
Wordfish scaling model, 155, 227n19
working group, 38–39, 67, 100, 207
working language, 4, 8, 21, 47, 66, 84, 86, 157–58, 207, 210, 211n5, 218n5; common/shared, 45–46, 61, 80, 112, 188; limiting the number of, 65, 95–96
working party, 57, 193, 208
World Trade Organization, 5
Wright, Sue, 19, 66, 68, 74, 128–30, 192, 212n16, 215n10, 223n37, 225n14, 225n16, 225n18, 230n23, 231n7
writing for translation (*see also* anticipation of translation or interpretation), 12, 161, 176–79, 189